THE GREAT BOOK OF
HANDICRAFTS

YOUR GUIDE TO:-

BASKET MAKING
LEATHERWORK   POTTERY
MARQUETRY   PRESSED FLOWERS
MACRAMÉ   TATTING   COLLAGE
TIE DYEING AND TRITIK
APPLIQUÉ
PATCHWORK QUILTING
FELT MAKING   PUPPET MAKING
BATIK
SILK SCREEN PRINTING
BEADWORK   QUILTING   SMOCKING
METAL THREAD EMBROIDERY
NEEDLEPOINT LACE
AUSTRALIAN CROSS STITCH
CANVAS WORK   WEAVING
CROCHET   KNITTING

All the techniques needed to tackle twenty-five traditional and modern crafts are explained in this new handicrafts book. Full instructions are also given for over a hundred original and exciting things to make. The projects are all illustrated in full colour with clear diagrams for the skills and stitches.

Written by practising crafts people, each craft is presented in the same order beginning with a description of the materials and equipment needed, followed by a 'Know How' section detailing basic and more complex techniques and continuing with the projects, which are graded in order of difficulty.

The book has been specially designed both for those wishing to start a new craft and for experienced workers looking for new ideas.

THE GREAT BOOK OF
HANDICRAFTS

Edited by
Ena Richards

Contents

First published 1980
By Sundial Books Limited

This edition published 1982
By Octopus Books Limited
59 Grosvenor Street
London W1

© 1980 Hennerwood Publications Limited

ISBN 0 7064 1763 1

Produced by Mandarin Publishers Limited
22A, Westlands Road
Quarry Bay, Hong Kong

Printed in Hong Kong

Introduction

Twenty-five practising craftsmen and women have described their skills and devised altogether over a hundred projects for this book. The presentation of the crafts has been designed to be of maximum use to readers whether they are complete beginners or experienced workers.

To help you identify and select what you need to practise the craft there is a photograph and description of all the relevant materials and equipment at the start of each new subject. Next comes a 'Know How' section, which takes you step by step through the basic techniques, stitches or processes involved, together with more specific details appropriate to the projects which follow.

For each craft there are three to four projects, starting with something for the beginner and progressing to an advanced project. We suggest that if you are completely new to the craft you should work through at least two of the earlier projects before attempting the last one, as this is generally larger in scope and a more complex interpretation of the craft.

The twenty-five crafts have been arranged according to the type of materials involved, so that if you enjoy working with, say, fabrics you will find patchwork, tiedyeing and tritik, batik, appliqué, silk screen printing, puppetry, felt and collage all grouped together.

Metric and imperial measurements have been supplied but, for ease of working, exact equivalents have not always been given. Therefore it is important that you use only one set of measurements throughout any project.

Two supplementary techniques to help you work from this book are given below.

How to enlarge a design

A design can be enlarged, or the overall shape changed, freehand but it is more accurate to use the squared system.

It is possible to buy squared up paper from a stationers, which simplifies the process, especially if you are working from a squared up original, as for many of the designs in this book. Number the squares on the original and number the enlarged version to correspond. Study each little square in turn on the original design. Note where the outline of the design crosses the grid lines and mark these on the enlargement. Then join up the marks to match the original. Slowly the picture will build up until complete (see Fig. 1).

If you are not working with squared up original and paper, divide the small design into sections yourself. First divide the top and bottom edges in half, then find the quarter marks and then divide the edges into eighths. Divide it again if working very small sections is preferred. Next draw vertical lines to join the marks. Repeat with the sides of the design.

Outline the area of the new and larger dimensions on a piece of paper. Divide this area in the same say as before making the same number of divisions.

Then proceed as before. By this second method you do not have to keep to a strict enlargement of the original, the new dimensions outlined can be made to alter the overall shape provided that they are divided up in the same way as the original.

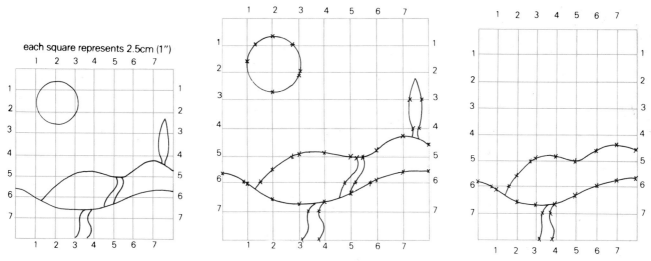

Fig. 1 **Left** The original design **Middle** Enlarging the original **Right** Altering and enlarging the original shape.

How to frame a picture

To calculate the length of moulding required, measure the top of the picture and add twice the width of the bottom of the moulding, plus 1 mm for an easy fit (see Fig. 2). Measure the side of the picture and add twice

Fig. 2

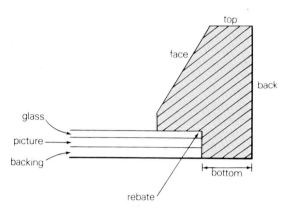

the width of the moulding and 1 mm as before. Add the two totals together and multiply by two. Finally add 40 mm for the eight saw cuts and any damage.

Use a mitre cutter and set it according to the manufacturer's instructions. Clamp it to the working surface. Put the moulding in with the rebate away from you, moulded face uppermost and the long length to the left. Using a tenon saw, always cut the mitres towards the rebate so that any splintering will be on the inner rebate edge and the bottom, neither of which will show on the completed frame. Make this first cut, leaving a small triangular piece of waste.

Remove the moulding and mark off along the back edge the length of one of the long sides plus twice the bottom width of the moulding and the 1 mm. Square the line across the back with a trysquare. Replace the moulding in the mitre cutter, using the right hand side, and make the saw cut on the waste side of the pencil line.

Remove the moulding, replace it on the left of the mitre cutter as for the first cut and make the third cut as at the beginning (Fig. 3).

Fig. 3

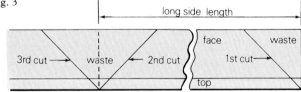

Place the mouldings back to back, with the tips of the mitres level and mark off the length of the first piece on the second. Replace the second piece on the right of the cutter block and cut to the pencil line.

Repeat for the two shorter sides. Clean off any splinters with a knife rather than sandpaper.

On a flat surface, fit the four sides together. Adjust a four corner cramp to fit, pulling the cord tight.

Slacken the cord, take out one side, glue both ends and replace. Do the same with the opposite side. Carefully reposition each joint so that there is no step on the inside and the tops are even. Pull up the cord as tightly as possible and lock.

Check with the trysquare then remove any surplus glue with a damp cloth. Leave to dry for two hours.

Remove the cramp. Stand the frame on edge and nail each corner with 2 cm ($\frac{3}{4}$ in) pins. Use a fine bradawl and hammer downwards.

Place the frame face downwards on the working surface. Lower the glass in place, then the picture and next a piece of hardboard for backing, cut to fit.

To hold the backing tightly in place against the glass, drive in 12 mm ($\frac{1}{2}$ in) pins at 10 cm (4 in) intervals halfway in to the side of the rebate. To avoid damage to the frame, hold a block of wood against the moulded edge opposite each pin as it is driven in.

Stick lengths of gummed paper round the sides to cover the joins.

Fit screw eyes between one third and one quarter of the way down from the top on each side. Thread nylon cord through.

To make a box frame

Use a moulding with a rebate of 25 mm (1 in) or more for a box frame. Make up the frame.

Fit the glass.

Measure the remaining depth of the rebate and subtract the thickness of the picture and backing board.

This measurement gives the depth of the pieces of wood required to hold the glass in the top of the rebate. They are called 'spacers' (see Fig. 4).

Fig. 4

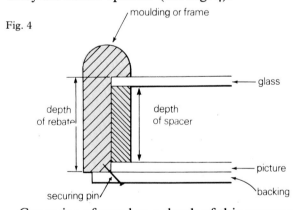

Cut strips of wood to a depth of this measurement and the length of the sides. Fit these spacers either with butt or mitred joints and hold them in place with a spot of glue.

Fit in the picture and backboard. Because the backboard fits flush with the bottom of the rebate, cut a small notch in the edge of the hardboard at regular intervals to take each nail.

SAFETY NOTE

Sharp knives are used in many of the crafts in this book. Handle them with great care and store them away immediately after use. Leather workers should be extra cautious when using the aniline dyes which are toxic. Rubber gloves should always be worn when using dyes.

Basket making

Basket making is one of the most ancient crafts in the world. From time immemorial man has interwoven the twigs, leaves, reeds and grasses which grew around him to provide his everyday needs. He has woven his huts, containers for his food, fences to protect his cattle and sheep, hives for his bees, granaries for his corn and winnowing fans and harvest baskets for his agriculture. He has made salmon and eel traps, lobster-pots, poultry coops, carts, coracles and chariots for transport in peace and war. He has even been wafted through the air, carried in baskets under hot air balloons. Indeed, baskets have supplied his wants literally from the cradle to the grave and beyond for basket-work coffins have been used through the ages and tiny food baskets have been discovered in Egyptian tombs and these were intended to provide refreshment for the little ornamental figures who accompanied the members of the royal household to the underworld.

It is worth noting that basketry is a craft which is still manual and one which has never been successfully imitated by machinery.

Materials and Equipment

Willow has always been the traditional material for basket making in this country. However, during the present century, centre cane has come to be used. This is particularly useful for beginners as it is sold graded into different thicknesses and in long lengths and is extremely flexible. All the projects in this section are made with centre cane.

Centre cane is the core of the rattan plant, a creeper which is found in the jungles of Indonesia. The plant grows to immense lengths, sometimes over 200 m (220 yd) although the average is 50 m to 100 m (55 yd to 110 yd). In spite of its length, however, the diameter is normally less than 3 cm ($1\frac{1}{4}$ in). Some cane is processed in Singapore but the higher quality cane used in this country is mainly processed in Europe and is known as continental cane, as opposed to Far Eastern cane. The outer glossy skin is stripped off and used for caning chairs, leaving the inner core of centre cane. This is passed through a machine which is fitted with cutting knives of various sizes which split the core into the diameters required. The cane is then graded and that which is considered too dark in colour to be sold as natural centre cane is bleached. Cane is normally sold in this country in 0.5 kg (1 lb) bundles and is obtainable in numbers 0 to 16, the smaller the number the finer the cane.

Handle cane is about 8 mm ($\frac{1}{3}$ in) in diameter.

Handle wrapping (or lapping) cane is also available. It is flat on one side and slightly rounded on the other and may be obtained with either matt or glossy surfaces.

A basketmaker's bodkin or awl is obtainable from most craft suppliers. However, it may be improvized by inserting a steel knitting needle into a wooden handle or by grinding the end of an old screwdriver into a point.

General items include side cutters or sharp secateurs, a sharp craft knife, a ruler – preferably a 2 ft wooden ruler or yardstick, round-nosed pliers and a few spring clothes pegs.

Know how

Preparation

Soak the cane in warm water for several minutes before use. As a general guide, soak for five to ten minutes for sizes 3 to 7, ten to fifteen minutes for sizes 8 to 12 and half an hour for handle cane. However, the time varies according to the thickness of the cane and also to the purpose for which it is being used. For instance, it is necessary to soak the cane much longer when working a border than when weaving the sides of a basket.

Chair cane and lapping cane need to be dipped for a few seconds only.

Do not leave the cane in water too long or it will become permanently discoloured. After soaking, it should be kept under a damp towel whilst working to prevent it drying out too quickly. After twenty-four hours, it must be dried very thoroughly or black mould spots will appear on the surface. Never leave damp cane in plastic bags.

Structure

Base sticks are used for the skeleton of the basket and are cut from thick cane.

Weavers are the canes used for weaving over the base sticks and are finer than the base sticks.

Bye-stakes are the same thickness as the side stakes and are used to give added rigidity to the sides of a basket.

Circular base

Different numbers of base sticks are used depending on the type of basket. To work a five by five base (i.e. a cross giving ten base sticks on which to work the base of a basket), cut ten base sticks. With the bodkin, make a slit in the centre of five of the base sticks. Using a sharp knife, sharpen one end of each of the other five sticks to a point and thread them through the slits of the first five to form a cross (Fig. 1). Take a length of weaver cane and fold it almost in half so that one end is a few centimetres (inches) longer than the other. This will avoid having two joins in one place later.

Take the cane round the back of the top vertical of the cross with both ends in front of the horizontals, to provide two weavers.

Take the left hand weaver across in front of the vertical, over the other weaver, round the back of the right hand horizontal of the cross and out at the front again (Fig. 2a). Weaving in this way with two ends of cane is called 'pairing'.

Turn the work a quarter turn anti-clockwise so that the right hand horizontal comes to the top. Take the new left hand weaver, as before, over the front of the canes and the other weaver, round the back of the horizontal of the cross and out to the front again (Fig. 2b).

Turn work round another quarter turn and continue in this way until each arm of the cross has been worked twice, keeping the tension firm and even. This is called 'tying in the slath'.

On the third round divide the arms to start forming a circle by gently easing apart the five base sticks of each arm in a two, one, two formation. Weave round the left hand pair, then the middle one, then the right hand pair, taking care that the weavers are kept very close to the previous row (Fig. 3). At the end of this round there will be a pair, a single cane and a pair on each of the four arms.

Weave another round on this formation.

Open out into single sticks to form a circle of twenty and work a round of pairing over the single sticks.

Pairing

Pairing is a weave which holds rods in place. It is worked in the same way as on the base with the weavers at the front of the work (Fig. 4).

Reverse pairing

Instead of starting the stroke with the weavers in front of the work, they are at the back.

Bring the left hand weaver each time to the front, round one stake and then take it to the back again. Bring the other weaver to the front, round the next stake and take it to the back of the work (Fig. 5).

Joining in new cane

When a new cane is required in pairing, leave the end of the worked one on the front. Pull it to the left and slip the new cane into the work between this end and the work (Fig. 6) so that the worked end protrudes at the front and the new one at the back. Make sure the ends are long enough to rest against a base stick or they will slip through to the other side of the work. After this, the two ends for pairing will not belong to the same cane.

Oval base

Cut three long base sticks and seven shorter ones. Make a slit in the centre of each of the short sticks and thread the three long sticks through (Fig. 7).

Use a length of chair cane to wrap the sticks together, tucking one end behind the first pair and working

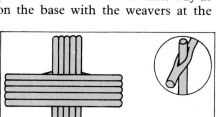

Fig. 1 Threading 5 base sticks through 5 others.

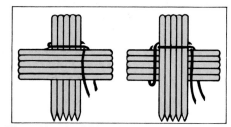

Fig. 2 (a) 1st and (b) 2nd stage of pairing.

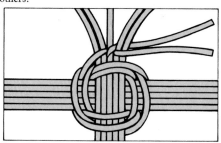

Fig. 3 Third round of pairing.

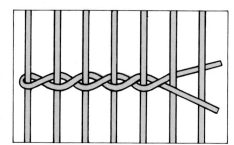

Fig. 4 Pairing.

Fig. 8 Wrapping the oval base.

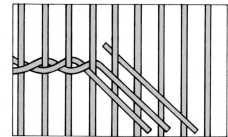

Fig. 9 Laying in a 3rd weaver for waling.

a cross over the right side of this pair.

Wrap the chair cane over the three long sticks, behind the next short stick then over the long sticks on the other side.

Continue in this way, making an equal number of wraps between the short sticks (Fig. 8). At the end make a second cross over the last pair of short sticks. Trim the end of the chair cane and thread it into the wrapping on the underside.

To help counteract the twist that occurs on an oval base, the weaving must have equal amounts of pairing and reverse pairing.

Three-rod waling
This gives a raised surface in contrast to pairing. It also strengthens the weaving.

Lay in a new weaver cane in the next space to the right of the pairing weavers, so that there are three weavers coming from consecutive spaces (Fig. 9). With a pen, mark the stick to the left of the first weaver. Take the left hand weaver to the right in front of two stakes, over the other two weavers, round the back of the next stake and out to the front again.

Weave the new left hand weaver in the same way (Fig. 10).

Continue round the base as far as the marked stake until there are three weavers coming out of the three spaces before the marked stake.

At the end of the round, take the right hand weaver (the one just worked) in front of two stakes, behind one and out to the front again.

Take the middle weaver in front of two stakes, behind one and out to the

front again.

Take the left hand weaver and work in the same way. This sequence is called a step-up and is worked at the end of each round. To begin the next round of waling, revert to the ordinary waling stroke of using the left hand weaver each time.

To complete the wale, do not work the step-up but take the left hand weaver in front of two stakes, round the marked stake and bring it back to the front. Cut it off leaving two or three centimetres (inches) of cane.

Take the next weaver (now the left hand weaver) in front of two stakes, behind the next and bring it to the front by passing it under the top weaver of the previous round. Trim.

Take the last weaver in front of two stakes, behind the next and bring it back to the front under two canes of the previous round. Trim.

Check that all three weavers are now lying under two other weavers.

Inserting bye-stakes
Point one end of each bye-stake and insert the pointed end immediately to the right of each stake, down into the weaving.

Working the upsett
The upsett is the name given to the first rows worked after inserting the side stakes into the base to form the sides of a basket. To ensure a firm beginning to the sides, it is usually worked in waling.

Fitching
This is a method of starting pairing again on the sides of a basket after a space in the weaving.

Loop a piece of cane round a stake

as for pairing. Grip both weavers between the thumb and forefinger of the right hand and twist them forwards, thus reversing the position of the weavers. Take the rear weaver behind the next stake on the right and front weaver in front of the stake. Repeat this twisting movement all round the basket (Fig. 11).

Randing
Unlike pairing, randing uses only one weaver and is generally used for the sides rather than the base. An odd number of stakes is necessary for this weave. Take the weaver in front of one stake, behind the next, in front of the next and so on. When joining in a new length of cane, leave both old and new ends inside the basket, resting against a stake.

Packing
This is a method of shaping. Rand with one weaver to and fro on the chosen stakes, bringing the weaver round one stake less at the end of each row, until the middle stake has been worked round (Fig. 12). Fasten off the end and leave it inside the work.

Trac border
This decorative border is made for the table mat with groups of four stakes worked together as one. It can also be worked with single border stakes.

Sharpen one end of each border stake. Trim off the ends of the base sticks close to the weaving.

Insert the pointed ends of two border stakes to a depth of 4 cm ($1\frac{1}{2}$ in) each side of every base stick.

Take one set of four stakes and bend it to the right about 4 cm ($1\frac{1}{2}$ in) beyond the pairing. Weave behind the

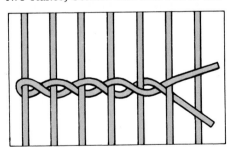
Fig. 5 Reverse pairing.

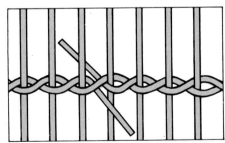
Fig. 6 Adding new cane in pairing weave.

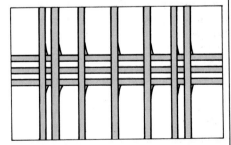
Fig. 7 Threading for an oval base.

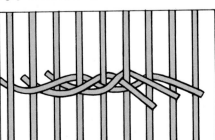
Fig. 10 3-rod waling.

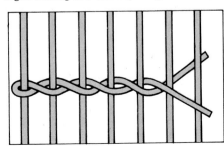
Fig. 11 Fitching.

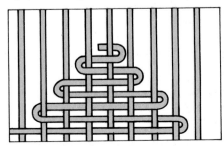
Fig. 12 Packing.

continued

next set of stakes to the right, in front of two sets (Fig. 13), behind one set, in front of one set, and tuck into the back of the work behind a group of border stakes. Secure them to the main work with a spring clothes peg.

Take the next upright set of four on the right of those just worked, bend to the right close to the previous set and work in the same pattern as before (behind one set, in front of two, behind one, in front of one) and tuck into the back. Move the clothes peg along.

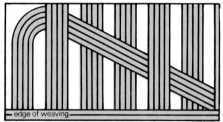
Fig. 13 Trac border.

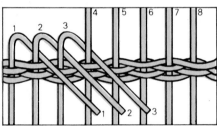
Fig. 14 (a) 1st 3 stakes of 3-rod plain border.

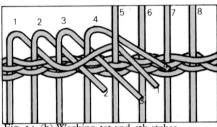
Fig. 14 (b) Working 1st and 4th stakes.

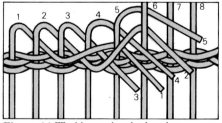
Fig. 14 (c) Working 2nd and 5th stakes.

Fig. 14 (d) Working 3rd and 6th stakes.

Continue in this way all round the border, threading the last few stakes in and out of the first stakes, keeping the pattern correct. Trim ends.

Three-rod plain border
Start anywhere on the border and number the stakes from one consecutively to the right. Squeeze them with round-nosed pliers about 6 mm ($\frac{1}{4}$ in) above the pairing.

Bend stake 1 down to the right behind stake 2 and out to the front. Bend stake 2 behind stake 3 and out to the front, bend stake 3 behind stake 4 and out to the front. There are now three single stakes lying to the front and pointing to the right (Fig. 14a).

Take the left hand front stake (1) in front of the other two (2, 3) and between the first and second uprights (4, 5) then out to the front to the right of the second upright. Bring down the next upright (4) behind its neighbour (Fig. 14c).

Take the left hand front stake (2) in front of the others (3, 1, 4) and between the first and second uprights (5, 6) and out to the front. Bring down the next upright (5) (Fig. 14c).

Take the left hand front stake (3) in front of the others (4, 1, 2, 5) and between the first and second uprights (6, 7) and out to the front. Bring down the next upright (6) (Fig. 14d).

The next left hand front stake is no. 1 which has already been worked. From now on count from the right to the 5th front stake. Take the 5th front stake from the right (4) in front of the others (2, 5, 3, 6) and between the first and second uprights (7, 8) and out to the front as before. Bring down the next upright (7) as before.

Continue in this way, taking the 5th front stake from the right and working as described above.

To complete the border, take the 5th stake from the right and thread it behind stake 1 and back to the front through the loop formed by stake 1. Bring down the last upright stake and thread it through to lie alongside.

Continue to thread in the remaining pairs in turn to complete the pattern, when all the ends of cane will be at the base of the border.

Four-rod plain border
This is worked in the same way as the three-rod plain border except that four stakes are brought down at the beginning, and they are woven in front of three stakes and behind one. Also, take the seventh stake from the right instead of the fifth.

Wall plaque or table mat

This can look most attractive as a backing to a knot of everlasting flowers or preserved leaves. At Christmas, substitute holly, or a suitable decoration with glitter, for a seasonal effect by fixing a small quantity of sponge-like flower arranging material on to the mat with wire.

You will need
● 28 g (1 oz) no. 8 cane for base sticks
● 43 g (1$\frac{1}{2}$ oz) no. 2 cane for weavers
● 71 g (2$\frac{1}{2}$ oz) no. 2 cane for trac border
● basketry equipment as given on page 9

Measurements
26 cm (10 in) diameter

Instructions
All the techniques required for this project are given on pages 10–12.

Make a five by five centre cross and work a circular base, continuing pairing until the diameter is 11.5 cm (4$\frac{1}{2}$ in).

Work three rounds of three-rod waling.

Work six more rows of pairing and secure by threading the weavers under one cane on the previous row.

Sharpen one end of each of the 80 border stakes.

Trim off the ends of the base sticks close to the work and insert two border stakes each side of every base stick to a depth of 4 cm (1$\frac{1}{2}$ in).

Work a trac border.

Trim the ends.

Breadroll basket

This useful and decorative basket achieves its unusual scalloped edge by means of wooden beads in two sizes.

You will need
● 57 g (2 oz) no. 10 cane for base sticks
● 85 g (3 oz) no. 8 cane for side stakes and bye-stakes
● 113 g (4 oz) no. 3 cane for weavers
● eight small and eight large macramé beads
● basketry equipment as given on page 9

Right The table mat is a suitable project for a beginner to basket making. The breadroll basket starts the same way but is then shaped with side stakes and wooden beads.

Measurements

Diameter at top of border 23 cm (9 in)

depth 6 cm (2¼ in)

Instructions

All the techniques required for this project are given on pages 10–12.

Cut eight base sticks each 18 cm (7 in) long, 32 side stakes each 30 cm (12 in) and 32 bye-stakes each 10 cm (4 in).

Base

Make a four by four centre cross and pair for two rounds. Then open the sticks out into pairs and pair for two rounds. Now open out the sticks into singles.

Work ten more rounds of pairing.

Work two rounds of waling without completing.

Make a point at one end of each side stake. Cut off the base sticks close to the weaving and insert a stake on each side of every base stick, pushing the stakes well into the weaving.

Work one more round of waling over each pair of stakes to cover where the base sticks are cut.

Sides

Separating the pairs into single stakes, work one round of waling without completing.

Gently bend the stakes up at an angle of about 45 degrees to form the sides of the basket, making sure the weavers are on the outside. Work two more rounds of waling.

Insert the bye-stakes.

Work three more rounds of waling, weaving round the stake and bye-stake together as one.

Omitting the step-up, *place one small bead, two large beads, one small bead on four consecutive stake and bye-stake pairs and rest them on the weaving. Miss four stakes. Repeat from * three times more.

Continue waling for six more rounds, working over the beads and pushing the weaving well down on the stakes between the beads. Complete the wale.

Cut off the bye-stakes close to the top of the weaving.

Border

Soak the stakes well before starting.

Begin with any stake, taking it behind two stakes, in front of two stakes and leave behind the next stake on the inside of the basket.

Take each stake in turn and work in the same way, threading the last four stakes into the first four to maintain the weave.

Trim all ends.

Peanut holder for garden birds

Both the container and the lid of this basket are worked from a circular base. Other techniques used include fitching and a four-rod plain border. The handle is formed by an extra long base stick. The lid is begun separately, then worked around the handle, thus fixing it to the bottom.

You will need

- 28 g (1 oz) no. 8 centre cane for base sticks, side stakes and bye-stakes
- 28 g (1 oz) no. 1 cane for weavers
- small piece of string
- plastic washing-up liquid container
- basketry equipment as given on page 9

Measurements

Diameter at base 5 cm (2 in)

height 14 cm (5½ in), excluding handle

handle 6.5 cm (2½ in)

Instructions

All the techniques required for this project are given on pages 10–12.

The base sticks and side stakes are all in one and referred to as stakes. Cut four stakes each 51 cm (20 in) long, one stake 87 cm (34 in) and ten bye-stakes each 23 cm (9 in).

Make a two by three cross with the stakes. The 87 cm (34 in) length should be positioned as the central one of the three threaded through the other two.

Work a circular base with three rounds of pairing over the central cross, then open the stakes out singly and pair to a diameter of 6.5 cm (2½ in). Fasten off the ends by threading them under the previous row.

Using a bodkin to make a space, insert each bye-stake into the base on the left hand side of the existing stakes.

Squeeze all the stakes with round-nosed pliers close to the last round of pairing, soak well, turn them up and tie firmly together at the top with string.

Side

Place the basket on its side, underside of base facing.

Begin the upsett by waling round the base very close to the base weaving, at the same time easing apart the stakes and weaving round them singly so that they are set equi-distant from each other instead of in pairs. Complete the upsett with two more rounds of waling.

Remove the string from the stakes.

Fasten off one end of cane by threading it through the previous row and with the two ends remaining work a continuous spiral fitch for $12\frac{1}{2}$ rounds, spaced a maximum of 1 cm ($\frac{1}{2}$ in) apart, otherwise the peanuts will fall out. After a few rounds, insert an empty plastic detergent bottle to keep the shape tight and upright.

Work the last half round of fitching to level off at 13 cm (5 in) from the base.

Remove the plastic container.

Work three rounds of three-rod waling.

Soak the ends of the long central stake and twist them together to make a simple twisted handle approximately 6.5 cm ($2\frac{1}{2}$ in) at its centre. Darn the ends away under the waling as shown in Fig. 15.

Border

Soak the stake ends and work a four-rod plain border close above the waling.

Lid

Cut ten stakes each 31 cm (12 in) long and make a 5 by 5 cross.

Work a circular base with three lines of pairing over the central cross before separating the stakes into a two, one, two formation. Pair for three rows, then separate into singles and pair to a diameter of about 6.5 cm ($2\frac{1}{2}$ in).

Slip the lid in place between the handles, ten stakes to either side, and continue to pair for three rounds round the outside of the handle. Check that the lid will move smoothly up and down the handle.

Squeeze the stakes with round-nosed pliers close to the last round of pairing, soak the ends well and turn them down towards the base.

Work four rounds of tight pairing. Fasten off the ends securely by threading them through the previous row.

Lid border

With single stakes work a trac border behind one and in front of two then tuck the ends behind the next.

Leave to dry, then trim.

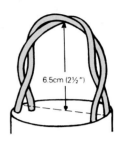

6.5cm (2½")

Fig. 15 Twisting the handle.

Left The fitching on the peanut holder has been spaced out to contain the nuts, whilst still allowing the birds to get at them. **Below** The cradle (instructions overleaf) is worked with an oval base and has a raised end to suggest a hood.

Doll's cradle

This doll's cradle has an oval base and it is advisable to have made at least three round based articles before attempting an oval. There are handles on the cradle so that it may be used as a carry cot.

You will need

- 56 g (2 oz) no. 12 cane for base sticks
- 84 g (3 oz) no. 10 cane for side stakes and bye-stakes
- 112 g (4 oz) no. 5 cane for side weavers
- 28 g (1 oz) no. 3 cane for base weavers
- 76 cm (30 in) no. 15 cane for handle bows and liners
- three lengths of no. 4 chair cane each 270 cm (9 ft) for handle and base wrappers
- two lengths of no. 2 cane for handle leaders
- basketry equipment as given on page 9

Measurements

Length at border 33 cm (13 in)
width at border 20 cm (8 in)
depth 15.5 cm (6 in) at head, 11.5 cm (4½ in) at foot
base 27 cm by 15 cm (10½ in by 6 in)

Instructions

All the techniques required for this project are given on pages 10–12.

Cut three base sticks each 30 cm (12 in) long and seven base sticks each 18 cm (7½ in).

Work an oval base.

Loop a base weaver round one end of the three long sticks and pair round the base for two rounds, keeping the weaving close to the long sticks.

Open out the long sticks and the two short sticks of the pairs into singles and continue pairing for 4 cm (1½ in). Change to reverse pairing and continue for 4 cm (1½ in).

Cut 29 side stakes: 18 each 40 cm (16 in) long, two 41 cm (16½ in), two 42 cm (17 in), two 43 cm (17½ in), two 44 cm (18 in), two 45 cm (18½ in) and one 46 cm (19 in).

Cut off the base sticks close to the weaving.

Point one end of each side stake. Pushing them up to the central wrapped stakes, insert one only by each of the five sticks on each side of the cradle and at the centre of the head of the cradle and one on each side of the remaining nine sticks. The longest stake goes at the centre of the head of the cradle, the next two longest on either side, and so on.

Squeeze the side stakes carefully with round-nosed pliers and bend them upwards. Using string, tie them up taking care to keep them in sequence. Use clothes pegs to keep the stakes separate.

Place the cradle on its side with the underside of the base facing. Insert four side weavers into the base and start the upsett with one row of four-rod wale. (This is worked as a three-rod wale, except that each weaver is taken in turn in front of three stakes and behind one stake.)

Discard the fourth weaver by taking it round the marked stake. Cut it off, leaving about 8 cm (3 in) and work the step-up with the other three weavers.

Work four more rows of upsett with three-rod wale and complete.

Thread the end of the fourth weaver, discarded after the first row of upsett, to the inside of the cradle.

Cut 29 bye-stakes: 18 each 10.5 cm (4 in) long, two 11 cm (4½ in), two 12 cm (5 in), two 13 cm (5½ in), two 14 cm (6 in), two 15 cm (6½ in) and one 16 cm (7 in).

Point one end of each bye-stake and insert one to the right of each side stake. The longest goes next to the longest side stake, the next two longest on either side and so on.

With one side weaver, rand for 5 cm (2 in).

Cut four handle liners each 15 cm (6 in) long and sharpen one end of each to a long point. Inserting the pointed end next to a stake, position each pair of liners about 10 cm (4 in) apart, centrally on the sides of the cradle.

Use six side weavers to insert two in each of three consecutive spaces near the foot of the cradle and work a round of double waling, without completing. Use double weavers in exactly the same way as single ones.

To pack the head of the cradle, rand with one weaver to and fro on the central eleven stakes round the head of the cradle. Bring the weaver round one stake nearer the head on each row to the last two stakes nearest the head of the cradle. Fasten off the end and leave it inside the work.

On the double waling weavers at the foot of the cradle, work a row of double waling as before and complete. Trim off the bye-stakes.

Soak the stakes well and work a three-rod plain border, leaving the handle liners in place and working round them. Ensure that the bent-down stakes are resting on the waling and not twisted or lying on top of one another.

To finish the border, take each end, one by one, to the inside of the cradle beyond the stake to its right. Trim off all ends.

Soak two handle bows each 34 cm (13½ in) long and shape into a curve with the fingers. Sharpen both ends to a long point.

Remove the handle liners and insert the ends of the handle bows in their place. Take a length of chair cane and, working from the outside of the border, insert about 15 cm (6 in) of it, wrong side up towards the inside of the cradle, under the outside of the border between the rows of double waling and to the right of the handle bow. Bring the short end up inside and over the border to the outside and diagonally to the left side of the handle and re-insert it between the waling as before. Leave it pointing upwards beside the handle bow (Fig. 16).

Bring over the long end of the handle wrapper and wrap it three times round the handle bow, including the short end of the wrapping cane.

Insert a handle leader about 14 cm (5½ in) long to keep the wrapping firm.

Continue wrapping the handle alternately under and over the leader (Fig. 17), ending with three plain wraps at the other end. Tie with a cross to match the beginning and weave away the end under the border. Make a hole with the bodkin diagonally through the handle bow just below the border and peg it by inserting a small length of no. 5 cane. Trim the ends close to the work.

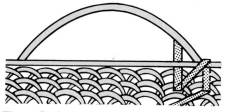

Fig. 16 Beginning to wrap cradle handle.

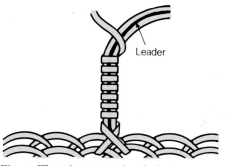

Fig. 17 Wrapping over and under leader.

Leatherwork

When man became a hunter he not only ate his kill but used the skins to clothe himself. Ever since, leather has been put to a huge variety of uses which today include furniture, clothes, shoes, handbags and other accessories, each requiring a different set of skills from the leather worker.

Leather comes in a variety of textures and thicknesses according to the animal it has come from and the treatment it has received.

This section concentrates on bags, one of which is carried on a belt. Each project introduces a new element whilst building on previously described methods of construction.

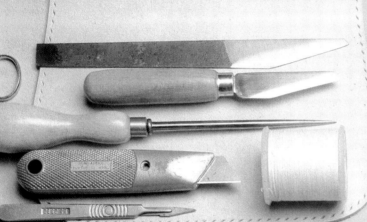

Materials and Equipment

Leather quality varies depending from which part of the animal it comes. The strongest part of the hide is the back, the belly is the softest. The outside of the hide is called the grain side while the reverse is the flesh side. Hides are only measured in metric units. Fig. 1 shows the various sections of a hide.

An oil stone and leather strap coated in oil and carborundum dust are used to keep the tools sharp.

Emery paper wrapped round a metal ruler is used to sharpen the recessed side of the edge beveller.

Shoe makers' knives and handymen's knives are particularly suitable.

A scalpel together with lino-cutting tools are used to make lino cuts.

A paring knife is used to skive (shave) down small areas.

A spoke shave is used for paring larger areas.

Edge bevellers come in various sizes and are used to round the edges.

A saddler's clamp or similar device can be used to keep leather in place while it is being stitched. Alternatively, hold the leather between the knees.

An adjustable screw-crease is used to make a continuous crease line on the grain side of the leather at a constant distance from the edge. This may be a functional line or a purely decorative line. Before use, one side of the tool has to be ground down for left- or right-hand working. It is applied when the leather is damp and is pulled towards the worker, who presses down at the same time.

Pricking irons come in various sizes. The teeth on each iron mark a specific number of stitches to the centimetre (inch) at the correct angle for sewing.

Races, double or adjustable, gouge a U-shaped groove and are used on the flesh side where the hide is to be folded or bent. As the tool is pulled towards the worker, the little semi-circular edge scoops out a groove.

Awls are used to make stitch holes.

Punches come in various shapes and sizes and should be hammered with a mallet on to a block of end grain wood.

Snap fasteners come in various sizes and each requires its own setting tool.

Harness needles have egg-shaped eyes and are blunt. They range in size from 0 (large) to 8 (small).

Linen thread is usually available in four colours. 18s/6 cord is a useful size and has been used with no. 3 needles in all the projects.

Powdered aniline dyes, used to stain the leather, are toxic. Wear rubber gloves and keep in screw top jars, away from food. Wash hands after handling.

Lino is used for lino cuts.

Neatsfoot oil is used to soften and waterproof the leather.

Hardboard is placed between the leather and a firm surface when cutting.

An ideal press is a book binding or copy press but a woodwork vice can suffice.

An anvil is used to set rivets and press studs.

A small piece of felt on the end of a stick is used to finish the edges.

Beeswax is used for drawing the thread through before sewing.

A shellac flakes and methylated spirits mixture is applied to edges of leather.

General items include hammer, scissors, dividers, a metal ruler, T square, pens and pencils, a rubber-based impact adhesive, soft polishing cloths, canvas cloth, cotton wool, card, tracing paper and a straight edge.

Know how

Making templates
Cut out the shapes of the pieces of leather required on card first.

Use a dotted line in ink to mark the centre line, the positions of any fastenings and the stitch lines.

Cutting the leather
Draw round the template on the grain side of the leather and prick through the position of any fastenings and centre line at the base of each piece. Mark this centre point with a pen when the piece has been cut out.

Place the leather over a piece of hardboard on a firm surface. Cut with a sharp knife keeping the blade vertical to avoid undercutting. Cut straight edges with a knife drawn along a metal ruler, taking care to keep fingers well out of the way. It helps to turn the leather whilst cutting round corners.

Marking
On the front piece of leather only, mark round the stitch line with a pricking iron. For curves, hold the iron up at an angle so that only a few teeth are used at a time.

Staining and polishing
Wearing rubber gloves, mix the powdered aniline dye. Start with 5 ml to 0.5 litre (one teaspoonful to $\frac{3}{4}$ pint) and allow to stand for five minutes for the powder to dissolve and the true colour to show. Increase the strength gradually until the desired colour is reached. An over strong solution will result in a metallic sheen.

Wet the surface of the leather with warm water. Print on any pattern (see below). Apply the stain with cotton wool while the leather is still damp. Using small circular motions, work horizontally from left to right across the work then back again from right to left immediately below the first line and continue in this way until the whole area has been covered. Repeat in a vertical direction until a uniform covering has been achieved. Build up the colour with several applications.

Polish with a piece of silk or soft cloth while the leather is still damp. Watch out for any pieces of grit which will scratch the surface.

Oiling
When the stain is completely dry, the leather is oiled with hand hot neatsfoot oil. Warm the neatsfoot oil in a tin over a flame. When it is warm and liquid, apply with a cloth. When oiling very light-coloured surfaces, start by wiping the grain side with a warm and barely oily cloth to get an even initial covering before applying a heavier coat. The flesh side can be heavily oiled. This improves the colour and makes the leather both more supple and water-resistant. Leave overnight to allow the oil to be thoroughly absorbed.

Glueing the edges
Lightly score the surfaces to be glued. Apply impact adhesive to both sides. When almost dry, line up the centre marks on each edge. Press together.

Sewing
The method traditionally used is with two needles. The double thread formation ensures strength and an even stitch on both sides.

Hold small items of work in position in a saddler's clamp or other improvized device or between the knees. Keep the awl blade horizontal as it is pushed through the leather.

Cut a piece of thread about three times the length of the seam and pull through a piece of beeswax. Cut the ends diagonally and flatten between the thumb and index finger before threading a needle on each end. To secure the needles, if necessary, thread a short length through the eye and,

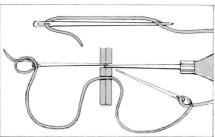

Fig. 1 Sections of a hide.

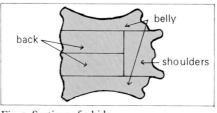

Fig. 2 Securing a needle and Fig. 3 inserting 2 needles.

Fig. 4 Formation of double stitching.

Fig. 5 Skiving.

holding the needle in the right hand, pierce the longer end with the needle point and pull the thread down over the needle (Fig. 2).

Push the awl through both thicknesses at the first stitch mark, following the angle made by the pricking iron. Put one needle through the hole and pull through until there is an equal amount of thread on either side.

Push the awl through the next stitch mark, place the left hand needle against the awl blade and keeping them together push the needle in as the awl is withdrawn (Fig. 3). Insert the right hand needle behind the left hand one so that both are in the hole at the same time then pull both needles through. Continue along the seam (Fig. 4).

Finish off by taking the threads round the end of the leather then sew back for three holes. Cut each thread close to its exit side of the third hole.

On small pieces it is easier to make the holes first before stitching.

Edging
Trim the edges and bevel them.

Using a piece of felt on the end of a stick, apply a thin coating of shellac dissolved in methylated spirits and mixed with a dark stain. Polish by rubbing hard with a cloth.

Moulding
Once all the seams have been completed, immerse the article in warm water until it becomes soft.

Run the fingers along the inside of the leather and along the seams, forcing the leather out into a curved shape.

Stuff with paper and leave to dry slowly in a warm place but not near direct heat.

Skiving
This process is used where two pieces of leather overlap to reduce the thickness so that there is no unsightly bulge.

Place the leather on top of a piece of scrap leather on the working surface so that the side to be skived is uppermost. Using a sharp paring knife, shave off thin layers of leather with sawing motions, so that the edge is shaped to an angle (Fig. 5).

Lino cutting
Draw the design on tracing paper and then transfer it to a piece of lino. The foreground of the design is cut out with a scalpel and the finished lino cut glued on to card.

When the leather is damp prior to staining, place the lino cut face down on the surface of the leather in the exact position for the design. Clamp the two together for a few moments in a press.

Purse

This small purse is made from two pieces of leather stitched together and makes an ideal first project.

You will need
Leather cut from the shoulder or belly of 3 mm russet skirt hide:
● front piece, 11 cm by 9 cm ($4\frac{1}{4}$ in by $3\frac{1}{2}$ in)
● back piece 11 cm by 18 cm ($4\frac{1}{4}$ in by 7 in)
● snap fastener and setting tool
● leather work equipment as given on page 17

Instructions
All the techniques required for this project are given opposite.

Draw the two templates (Fig. 6) enlarged to their full size and cut out. Mark the position of the snap fastener.

Place the smaller template over the larger one and mark with a dot on either side at the top edge of the smaller one to show where the stitching begins and ends. Mark the stitch line about 3 mm ($\frac{1}{8}$ in) in from the edge.

Draw round the templates, pricking through the position of the snap fastener and the centre marks.

Cut out and indicate the base centre marks on the edges with a pen. Bevel all the edges not to be stitched together with a no. 2 edge beveller on both flesh and grain sides.

Make a stitch line with the dividers round the edge of the front and mark the stitches with a no. 4 or no. 6 pricking iron. Wet, stain and polish.

While the leather is still damp, make a crease line along the top of the front of the purse and around the flap with the adjustable screw-crease.

When completely dry, oil and leave over night.

Apply shellac to the bevelled edges and polish with a piece of canvas.

Punch the holes for the snap fastener fittings and set them in.

Glue back and front together.

Stitch, making the first and last stitches a double one over the top edge of the front piece.

Mould the purse in warm water so

that the stitched part of the purse is curved in a three-dimensional shape. Stuff with paper and leave to dry.

Finish the stitched edges by trimming them with a sharp knife. Bevel back and front, apply shellac and polish.

Braided belt

This belt is made from one strip of leather. The width of the belt is determined by the buckle, which is measured in imperial units, so only imperial measurements are given.

You will need
Cut from the back of 3 mm russet skirt hide:
● belt piece, $1\frac{3}{4}$ in by length required
● buckle piece 6 in by $1\frac{1}{4}$ in
● loop piece $\frac{5}{8}$ in by $4\frac{1}{2}$ in
● buckle with bar measuring $1\frac{1}{4}$ in
● leatherwork equipment as given on page 17

Instructions
All the techniques required for this project are given on page 18.

Draw the two templates (Fig. 7) enlarged to their full size and cut out.

Check the buckle for its exact width. Mark a slot along the centre line of the

The purse and belt make ideal first projects.

template to take the buckle prong by punching two holes the correct size and distance apart, then cut a slot between them.

On template B, punch six holes 1 in apart along the centre line, starting 3 in from the shaped end.

Using a metal edge and knife, cut a strip of leather exactly $1\frac{1}{4}$ in wide and to the length required remembering that the braided part will shrink to approximately three-quarters its original length when completed.

Leaving the first 10 in of the better end uncut, split the rest of the belt into seven $\frac{1}{4}$ in strips.

Using a no. 1 beveller, bevel the grain and flesh sides of the thongs.

Cut a strip $\frac{5}{8}$ in wide and approximately $4\frac{1}{2}$ in long for the loose loop.

Bevel the longer edges, back and front.

Draw round and cut out the buckle piece A, including the buckle slot. Make a stitch line round the edge, then, using a no. 6 pricking iron, mark a line of stitches on what will be the front side when folded over the buckle. Make the first stitch mark on a line with the end of the slot and continue down, along the bottom and up the other side, finishing exactly opposite the first stitch.

Bevel the grain edge only. Skive $\frac{3}{4}$ in at either end on the flesh side.

Wet and stain all pieces, including the flesh side and all the edges. Polish the grain side.

Mark the edges of the loop with a screw-crease.

When completely dry, oil on both sides and leave to dry.

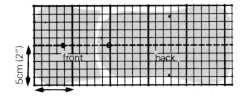

Fig. 6 Purse templates.

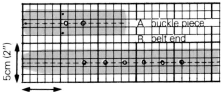

Fig. 7 Belt templates.

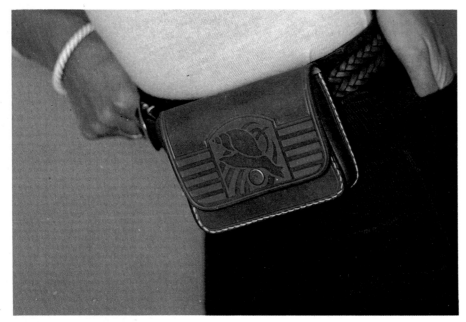

Fig. 8 Braiding for belt.

Finish the edges with shellac, including the buckle slot but not 10 in of untrimmed belt end.

Submerge the thongs in lukewarm water then braid (Fig. 8) as follows:

take D over E; B under C and E; G over F and under D and B; A over C and under E and G; F over D and under B and A. Continue as shown in Fig. 8, following the basic pattern of passing each outer thong over one thong and under two. Keep the braid as tight and even as possible, re-soaking if necessary to keep leather soft.

When finished, tie the ends together and hang up to dry. When completely dry, work the braid by pulling and bending to make it more supple and even.

Using template B, mark out the belt end and trim it, taking care to curve the edges out slightly to meet the braided part. Do not trim down the two outer thongs.

Punch the holes, soak the end and mark round the holes with a screw-crease.

When dry, bevel the edges back and front, shellac and polish them.

Cut the open end of the braid straight across at the required length,

The belt pouch with a lino cut decoration.

after adding an extra ¾ in.

Unravel the last couple of inches of the braid and skive ⅝ in of each thong on the flesh side, then re-braid.

Apply warm water to both sides of the buckle piece fold to avoid cracking.

Score and apply glue to the flesh side of the buckle piece and to both sides of the last ⅝ in of the braid. Fold the buckle piece around the buckle and press the two halves together, sandwiching the last ¾ in of the braid between the two ends and making sure the edges correspond exactly.

Sew, making a double overstitch over the side edges near the buckle to hold it securely and continue round the buckle piece, finishing with a double overstitch on the other side.

Bend the loop strip around both the braid and the end of the belt to find its correct length, allowing an overlap.

Splice the overlap together by skiving the flesh side of one end and the grain side of the other. Glue and sew up the loop making two rows of awl holes over the splice before stitching.

Polish the stitching and the rest of the belt with a soft cloth.

Belt pouch

This pouch is made from four pieces of leather and is decorated with a lino cut.

You will need

3 mm russet skirt hide from the shoulder:
• back piece, approximately 17 cm by 23 cm (6½ in by 9 in)

• front piece, approximately 16 cm by 12 cm (6¼ in by 4¾ in)
• belt loop, approximately 8 cm (3¼ in) square
2 mm thick hide from the belly:
• gusset, 4.5 cm (1¼ in) wide
• leatherwork equipment as given on page 17

Instructions

All the techniques required for this project are given on page 18.

Draw templates (Fig. 9) enlarged to their full size and cut out.

Cut the gusset long enough to go round the edge of the front of the pouch with an additional 1 cm (½ in) overlap at either end. Leather which is thicker than 2 mm can be reduced with a spoke shave or paring knife.

Make two grooves on the flesh side of the gusset with an adjustable race, the first 5 mm (³⁄₁₆ in) in from edge A, the second 12 mm (½ in) from edge B (Fig. 10). Mark the centre on both edges.

Cut out the back, front and belt loop and make the centre marks.

Make the lino cut (Fig. 11).

Prepare the leather for staining and press the lino cut on the front flap. Mark the front and round the flap and back section with a double crease line, using a screw-crease and omitting the outer crease line at any stitch marks. On the flap the double groove separates for the inner one to go over the

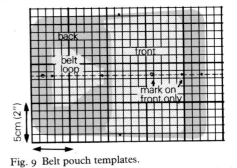

Fig. 9 Belt pouch templates.

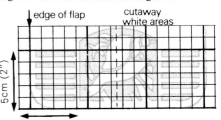

Fig. 10 Grooves on flesh side of gusset.

Fig. 11 Lino cut design.

top of the lino cut imprint and the outer one round the edge.

Stain and polish all the pieces.

Oil the pieces then apply shellac and polish the bevelled edges.

Attach the belt loop to the back of the pouch, stitching along the top edge on the flesh side of the loop, bend it over and sew along the bottom as shown in Fig. 12.

Set in the press stud.

Lay the gusset, grain side up, on the work surface and bend up edge A along the groove on the flesh side. Fold edge B in the opposite direction.

Bend the gusset into the correct shape, using the front of the pouch as a guide (Fig. 13).

Apply glue to the turned-over edge B of the gusset and under the front edge of the pouch. When almost dry, lay the gusset on the bench and press the front on to it, lining up the centre marks and working out to either corner.

Turn work face down and slip a piece of scrap leather between the gusset and the front. Snip out several notches at the corners of edge B. Remove the scrap of leather.

Press the rest together firmly. Trim off the excess gusset and finish the end edges by bevelling, applying shellac and polishing.

Stitch the front to the gusset, one half at a time, starting at the centre and working outwards. End by making a double stitch over the top edge of the front and the gusset, finish off.

Glue the back of the pouch on to the turned-out gusset edge, lining up centre marks.

Press on to the gusset, one half at a time, leaving the gusset edge protruding by about 2 mm ($\frac{1}{8}$ in).

Sew from the centre out, ending with a double stitch over the edge of the gusset before finishing off.

Immerse the pouch in warm water and mould it into shape. Stuff the pouch with paper and leave to dry.

When dry, carefully trim away the overlapping gusset edge plus a fraction of the back of the pouch to remove any bits of glue. Bevel the gusset edge, apply shellac and polish.

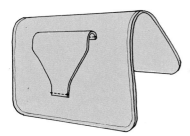

Fig. 12 Stitching belt loop.

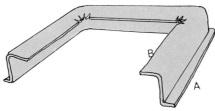

Fig. 13 Bending the gusset.

Always in fashion – a bag in real leather.

Shoulder bag

This bag requires eight separate templates, one of which is only used to mark the position of the pocket.

You will need
● 11 pieces of leather: the main pieces, i.e. the back, front and pocket front should be cut from a piece from the shoulder of a 3 mm russet skirt hide; the gussets from a softer bit of belly. See Fig. 14 for measurements
● two D rings
● four rivets
● buckle with bar 2 cm ($\frac{7}{8}$ in) wide
● leatherwork equipment as given on page 17

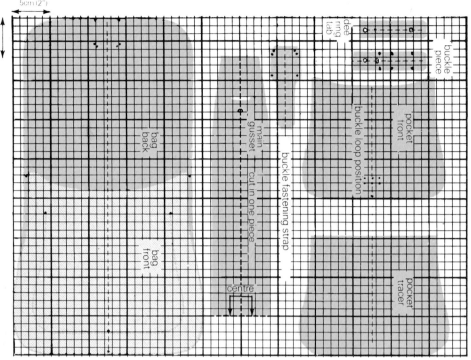

5cm (2")

bag back

bag front

main gusset cut in one piece

centre

buckle fastening strap

buckle loop position

dee ring tab

buckle piece

buckle piece

pocket front

pocket tracer

Fig. 14 Bag templates.

Instructions

All the techniques for this project are given on page 18.

Draw the templates (Fig. 14) enlarged to their full size and cut out. The bag front is drawn on top of the bag back in Fig. 14. Cut the pocket tracer 3 mm ($\frac{1}{8}$ in) larger round all the edges except the top one, to accommodate the turned out gusset. On the front template mark the position of the pocket tracer with dots at its top corners and centre base. Indicate the position of the buckle loop on the template for the pocket front. Show all other relevant information on the templates.

Allow a small surplus at either end of the gusset to be trimmed off after glueing to the flesh side of the front. Make a slot at each end of the gusset to accommodate the D ring tabs, positioned sufficiently low to prevent the riveted ends of the bag strap protruding over the top of the gusset. Punch a hole approximately 12 mm ($\frac{1}{2}$ in) below each slot to take a rivet.

Cut out all the pieces as well as a shoulder strap to fit the D rings, a short length for the buckle loop and a strip approximately 4.5 cm ($1\frac{3}{4}$ in) wide for the front pocket gusset. This should be long enough to fit round the front pocket piece plus an extra 12 mm ($\frac{1}{2}$ in) at each end. When cutting the front template, prick through the dots marking the top corners and centre base of the pocket.

Make the stitch marks on all pieces.

Bevel on both the flesh and grain sides all the edges of the unstitched part of the back piece, the top edge of the front piece and all the edges of the pocket front.

Wet, stain and polish all the pieces. While still damp, mark a double crease line with a screw-crease all round the flap, and across the tops of the pocket and the front. When dry, oil all the pieces and leave overnight. Apply shellac solution to these edges and polish with canvas.

Using a no. 6 pricking iron, mark the lines of stitches on the buckle piece. Bevel the grain edge only. Apply warm water to both sides of the buckle piece. Fold the strip over the buckle so that there is 2.5 cm (1 in) behind it. Skive the flesh side of the edge of the small folded piece. Make a stitch over the edge as near to the buckle as possible then stitch away from the buckle for the required number of stitches. Take both needles behind the buckle piece and twist the two threads together across the back before sewing up towards the buckle on the other side. End with a stitch over the edge to correspond with the other side.

Form the strip for the buckle loop over the combined thickness of the fastening strap and the buckle piece just below the buckle, allowing an overlap. Splice the overlap by skiving the flesh side of one end and the grain side of the other and glueing together. Stitch the loop on to the front of the pocket in the position marked.

Make two grooves on the gusset for the front pocket as shown in Fig. 10.

Make a line of stitch marks along the turned-out edge A. Bevel, apply shellac and polish the edge. Referring back to Fig. 13, form, glue and stitch the gusset for the front pocket.

Attach the buckle to the pocket by passing the end of the buckle piece through the loop and stitching it on to the underside of the gusset.

To attach the pocket, first place the tracer on the bag front, lining it up with the three marks pricked through from the template. Lightly draw around the two sides and bottom of the tracer. Using the point of a knife, carefully scratch a wide line round the inside of the tracer line for glueing on the gusset, but do not scratch too near the tracer line, as it might show.

Apply glue to the scratched area and the edge of the gusset. Take care to glue the gusset down evenly using the line as a guide and starting by positioning the gusset ends and base centre marks. When glued in position, run the back of a spoon handle over the stitch marks to press down firmly.

Stitch on the pocket.

With an adjustable race, make a groove 2 cm ($\frac{3}{8}$ in) in from each edge of the gusset on the flesh side. Make a corresponding line on the grain side.

Punch the D ring slots and rivet holes on the main gusset, staining the insides of the slots. Fix the D rings in position by folding the prepared tabs over them, lining up the two rivet holes and passing the tabs through the slots before riveting to the inside of the gusset.

Immerse the gusset in warm water to soften it and lay flat, grain side up, to bend the edges at right angles. Form it into the correct shape. Leave to dry.

Apply glue to one side of the gusset edge and to the bag front on the flesh sides. Glue together pressing the bag front on to the gusset, starting with the centre marks and working outwards. The edge of the gusset should protrude slightly. Cut the surplus at either end, bevel, apply shellac and polish.

Start stitching from the centre outwards ending with a double stitch over the top edge. Do not finish off.

Trim, bevel, apply shellac and polish the last 2.5 cm (1 in) of the gusset and front of the bag then work two double stitches over the side of the bag before finishing off.

Sew up the back in the same way.

Immerse the bag in warm water, mould and stuff with paper.

When dry, trim, bevel, apply shellac and polish the edges. Sew the buckle fastening tab in position, punching a hole in the appropriate place.

Rivet the strap on to the D rings.

Pottery

Because of the recent introduction of self hardening clays, pottery is now a craft which can be done at home without complicated equipment. This new type of clay can be decorated with almost any paint, pen or crayon. However, it is not as hard-wearing as fired pottery and cannot be used for food containers, put in the oven or washed.

Materials and Equipment

The clay ought to be one of the several varieties available which contain natural clay and are water soluble (for example ColdClay). The techniques given here require clay which can be mixed with water, rolled, cut and coiled.

The working surface must be smooth and hard wearing, so that the clay can be scraped or sponged off it.

Tools can include ordinary household items:

Redundant kitchen knives for cutting; a length of wire or fishing nylon with a toggle at either end, to slice through lumps of clay; a thick sewing needle set into a piece of cork for cutting, marking and trimming; a sponge for smoothing over surfaces; water containers; a rolling pin for rolling out slabs of clay; hessian, polythene or newspaper on which to roll the slabs; short pieces of wood about 5 mm ($\frac{1}{4}$ in) thick; paint brushes for applying slip and for painting; paints, either poster, acrylic and powder colours, oils, spray paints, wax crayons and pastels, or even household paints.

Varnishes such as polyurethane can provide a water resistant finish and increased gloss.

Special purchases include box wood modelling tools, available in a wide variety of shapes; wire-ended tools for paring down or hollowing out models, although these can be improvized by bending a piece of metal wire over the end of a piece of wood and securing with string; a banding wheel which is a turntable, allowing a pot to be turned as it is worked on, without actually being moved – a cake icing stand would suffice.

Know how

There are only a few techniques in hand built pottery. These take advantage of the fact that clay is soft and pliable. However, it cannot be forced to do things not in its nature such as taking a lot of strain or being used in long lengths without support. Do not overwork the clay or it will become 'tired' and will crack or even collapse. Each technique should be practised and experimented with.

Clay

A self hardening clay containing natural clay will become hard if left unwrapped but can be softened again with water, provided the surface has not been decorated with paints or varnish.

The clay can be prevented from drying out by wrapping in polythene.

Slip

Whichever method of modelling is used, it is more than likely that at some stage two or more pieces of clay will have to be joined. This is done when the clay is leather hard (see below). First score the edges lightly with a knife in a criss-cross pattern, called cross-hatching.

Make some slip by mixing water and clay to a paste of about the consistency

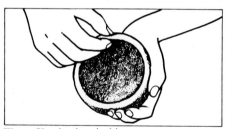
Fig. 1 Shaping by pinching.

of double cream. Spread the slip over the edges and press them together. Smooth the join, wiping away any slip which oozes out.

Leather hard

When the clay is half way between soft and hard this is called leather hard or, sometimes, cheese hard. It is at this stage that any carving or scraping is done.

Shaping

Pinching. Pinching is a good shaping technique to learn first as the clay is worked in the hands and will therefore give the beginner a knowledge of the material. This seemingly simple technique often requires practice.

Take a ball of clay which fits comfortably in the palm of the left hand (the reverse for left handers). Push the right thumb gently into the centre of the clay, but not right through. Pinch the clay between the thumb and first two fingers of the right hand, gently forming the walls of the pot. Keep the clay moist by wetting it occasionally (Fig. 1).

Turn the ball slowly, pinching the walls and gradually opening out the pot. Continue rotating and pinching until the walls are the desired thickness. Try to keep the sides an even thickness. The basic shape formed by this movement will be a small bowl shape.

This simple hollow form has many uses. For example, two bowls with the same diameter at the rim can be joined together to make a spherical shape. To do this the rims should each be scored, moistened, then gently pressed together (Fig. 2) and the join smoothed over with a wooden modelling tool

(Fig. 3). The sphere can be further shaped whilst leather hard by patting it with a ruler and then cutting out sections with a knife (Fig. 4).

Coiling. Coils are rolled out and then secured one on top of another to build up a shape. Shapes can be circular, geometric, irregular or a combination of these.

Take a small lump of clay and roll it gently into a sausage shape. Place it on the working surface and, starting with the tips of the fingers of both hands, roll the sausage into a long, thin coil (Fig. 5).

Make several coils of moderate length as long coils tend to break when picked up. Keep the clay moist by wetting the hands.

To build up shapes, start with a flat piece of clay for the base. The shape of the base will depend on the shape of the finished pot.

Lay one coil around the circumference of the base. Break the coil and form a complete ring. Using the forefinger, make sure that the two are firmly attached by pressing clay at the bottom of the coil on to the base, both inside and outside the pot.

Make a second coil on top of the first. The second coil is joined to the first by pressing the soft clay from the bottom coil upwards to the top coil with the thumb on the outside of the pot, supporting both coils on the inside with the fingers. Then on the inside, press the newly added coil downwards with the thumb, supporting the outside with the fingers. This ensures a good join and a wall of parallel thickness, with the join smoothed out.

Continue adding coils until the pot

Fig. 2 Scoring the edges.

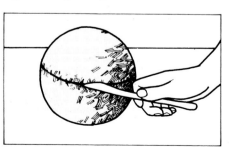
Fig. 3 Smoothing over the join.

Fig. 4 Cutting out designs from sphere.

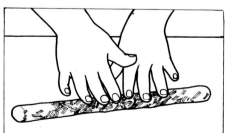
Fig. 5 Rolling out a coil.

Fig. 6 Cutting slabs using a template.

Fig. 7 Scoring the edges.

is as tall as required. The cylinder is made by making each new coil ring the same diameter as the last. For an open shape, make each new coil slightly larger than the last; to close in the shape, make each coil smaller than the last.

Smooth over the rim of the pot with a damp sponge.

Joining coils. To join two pieces within one coil, overlap the ends. Place fingers over the join and roll together until the join is the same thickness as the rest of the coil.

Slabbing. For this technique the clay is rolled out into slabs and partly dried so that it will stand up. It can then be joined to other pieces. This is useful for making straight, vertical sides for a square, rectangular, or geometrically shaped base.

Cover the working surface with newspaper or hessian. A porous surface is necessary so that it can be peeled off the clay easily.

Place a lump of clay on this surface and roll it out with a rolling pin. To ensure an even thickness, place the clay between two pieces of wood 5 mm ($\frac{1}{4}$ in) thick and roll over the clay and the wood.

Leave the slabs to dry out a little. When leather hard, mark and cut to size with the knife, using a ruler or template to ensure straight edges (Fig. 6).

To join two pieces, score the edges which will come into contact with each other lightly with a sharp knife (Fig. 7), then moisten with slip. Press the two edges gently but firmly together and smooth over the join with a modelling tool.

For a cylindrical shape, cut a circle for the base. Cut the sides in one piece with one side the measurement of the circumference of the base and the adjacent side the measurement of the height of the pot. Do not leave the clay to dry but prepare the edge of the slab at the outside of the circular base as before. Also score and moisten both ends of the rectangle. Form it into a cylinder round the base, smoothing all joins. Use a cardboard tube or a jam jar (covered with newspaper to prevent sticking) as a support inside if desired, but remember to remove the support before the clay dries on to it.

Combining the techniques. Once each technique has been thoroughly mastered they can be combined. For instance, a pot with a slabbed base could be finished with a coiled neck

and rim. Pinch pots can be completed with coils and, conversely, a coiled pot can have a fine, pinched out rim which can be frilled or pleated.

It is best to experiment to find all the possible permutations.

Decoration

There are many ways of decorating pottery, carried out at different stages of the drying process.

Impressed. When the clay is leather hard it can be cut, scraped or carved and have things like beads pressed into it to make patterns.

Relief. Relief decoration involves adding pieces of clay to the surface using slip.

Piercing. This is a form of decoration made by cutting shapes out of the clay.

When the clay is leather hard, draw out the shape on the clay with a needle, either freehand or round a template.

Use either a sharp knife with a thin, pointed blade or, for round holes, a special hole cutter or a piece of hollow tubing. Push the cutter gently at right angles through the clay, supporting the clay from behind. Turn it gently whilst pushing. With a knife, work in a stabbing motion all along the design, taking it out of the clay completely before moving further along and repeating. Never use a sawing motion.

Remove any shavings with a dry brush before sponging smooth. Piercing can also be worked through relief decoration.

Painting. The clay is painted when completely dry using any of the paints mentioned on page 23. Water colours are no use because they sink into the surface of the clay. Varnish as a last coat gives an increased gloss and a waterproof finish.

Surface treatments. One unique feature of ColdClay is that it is sensitive to light. If left to dry in the light it dries a matt black colour; if covered it dries a light grey. This feature can be used as decoration. Cutting a stencil and sticking it to the surface until the pot has hardened creates a pale grey area surrounded by the black. Black areas can be further emphasized by rubbing over them with black boot polish to produce a strong contrast.

The surface can also be burnished to produce a smooth, dark, somewhat metallic finish, particularly suitable for models and sculptures. Use the back of a spoon to rub over and over the surface of the dried pot until it is shiny. Use a circular movement.

Badges

Badges are particularly appealing to children and many of them, even quite young ones, will enjoy making clay badges for themselves. A little help may be needed with rolling out the clay. Then they could dream up all sorts of decoration – perhaps their own name, or crazy coloured patterns.

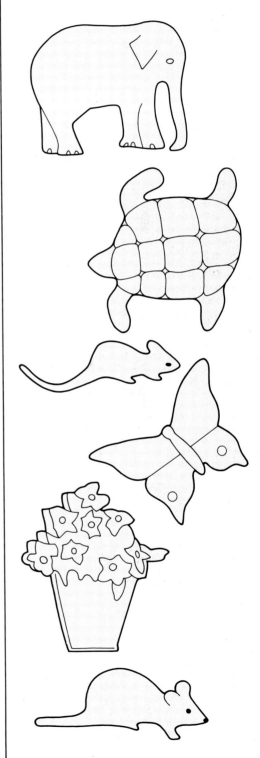

Fig. 8 Templates for the badges.

These badges are quick and easy to make so several can be made and then worn together.

Pomanders

Pomanders are always a welcome addition to any room, releasing the fragrance of the dried flower petals that they contain. Those illustrated here are made by the pinching method and have simple basic shapes.

You will need
- Self hardening modelling clay
- card
- scissors
- glitter
- glue
- brooch mounts
- modelling equipment as given on page 23

Instructions
All the techniques required for this project are given on pages 24 and 25.

Prepare the working surface and place the two wooden guides about 30 cm (12 in) apart with the ball of clay in the middle. Roll out the clay and leave for five to ten minutes to harden slightly.

Draw the outlines of the badges on the card and cut round to make templates (Fig. 8). Place the templates over the clay and cut round them with a knife. Smooth over the rough edges and leave the badges to dry out for one day.

When the badges are dry they can be decorated as desired. To add some glitter, paint the surface and the sides and when completely dry, spread some glue over the surface and sprinkle on the glitter.

Leave to dry.

To waterproof the badge, paint a layer of varnish over the decoration. Make sure all the surfaces are covered. Leave to dry.

Finally, glue a brooch mount to the back of the badge.

You will need
- Modelling clay
- dried flower petals or dried lavender
- modelling equipment as given on page 23

Instructions
All the techniques required for this project are given on pages 24 and 25.

Take two equally sized lumps of clay and form each into a ball which will fit comfortably in the palm of the hand. Beginners will find it easier to work on a small shape.

Work each piece of clay into a half sphere shape by pinching, making the rim fairly thick.

Join the half spheres together. Do not worry about the overall shape at this stage.

Roll out a thin coil, moisten and wind it round the sphere over the join. Smooth the coil over the join.

The air sealed inside supports the ball so that it can be gently rolled on a flat surface to even out any lumps and bumps. If necessary, leave the clay to harden for a few hours and roll again until a good shape is achieved. Once the clay is leather hard it will keep its shape without the air trapped inside.

Use a knife to cut it in half. Do this in either a straight line or in a petal shaped design as illustrated. Smooth over the edges.

Thin the insides of the pomander by gradually scraping the clay away with a wire-ended tool. Support the outside walls with the fingers. They should be about 5 mm ($\frac{1}{4}$ in) thick.

Finally, smooth over the insides with a modelling tool.

Holes through which the perfume can escape are an essential aspect of the design. When leather hard, work a pierced decoration.

The surface pattern could also

Below left In the foreground the two halves of the pomander have been cut following the petal shapes. Both pomanders have pierced and painted decoration. **Top right** The various coils making up the night light holder have been picked out in two shades of blue. **Below right** Hills and fields are suggested by the front and middle sections of the letter rack and clouds by the back.

include relief and impressed decoration. Small modelling tools can be used when pressing patterns into the soft clay, or metal tools for carving the clay when leather hard.

When the clay is dry, paint the pomanders.

Night light holder

This holder is designed to take either an ordinary candle or a night light. It is built up from coils of clay which form an attractive lattice for the candle light to shine through.

You will need
- Modelling clay
- two wooden guides
- candle or night light
- paint in two different colours
- modelling equipment as given on page 23

Instructions
All the techniques required for this project are given on pages 24 and 25.

Roll a small ball of clay into a slab. Cut it into a square, measuring 14 cm square (5½ in square). Set aside for four hours or until leather hard.

Cut out two paper discs, one 11.5 cm (4½ in) in diameter and a smaller one, 9 cm (3½ in). Mark out the discs into 5 sections (Fig. 9). These are the guides for the star-shaped coils. The base takes four large stars and the lid four smaller ones.

Roll out several coils, some about 6 mm (¼ in) thick and some 8 mm (⅜ in). With the first thicker coil, form the inner star as shown in Fig. 9. Pinch the curves at the centre of the star to neaten.

Next take a second thicker coil and lay it round the outside of the star following the shape in and out, as in Fig. 10. Make sure that the coils have stuck together at the joins.

Remove the shape carefully from the paper disc and set aside. Leave it in the warm to dry out and harden. Do the same for the remaining 3 large stars and 4 small ones.

Assembling the base
Place each large star in position on the base (see Fig. 11) and mark the base where it touches, lightly with a needle. Remove the stars and score the points of contact with a knife or needle, then apply some slip to this area. Assemble the four sides of the bottom by pressing each larger star into its position on the base. Brush on a little slip at the

place where the upper points of the stars touch each other.

To make the construction more stable wind another coil inside the base and loop it to fill in the corner spaces.

Spread some slip over the top edges of the sides. Lay a coil over the tops of the stars, following the points up and down. Press down firmly (Fig. 12).

Trim small triangles from the corners of the base to fit the position of the stars.

Assembling the lid
First fill the base with loosely-rolled newspaper so that it forms a dome above the sides. Lay a coil on top of the last coil on the base, following it exactly, but not sticking to it. (If it does stick, it can be cut later on.)

Position the four small stars on this coil as shown in Fig. 13. Fix them to each other and to the coil with slip. Three further coils are needed to fill in the space at the centre of the lid. The first follows the outline of the stars, the next is slightly smaller and the third is almost circular (see Fig. 14). Join them all together with slip.

Finally, to make a round knob, wind a coil into a ring. Set it upright and attach it to the centre with slip.

When the clay has hardened enough to be handled, smooth over the inside to strengthen the joins. Smooth over any rough surfaces with a moist sponge. Paint in the colours of your choice. Varnish. Place a candle inside.

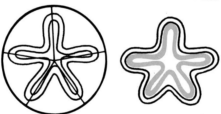

Fig. 9 Forming inner star over paper disc.
Fig. 10 Laying second coil.

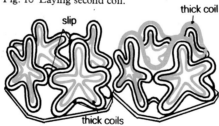

Fig. 11 Positioning large stars on base.
Fig. 12 Laying coil at top of base.

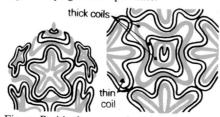

Fig. 13 Positioning 4 stars for lid.
Fig. 14 Finishing the lid.

Letter rack

The letter rack is made using the slabbing technique with a landscape theme of clouds, hills and fields.

You will need
- Modelling clay
- two wooden guides
- stiff paper
- modelling equipment as given on page 23

Instructions
All the techniques required for this project are given on pages 24 and 25.

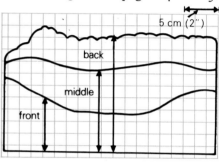

Fig. 15 Templates for letter rack.

Make paper templates of the landscape shapes by enlarging Fig. 15.

Roll out the clay into sufficient slabs for all the pieces so that they can dry evenly. Cut out a base 30 cm by 12 cm (11½ in by 4½ in), two sides each 12 cm by 16 cm (4½ in by 6½ in) and three vertical sections, each 28 cm by 18 cm (11 in by 7 in).

Allow all six rectangles to dry out for about four hours.

Place the templates over the clay and mark out the shape with the point of a needle. Cut away the unwanted clay with a knife.

Paint the landscape features on the middle and back vertical sections. Paint the remaining sections in the colour of your choice.

Assemble the letter rack, first preparing the edges which are to be joined.

First fix the front vertical section on top of the base, leaving a 5 mm (¼ in) gap at either end for the sides.

Next position the two other vertical sections, then the sides. Reinforce all the vertical joins and along the base of the first and middle vertical sections.

Drape a damp cloth or sheet of polythene over the letter rack so that it dries slowly and evenly. When leather hard, smooth the joins.

Leave to dry in a warm atmosphere for two or three days.

Varnish when completely dry.

Pressed flowers

Flowers preserved by drying and pressing have a delicacy which adds another dimension to the pleasure of keeping a permanent record of flowers and grasses from the garden.

It is a craft which requires careful preparation and patience while the flowers are being pressed and dried – the longer the flowers are kept in the press the better the result will be. Once a collection of pressed flowers has been accumulated, skill and imagination can be used to display them in many different arrangements.

Materials and Equipment

Sheets of white blotting paper.

Whole newspapers should be kept in plentiful supply.

A pointed knife.

A pair of scissors.

Heavy, even weights can be improvized by using large books.

An iron.

Two pieces of hardboard each half the size of the newspapers.

Flowers, leaves, ferns: most types can be pressed, although some keep their colour better than others – white flowers have a tendency to go brown. Bulky flowers cannot be pressed whole.

Glue which dries clear.

Cocktail sticks are useful for applying glue.

Fine paint and pastry brushes are useful for moving the pressed flowers when assembling a design.

Card, perspex, transparent seal, glass, hardboard, felt, handles and picture frames are also used to make up the projects on which pressed flowers are displayed.

General items include cartridge paper, pens, pencils and a ruler, Sellotape and double-sided Sellotape.

Know how

Making a pad

Flowers are pressed on top of a firm but resilient pad. Start with a piece of hardboard half the size of the newspaper.

Make sure newspapers are dry by ironing and storing in an airing cupboard for a few days, then make a thick layer with two whole newspapers folded in half.

Fold the blotting paper in half and lay one half of the blotting paper on top of the newspaper pad.

Picking the flowers

Always pick flowers at their best, when they are fully open. Try, too, to pick them when they are at their driest; the middle of the day is usually best as the dew has evaporated by this time. Press them **immediately** after they have been picked.

Preparing the flowers

Remove any stems or leaves from the flowers. These can be pressed separately if needed.

Flat leaves and flowers, for example pansy, poppy, buttercup, daisy and primrose, are easiest to press. Remove any stalk from the flower and place it face down.

For daisy-like flowers, some of the thickness underneath should be removed as shown in Fig. 1a. Alternatively, flat flowers can be folded in half before pressing to give a side view.

Small flowers such as lily-of-the-valley, forget-me-not and scilla can be pressed whole.

Cupped flower heads such as tulip, narcissus and hyacinth are cut in half and each half pressed separately. Cut through the stem and the flower, remove the stamens, stigma and style and then place both halves on the pressing pad (Fig. 1b).

Bulky flower heads like carnation and chrysanthemum have to be separated into single petals before they are pressed. Roses and fuchsia should be cut through the thickest part and pressed separately. Squeeze these gently between the thumb and forefinger before placing on the blotting paper.

Pressing the flowers

Always press more flowers than you expect to use.

Keep similar flowers in one layer, making sure that they do not touch each other. Do not mix thicknesses of flower.

Lay the flowers at different angles, some face down and some sideways. Allow space for each bloom to spread when flattened.

When the blotting paper is covered, fold the other half over the top. Great care is needed at this stage to avoid unwanted creases. Sellotape the edges of the blotting paper together.

Cover the whole sheet of blotting paper with one whole newspaper folded in half. Continue in this way if there are more flowers to press to a maximum of six layers of flowers. Finish with two newspapers folded in half and topped with a second piece of hardboard.

Place an even weight on top, for example, large books, a sewing machine or something heavy. Apply extra weight for thick flowers.

After two days

Remove the weights and carefully lift the layers of damp newspapers from the pile without disturbing the contents of the blotting paper.

Replace the newspapers with dry ones and position the weights once again.

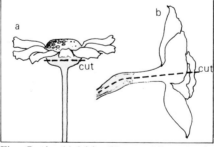

Fig. 1 Cutting (a) daisies, (b) cupped flower heads.

This should be done three times more. Without changing the newspapers, the flowers could go mouldy.

After six weeks

Remove the weights. Look at the flowers. If they are creased or mis-shapen, throw them away.

Change the newspapers and put flowers in the airing cupboard or somewhere dry for at least a further six weeks. Keep them in a pile with a small weight on top, just to keep them flat.

The longer they are left to dry the more reliable the colour will be. Discard any flowers which turn brown or have become colourless as they will only deteriorate.

Making pictures

Use cartridge paper cut to the required size, to plan the design. Decide which flowers, stems and leaves you are going to use.

Use a pointed knife to lift the flowers to save damaging them and a fine paint brush to move them around whilst arranging them.

When mounting the design, use only a little quick drying glue which does not stain in the centre of each flower. Leaves can be half covered with glue but never put it close to the edge or it will show. Apply the glue with a cocktail stick then press each flower or leaf into place with the fingers.

If it is necessary to stop before the picture is complete, cover it carefully with clean glass or Perspex to protect it. The flowers are very delicate and will spoil easily. Use a pastry brush to tidy up the design before framing.

Storing

Pressed flowers are best stored in the blotting paper in which they were pressed. It is helpful to date and name the flowers contained within the paper. For example: Pansies (yellow), 4.6.80. This will avoid unnecessary disturbance later when you come to use them. The flowers must be kept dry at all times and will absorb moisture if left unprotected.

Gift tags

This is a useful introduction to the art of pressed flowers because it uses a simply shaped flower. A gift tag such as this adds a thoughtful and personal touch to the present.

This basic idea extends well to greetings cards for all occasions – to wish a sick friend well or simply to say a specially thoughtful thank you.

You will need
- White card
- cord, 22 cm (9 in)
- gold paint
- fine water colour paint brush
- filing punch
- pansies approximately 5 cm (2 in) across
- flower pressing and mounting equipment as given on page 29

Instructions

All the techniques required for this project are given above.

Cut the card to size 10 cm by 7 cm (4 in by 2¾ in) for each tag unless the flowers are more than 5 cm (2 in), in which case make the card bigger. The flowers should be less than half the width of the card.

Draw a line in pencil around the card 4 mm (⅛ in) from the edge. Draw a second line 2 mm ($\frac{1}{16}$ in) from the first.

Fill in the double line with gold paint using short strokes and applying at least two coats of paint to give an embossed effect.

Place the pansy face down on the backing of the transparent seal. Draw a line round the pansy 4 mm ($\frac{1}{8}$ in) away from the general outline of the bloom as shown in Fig. 2.

While the pansy is upside-down, put some glue in the centre where it is thickest and smear some on the petals. Turn it over and place on the card at the left hand corner, allowing 4 mm ($\frac{1}{8}$ in) space between the outside of the pansy and the inside edge of the gold line.

While the glue is still wet, smooth the petals flat and adjust the pansy with a paint brush.

Leave to dry.

Cut out the seal round the pencil line and check that it fits. Starting at the top left, 4 mm ($\frac{1}{8}$ in) from the flower, and working diagonally across it, peel off the paper backing while sticking the seal on to the card. Static in the plastic may lift the petals in which case slip the pointed knife under the seal and flatten them.

Rub down and smooth the transparent seal into place, easing out any air bubbles.

Make a hole in the top left hand corner of the card with one side of the filing punch. Push the doubled cord through and then pull the ends through the loop.

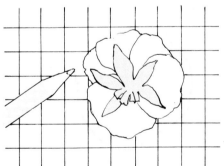

Fig. 2 Cutting line for transparent seal.

Finger plate

The wild flowers used for this design bring a pleasant reminder of the countryside into the home. The flowers and leaves used are not complicated to press.

Top A tag which is a gift in itself. **Bottom** Pretty wild flowers with a practical purpose to protect the paintwork on a door.

You will need

- Perspex finger plate, 9.5 cm by 25.5 cm ($3\frac{3}{4}$ in by 10 in)
- three paper handkerchieves
- filing punch
- fine water colour paint brush
- flowers: wild flowers such as two poppies and their leaves, two small stems of cow parsley, a spray of blackberry leaves, a head of lady's slipper, one buttercup, two little white flowers, two yellow flowers
- flower pressing and mounting equipment as given on page 29

Instructions

All the techniques required for this project are given on page 30.

All these flowers can be found by the roadside and are very common. The poppies should be pressed whole with the stem attached, without opening out the petals. Press some of the poppy leaves, too.

Cut the cow parsley into small sprays before pressing and add some leaves.

Remove the stems from the buttercups and lay them face down.

Lady's slipper, any little white flowers, yellow hawk's beard and blackberry leaves need no preparation and press easily.

Cut cartridge paper to size, a little bit smaller than the finger plate. Draw a double line in pencil about 5 mm ($\frac{3}{16}$ in) from the outside edges.

Using one side of the filing punch make holes in the paper to correspond with the screw holes in the finger plate.

The order of glueing and fixing the flowers is shown in Fig. 3. Whatever their size, take the smaller poppy first. Try it on the card and trim the stem if it is too long. On the reverse of the poppy put a dab of glue at the thickest part of the flower where it joins the stem. When in position on the card, slide a tiny amount of glue under part of the stem, allowing the stem to follow its natural shape. Press down. Follow the same procedure with the second poppy.

Trim off any thorns on the blackberry leaves and the thick part behind the leaves. Leave them joined together. Spread glue more liberally than with flowers, but not too close to the edges. Press into place at the bottom of the design. These, together with the poppies, give the basic shape.

Try the trimmed cow parsley for size on the design. When satisfied, lightly glue the reverse. Position the cow parsley from the top, working down

and slipping the lower pieces partly under the large leaves near the base. Press down.

Now there is an outline, the precise order for finishing is not important. Fill in the design, finishing off with the daisies and buttercup on the centre of the blackberry leaves.

When complete, cover with a clean sheet of glass and leave the glue to dry.

Secure the design to the Perspex with transparent seal to make it airtight. Turn the finger plate and design over, holding them tightly together, and cover with plastic seal, removing paper backing diagonally.

Three paper handkerchieves, folded and trimmed a little smaller than the design, are fixed to the back using double-sided Sellotape. This will allow it to 'bed down' when fixed to a door.

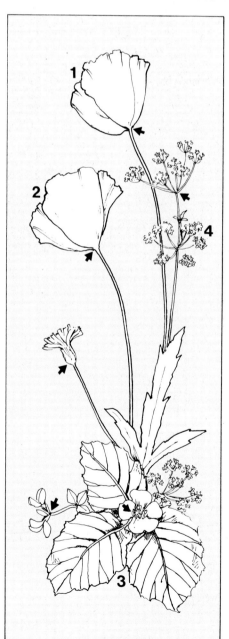

Fig. 3 Order and position of glueing.

Breakfast tray

The flowers making up the design for this tray have been picked from the garden in spring time. Using flowers which all bloom at the same time captures and preserves a natural scene. Here they have been mounted on velvet which gives a rich texture to the background and in a subtle shade of green is reminiscent of a well-tended lawn in keeping with the floral theme.

You will need

- Suitable frame made to measure with straight sides to take the handles
- heavier than the usual picture glass cut to fit frame
- waterproof plastic seal, available in a tube
- panel pins
- pair of handles and their screws
- thick cardboard to fit in the frame
- background fabric to cover the cardboard
- cardboard packing
- hardboard to back the frame
- felt the same size as the hardboard
- flowers: yellow narcissus, white narcissus, small tulip, helleborus, pink hyacinthus, forget-me-not, wallflower, scilla (sibirica), yellow and purple primrose, decorative leaves
- flower pressing and mounting equipment as given on page 29

Measurements

Inner edge of frame 34 cm by 23.5 cm ($13\frac{1}{4}$ in by $9\frac{1}{4}$ in)

Instructions

All the techniques required for this project are given on page 30.

Remove all the stem from one of the primroses and lay it face down on the blotting paper, fold others sideways with the stems still attached.

For the open tulip in the centre of the design, remove all the centre (stamens, style and stem) and spread out flat in a circle.

The other tulips in the design are

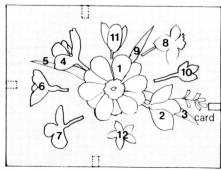

Fig. 4 Shape of design and order of glueing.

Top left Narcissi, tulips, hyacinths and primroses make up the main elements of this display. Smaller flowers such as helleborus, scillas and wallflowers add the details. **Top right** A sample of flowers, ferns and ribbons preserved from a bouquet and rearranged against silk background material as a permanent memento of a special occasion.

cut in half, leaving about 3 cm (1¼ in) of the stem still on the flower. Press them both – one will go to the right, one to the left.

The yellow narcissus is split through the middle in the same way.

Cut off everything behind the bloom of the white narcissus and press flat, face down.

Press the helleborus flat. The stems may remain.

Cut through the middle of the hyacinthus and press.

Press all the other flowers as they grow.

Cover the cardboard with glue. With a thick background fabric, place the fabric on the glue while it is wet. A thinner fabric, such as silk, should be placed on top when the glue is tacky and almost dry, and then pressed under a cloth with a warm iron. Be careful to keep the weave of the fabric straight. Trim the edges flush with the card.

Find the centre by measuring half way down two opposite sides and joining the points with a length of cotton, horizontally and then vertically. Where the threads cross is the centre.

On the reverse of the largest tulip put a dab of glue and press into the centre point, under the threads. Then remove the tacking threads.

Make the general shape of the design, working the corners diagonally in the order shown in Fig. 4. Bear in mind that the design must fit centrally in the finished tray without coming right to the edges.

Cut a piece of card to the depth of the border space and use it to check that the design is even as work progresses (Fig. 4). Also bear in mind that, unlike a picture on the wall, a tray will be seen from all angles. Although a symmetrical design will not look completely natural, it is important to create an all round effect. The border space must match on opposite sides but does not have to be the same on all four sides.

Once the basic shape of the large flowers is established, the order of filling in with leaves and small flowers is not important.

Trim unwanted bits off stems and leaves with scissors, trying the flower or leaf on the design to estimate the finished effect. Overlap petals and leaves for a natural look. Do not let a flower base end visibly but cover with a leaf or small bloom, tucking the stems out of sight. Trim off any pieces that will lie more than 2 mm (1/16 in) under a flower, because, in time, they will show with the pressure of the glass.

Keep the completed design under the glass for a day to allow the glue to dry. Take care when placing the glass in position, as the petals may break or the pollen spread.

Bind the design to the glass with Sellotape. Put waterproof seal round the inside rebate of the frame. Seal by putting the design and glass in the frame, making sure no seal is visible and press the design into the frame.

Lay a sheet of thick card over the back of the design and secure it to the frame with panel pins. Lay further sheets of card over the back until they are flush with the frame, pinning them in position. Place the hardboard in position, glue and pin it to the frame (Fig. 5).

Cover the hardboard with felt to avoid scratching any surface the tray may come in contact with.

Screw on handles to the short sides of the frame.

Sentimental souvenir

The preparation of the pressed flowers for this project is more ambitious than usual but very worthwhile because it is a way to have a permanent souvenir of an important occasion such as a wedding.

As the flowers will be past their best when pressed, the final result may not be as good as one would wish. But the sentimental association will be the important thing.

You will need
● Picture frame
● hardboard cut to fit the picture frame
● fabric a little larger than the hardboard, perhaps from the bride's dress or something similar
● white paper of a similar size
● the bouquet – flowers used here are sonia roses, gladiolus, stephanotis, lily-of-the-valley and asparagus fern
● flower pressing and mounting equipment as given on page 29

Instructions
All the techniques required for this project are given on page 30.

Draw or photograph the bouquet. Start work as soon as the bride will part with the bouquet. The flowers will be just heads attached by wire to the arrangement. Concentrate on the heads, snipping the wire and pulling it back through the head, to release the flower. Often only part of the bloom is used and this may be wound round with wire. Also take some fern or leaves from the bouquet.

As work has to begin away from home to avoid delay, use a small press made in the usual way but of smaller pieces of hardboard, newspaper and blotting paper. Once home, transfer the blotting paper to the full sized press.

Press all the flowers in the bouquet, although they may not all be required in the final arrangement.

Slice rosebuds through the middle and remove as much as possible from the centre such as seeds and some petals (Fig. 6). Cut the flower where the wire has gone through, otherwise a rusty hole may appear in the finished picture. As they are bulky, press roses separately. Lay the rose, cut side down, on the blotting paper.

Press the blooms of gladiolus flat. Cut buds in half lengthways and press them down on blotting paper.

Cut behind the circle of petals of the stephanotis flower as shown in Fig. 7. Lay the flower face down on the blotting paper. Cut the long white trumpet shaped piece behind the petals in half and press. Also press the little green leaves.

Pieces of carnation wired to fern are pressed flat.

Lily-of-the-valley presses whole quite easily. They turn brown but keep their lovely shape and outline.

Lay asparagus fern and rose leaves flat on the blotting paper.

When the required time has passed, look at the pressed flowers. Only a small picture may be possible as the spoilage may well be considerable because the flowers have been handled a lot and have been cut at least 48 hours before the wedding. Sentiment will compensate, but hopefully it will be possible to represent the original bouquet.

Prepare the background. Keep the frame, without its glass, and the sketch or photograph nearby.

Make up the picture on paper first. Begin with the fern, making the general shape as shown in Fig. 8. Place the frame over the design to ensure the picture does not fill the frame. Leave about 2–3 cm ($\frac{3}{4}$ in) clear round the edge and keep the design within the fern outline.

Place any ribbon or lace in position.

To recreate the effect of a bouquet there must be depth. This is achieved by adding one flower, or half of one, on top of another.

Balance the design as it progresses, working away from the centre and using less material towards the edge, giving a round, light effect. Small flowers and leaves help here. Begin with the roses at the centre, then the

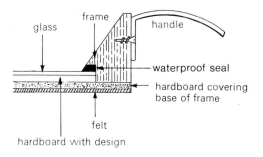

Fig. 5 Cross-section of make up of tray.

Fig. 6 Cutting through centre of rose.

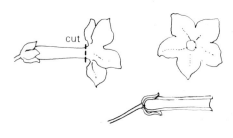

Fig. 7 Cutting petals and trumpet of stephanotis.

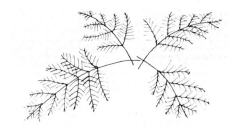

Fig. 8 Suggested basic shape made with ferns.

stephanotis, keeping a note of the order of the construction.

When happy with the design on paper, make the shape again on the prepared background with some more of the pressed fern. Any pieces of lace or ribbon must be glued in place.

Transfer the flowers from the pattern to the fabric on a pointed knife. Lightly glue the back of the flowers and work in the same order as the pattern.

Cover the completed design with a clean piece of glass and allow a day or two for the flowers to dry out and stick firmly. During this time it is possible, with care, to add a little or take away.

When satisfied, fix in the frame in the usual way, making sure the back is well sealed to make the picture airtight.

Marquetry

Marquetry is the craft of using wood veneers to decorate a wooden surface. It is an ancient craft which, nonetheless, is capable of a modern interpretation.

It is becoming increasingly popular as a hobby. This is partly due to the fact that the veneers have become available from many parts of the world. Although some veneers such as holly, magnolia and even horse chestnut have become scarce, new veneers continually take their place and can form the basis of the most beautiful contrasting pictures in natural wood.

Materials and Equipment

A cutting board of plywood, about 30 cm (12 in) square.

A medical scalpel makes the best cutting knife – number 3 handle with number 10A blades, or a craft knife with a supply of blades.

An oil stone, coarse on one side and fine on the other, is used to keep the blades sharp.

Adhesives such as PVA woodworking adhesive are used for butt joining veneers. Also contact glues are used for mounting a picture to a base board. If a press is used, a cold water glue is best.

Brown paper gummed strip 2 cm (1 in) wide.

A press is used to glue veneers to a base board. An old letter press is ideal but alternatively improvize with chipboard and G clamps. Weights like a pile of books will not make a satisfactory press.

Steel ruler – non-slip, if possible.

Black carbon paper for tracing the design. Do not use blue carbon paper as this stains the wood.

Garnet paper for sanding (sizes 3, 6 and 9).

Cork block is used to wrap the garnet paper round to keep work level.

Hardset or French polish (white).

Veneers, available in packs of mixed sheets.

A tenon saw for cutting plywood.

A base board for pictures is usually made of plywood, either 5 or 7 ply, but blockboard or chipboard can be an alternative. Avoid solid wood boards.

General equipment includes pencils, tracing paper, a T-square or set square, an iron, brown paper and silver foil.

Marquetry

Know how

Veneers

Different veneers are suitable for portraying different features because of their varied colouring and grain. The most useful of all dark veneers is European walnut and the only white is sycamore. Red mahogany with its fiddle-back grain is used for covering boxes. Sapele is good for backing pictures and for borders. Yellows are provided by avodire (mottled grain), afara (wavy grain) and obeche. Ash and olive are cream with wild brown markings and aspen is cream to pink, all are good for water and sky effects. Also creamy pink are Canadian birch (close grain for portraits), Masure birch (dark markings for roads, rocks, beaches, etc) and birdseye maple (with tiny eyes for costumes and small portraits). Lacewood is biscuit-coloured with radiating marks (for stonework, bridges and beaches). The only orange comes from opepe (for cornfields, flowers and sand), whilst rosa peroba is orange-red (for winter skies, robins and clothing). African mahogany is a mottled dark red suitable for portraits, shadows and horses. Harewood is a treated sycamore, silvery-grey coloured and useful for birds. Zebrano with its close light and dark stripes has many uses. Useful burrs for trees and bushes are ash, elm, maidu, vavona and walnut.

The window method

This name is given to a particular method of building up a marquetry design which encourages accurate cutting. From a piece of waste veneer, spaces are cut out, one at a time, and filled with selected veneers until all the original veneer has been replaced. Cardboard can be used instead of waste veneer.

Transferring the design. First choose a design from a sketch or photograph. Trace it or re-draw it to the exact size of the finished picture desired, leaving a border all round of about 2 cm ($\frac{3}{4}$ in). Draw an outline round the picture to mark off the border area, as shown in Fig. 1.

Cut a piece of waste veneer or cardboard (from an empty breakfast cereal packet, for example) to the same size as the picture, with the border. Fasten the drawing, picture side up, along the top edge of the veneer or cardboard using gummed tape. Place a piece of carbon paper in between, carbon side down (Fig. 2), and draw over the main features of the design (Fig. 1). The more intricate details are added later.

Cutting the templates. Raise the line drawing and remove the carbon, to check that the outlines of the drawing have transferred to the veneer or cardboard (Fig. 3).

The sequence of cutting out the shapes is top to bottom. Using the scalpel, cut out the first area. Discard the piece cut out of the waste veneer.

Place a suitable veneer under the hole and move it around until the direction of the grain and the colouring of the veneer make a suitable representation for the section.

Fix the veneer in position by placing gummed paper strip at either side of the cut out hole or 'window'. Use gummed paper sparingly although making sure the veneer is secure.

With the scalpel, prick round inside close to the edge of the window without attempting to cut through. The accuracy of the piece will depend on this marking.

Cut the tape holding the veneer and place the veneer on the cutting board.

Cut out the piece, keeping exactly in the groove made by the scalpel mark. Hold the knife vertically and make small cutting movements. For difficult contours, it is better to prick rather than to draw the knife round. It may be necessary to go round the shape several times, especially if using a hard veneer.

Carefully remove the piece without forcing it and place in position in the window left in the waste veneer to check that the shape is correct. Turn the waste veneer and piece upside down together.

Glueing in the veneer. Spread a little adhesive such as PVA around the join, as shown in Fig. 4. Rub it gently in until dry. Turn to the right side, mop off any surplus glue and press well into the window with the handle of the scalpel. The glue dries within minutes but if large pieces do not hold, use a little gummed strip on the wrong side.

Continue in this way, cutting out and glueing each shape separately.

Adding the details. When all the background pieces have been cut, place the tracing back over the picture, lining it up with the veneers underneath. Carefully slip a piece of carbon in between.

Draw round the outlines of the smaller details.

Cut the pieces out one by one from the picture veneers, working from top to bottom as before.

Trimming

Use the metal ruler and cut off the top border of waste veneer or cardboard, trimming the picture to a true edge.

Using a T-square, trim the rest of the waste veneer from the picture, making sure all corners are right angles.

Damp any gummed tape left on the picture and scrape off using the scalpel. Examine the picture critically for faults in the cutting or for a wrong grain direction. At this point it is a simple matter to cut out a piece and replace it if necessary.

The base board

Measure the veneer picture and add on 2 cm ($\frac{3}{4}$ in) all round for a border.

Use these measurements to cut the

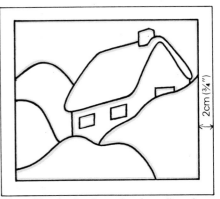

Fig. 1 Showing border and main outline of design.

Fig. 2 Attaching to waste veneer and inserting carbon.

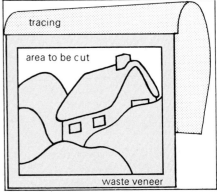

Fig. 3 Showing 1st area to be cut.

36

base board from plywood, blockboard or chipboard, on which the veneer picture will be fixed. Cut with a tenon saw and square up accurately with a T-square.

Try the veneer picture on top of the base board to make sure borders are equal all round and trim board if necessary.

The back. First veneer the back of the board by cutting the veneer a little larger all round than the board to allow for mistakes in sticking. When short of veneer use up odd pieces by making an abstract design.

If using a press, use a cold water glue. Its disadvantage is that if blisters form they cannot be rectified once the glue has dried.

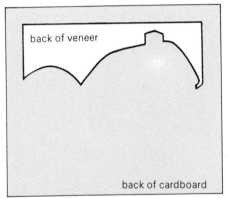

Fig. 4 Glueing the joins from the back.

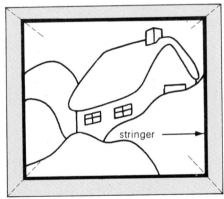

Fig. 5 Pencilling in the mitre lines.

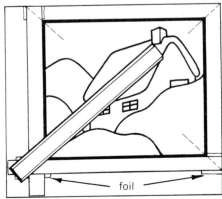

Fig. 6 Cutting the 1st mitre.

Where no press is available, contact glues are the answer. Bubbles can be smoothed out using an iron over brown paper.

Put glue on the veneer and the board then wait until both surfaces are finger dry for the time given on the manufacturer's directions.

Lower the base board on to the veneer, being careful to centre it. Press down well, especially round the edges.

Sand round all the edges so that they are flush.

The sides. After veneering the back of the board, cut strips for the side edges. Measure the sides of the base board one by one and cut the four strips slightly wider and longer.

Glue as before, starting with the top and bottom edges.

As each veneer is fixed, wait until the glue has dried then trim the edges and sand back, flush to the board.

Stringers
Thin pieces of veneer are inserted between the border and the picture and can be dark or light. Usually they are made of sycamore and are 2 mm ($\frac{1}{16}$ in) wide. Cut them a little longer than the sides of the picture.

Stick them one at a time to the edges of the picture with PVA glue, overlapping at each corner.

Mitre the corners of the stringers by cutting through both layers at an angle of 45 degrees.

Mounting the picture
Lay the picture on the un-veneered side of the base board. Centre it carefully by measuring an equal border all round.

Draw a pencil line round the picture, then remove the picture.

Apply glue from the middle of the base board, up to and slightly over the pencil line.

Apply glue to the back of the picture.

Wait fifteen minutes until touch dry and put the top of the picture to the top pencil line. Gently lower the picture, making sure that the sides are even with the side pencil lines. Press firmly with the hands.

Borders
The borders of the picture are also cut in four strips, two for top and bottom and two for sides.

Cut them from straight grained veneer. Mahogany is usually best, especially Sapele. These should again be cut a little wider and several centimetres (inches) longer than needed.

Using a ruler, draw a diagonal pencil line from each corner of the base board

through the corner of the stringer and continue, very lightly, on to the picture for about 5 cm (2 in) as a guide (Fig. 5).

Apply glue to the border strips and the rest of the base board. Leave the glue to dry.

Cut some small pieces of foil or tracing paper just large enough to fit where two border strips overlap at each corner. These will prevent the pieces from sticking while the mitre is being cut.

Lay one border at a time, moving round from the bottom left hand corner anti-clockwise. Put foil at the first and second corners. Lay the first border, making sure that it makes contact with the picture. Press it down only in the middle.

Lay the second border close to the picture, overlapping the first border at the corner. Press it down only in the middle.

Put foil under the third corner.

By lining up the ruler with the line on the picture of the second corner, cut the mitre (Fig. 6). The top triangle of surplus border will come away immediately but it will be necessary to wriggle out the second piece, taking care not to break it as this will make it very difficult to remove.

Make sure all foil and surplus veneer have been removed from the mitre. If not, lift the border with a table knife to remove it.

Press down the corner.

Lay the third border and place foil underneath the fourth corner.

Cut the third corner as before.

Lay the fourth border and cut the fourth corner.

Finally, mitre the first corner.

Press hard all round, especially edges.

Trim and sand all veneers back flush with the board.

Allow 24 hours in a press if possible for the glue to harden.

Polishing
Sand all surfaces using garnet paper no. 3 wrapped round a cork block.

Sand again with nos. 6 and 9 until it is as smooth as glass.

The surface, back and edges must be polished with French polish or Hardset or with wax polish, which gives a good matt finish and the picture must be perfectly cut for this to look well. Give several coats of polish for the best effect, allowing each coat to dry overnight and sanding before re-polishing.

Above The completed picture.

Below Fig. 7 Veneers key and trace pattern.

Above The chessboard in use.   **Below** Workbox with abstract design.

Picture

This charming picture gives a chance to practise all the skills described in the Know How. A specific pattern is provided but this can be adapted or enlarged to suit individual taste.

You will need

Veneers (see Fig. 7): The following have been used in the picture, but any other veneers of the same shades could be used
- 1. aspen or sycamore
- 2. light walnut
- 3. medium walnut
- 4. dark walnut
- 5. pink burr or pear
- 6. pink lacewood
- 7. horse chestnut or sycamore
- 8. mahogany for the borders, edges and back
- base board 21.5 cm by 16.5 cm ($8\frac{1}{2}$ in by $6\frac{1}{2}$ in)
- copper screw eyes with rings and string for hanging
- marquetry equipment as given on page 35

Instructions

All the techniques required for this project are given on pages 36 and 37.

Trace the line drawing in Fig. 7. The numbers indicate which veneers have been used (see above) and the arrows show the direction of the grain.

Cut a piece of cardboard or waste veneer 21.5 cm by 16.5 cm ($8\frac{1}{2}$ in by $6\frac{1}{2}$ in) and transfer the design to it.

Cut and insert the veneers in the sequence given in Fig. 8.

Fill in the details of trees, chimney and windows.

Prepare the base board, then mount the picture and border.

Press and polish.

To hang the picture, fix two copper screws with ring attachments a third of the way down the back of the picture and thread through some string.

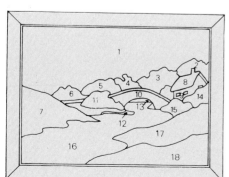

Fig. 8 Cutting sequence for picture.

Chess board

Board games make an attractive subject for marquetry and the pride of craftsmanship will give added pleasure to the game.

The cutting for this chess board is straightforward.

Instead of making a separate board, the chequered veneers could be stuck to a table top or used to decorate the lid of the box in which the chessmen are kept.

You will need

- Sycamore or a pale, straight grained veneer
- mahogany, or a dark, straight grained veneer
- medium walnut for the borders, edge and base
- a base board either 35 cm ($13\frac{1}{2}$ in) *or* 23 cm (9 in) square
- for plywood jig board one piece 50 cm (20 in) square and another 50 cm by 3 cm (20 in by 1 in)
- screws for the jig board
- steel ruler, either 2.5 cm (1 in) wide for the smaller board *or* 4 cm ($1\frac{1}{2}$ in) wide for the larger board
- marquetry equipment as given on page 35

Instructions

All the techniques required for this project are given on pages 36 and 37.

First make the jig as shown in Fig.

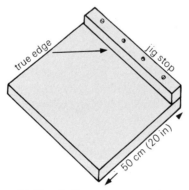

Fig. 9 Making the jig stop.

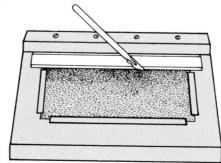

Fig. 10 Cutting the 1st strip on the jig.

9. Screw the strip of plywood firmly along the top edge of the square. The strip must have a true edge as it forms the jig stop.

Place the light veneer on the jig board and trim one edge with the grain to a straight edge.

Place this straight edge against the jig stop. Lay the ruler on top of the veneer, also firmly against the jig stop. Using a sharp knife, cut a strip the width of the ruler (Fig. 10) taking care to keep fingers clear of the knife.

Remove the strip and push the remaining veneer up against the jig stop. Replace the ruler and cut another strip as before.

Repeat until four strips have been cut in all.

Cut four strips of the dark veneer in the same way.

Place all the strips on the jig board, alternating light and dark. Tape with gummed strip on the right side.

Using a set square, cut the left hand edge to make an exact right angle at the top left hand corner (Fig. 11).

Turn all the strips round in one piece so that the straight edge is against the jigstop.

Cut eight strips as before (Fig. 12).

Alternate the pieces for a chequered effect and tape together.

Prepare the base board and mount veneer, glueing the unpapered side.

Add stringers (optional) and borders.

Remove the gummed paper.

Sand all surfaces until smooth, press and polish.

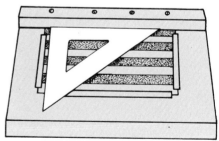

Fig. 11 Squaring the edge.

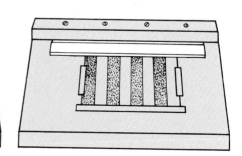

Fig. 12 Cutting chequered strips.

Work box

Most marquetarians are not cabinet makers and so veneered boxes such as this one usually begin as a plain purchased box. New boxes can be used as found but old boxes must first be prepared by sanding down to the natural wood before veneering. Remove paint with paint stripper, wash the box thoroughly and sand when dry.

Remove hinges and fastenings where possible, to be refitted when the box is veneered.

The abstract design which decorates this box offers wide scope for using up a large variety of oddments of veneers. The skill is in the way they are put together.

You will need
● A purchased box
● mahogany veneer for the sides and bottom of the box and for the background of the picture.
● a selection of veneers including sycamore
● marquetry equipment as given on page 35

Instructions
All the techniques required for this project are given on pages 36 and 37.

Cut pieces from the mahogany veneer for the bottom, front, back and sides of the box, each slightly larger all round than the actual measurements.

Cut pieces from the same veneer for the four sides of the lid, also larger than the actual dimensions.

Stick the bottom veneer first using impact glue and sand back to the box.

Add the two sides to both the base and the lid. Sand these flush with the box.

Add the back and front to the base and the lid, sanding again to join up with the sides.

Line the box with veneers in the same order as the veneering for the outside, adding a piece for the inside of the lid.

An alternative would be to make a lining from fabric which would be first stuck on to thin white card or from self adhesive covering. For a fabric lining, cut the card to the exact dimensions of the inside of the box but cut the fabric 1 cm (½ in) larger all round. Glue it to the card folding the excess to the back.

Trace the line drawing given in Fig. 13 and transfer it to a piece of the mahogany veneer cut slightly larger than the dimensions of the box lid and with the grain horizontal. The shaded areas are left in this background veneer.

Cut the other shapes from a selection of veneers. Spread the different colours equally over the design so that veneers of the same tone are separated. Sycamore, being light, is good for dividing up other colours.

Once the design is complete, mount it on the lid and sand back to sides. Sand and polish all areas.

Replace any hinges and fastenings on the box.

Fig. 13 Trace pattern for box top.

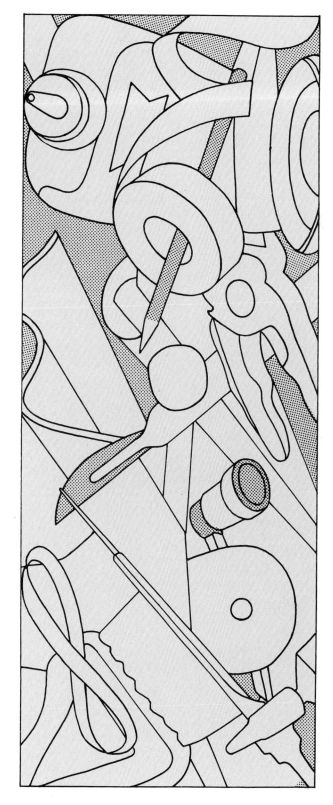

Miniature

Marquetry miniatures are a class on their own. The Marquetry Society ruling is that a miniature must not exceed 7 cm by 10 cm (12 square inches) including any border. As the detail is small it follows that these little pictures are more difficult to cut.

The size lends itself particularly to birds and small animals. There are many shades of veneers available so that, with the exception of green and blue, every colour can be found in natural wood. For this reason it is best to choose a picture which can be interpreted in natural wood colours.

One wood which has been used for over a century is harewood. It is a chemically treated sycamore and varies from silver grey to dark slate grey and when used next to brown veneers gives the illusion of being blue.

Below An intricate miniature which has a built-in stand.

You will need
● Harewood veneer for the background
● silver grey harewood for the wings
● a selection of other veneers for the rest of the bird and the tree
● walnut veneer for the base board and stand.
● a base board 7.5 cm by 9.5 cm (3 in by $3\frac{3}{4}$ in)
● stand of same material as base board 6.5 cm by 6.5 cm by 3 cm by 1.5 cm ($2\frac{1}{2}$ in by $2\frac{1}{2}$ in by $1\frac{1}{4}$ in by $\frac{5}{8}$ in)
● marquetry equipment as given on page 35

Instructions
All the techniques required for this project are given on pages 36 and 37. There are, however, a few differences for a miniature and these are given in detail as they arise.

Firstly cardboard or waste veneer is not used. Instead, the drawing is traced using black carbon straight on to the background veneer (Fig. 14). Secondly, all the pieces, with one exception, are cut out piece by piece rather than adding the more intricate details at a later stage. The exception is the bird's eye. The eyehole is cut first and glued in position, then the iris is drawn and cut leaving grey ring. Finally, make a hole in the centre of the black with a pin then glue and drop a tiny white veneer into place. This miniature has no stringers or borders.

Prepare the base board by veneering the back only with the walnut veneer, then glue the picture to the front. The sides are veneered in the usual order of top, bottom, right then left.

Cut a wedge of plywood using Fig. 15 as a template.

Using walnut, veneer the sides and two of the edges, leaving one long edge un-veneered. Glue this edge in position so that the short edge is flush with the bottom of the picture, as shown in Fig. 16, and using impact glue.

Fig. 14 Trace pattern.   Fig. 15 Template.   Fig. 16 Wedge in place.

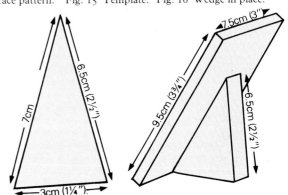

Macramé

Macramé is a very old craft of obscure origins. The name comes from an Arabic word which means ornamental fringe.

In 16th century Italy and Spain, 'macramé borders' were made for ecclesiastical linen. Sailors made macramé items on their long sea voyages, either selling or using them for barter in foreign ports, thus spreading knowledge of the craft around the world.

Macramé was particularly popular in Victorian and Edwardian times, when instruction books were written in French and German since the craft was widely practised in those countries. There is currently a popular revival of the craft and once the basic knots are mastered it is fascinating to make up either from instructions or to an original design.

Materials and Equipment

Use any thread with a firm, smooth twist to it, but avoid anything which stretches. A thread with a rough texture would be uncomfortable to work with. The traditional thread was of smooth linen in natural colour, but many different types and colours are used today. Natural fibres are best to work with, but most synthetics can be successful. String, rope and twine of all thicknesses are ideal for sturdy articles, whilst finer, more delicate items require something such as a crochet cotton which produces a beautifully soft macramé.

A knotting board is the surface on which the macramé is worked. It should be soft enough to take pins: about 30 cm by 45 cm (12 in by 18 in) would be a good size. Buy a special board or improvise with cork board or cork tiling.

T pins or coloured glass headed pins are used to hold the work in place on the board.

Rubber bands are advisable when working with particularly long threads. The threads are wound into a figure-of eight and secured.

Needles for sewing ends back into the work must have an eye large enough to take the thread being used.

Pliers can be useful for pulling the needle through the work.

General items include scissors, tape measure, fabric glue, sewing thread and a note book and pen to keep a record of how different threads work up, for future reference.

Know how

Macramé is based on two knots – the flat knot and the half hitch.

Foundation (or holding) cord

Tie a knot at each end of a length of thread and pin through each knot so that the cord is taut on the working surface.

If, instead of being separate, the cord is an integral part of the work, the knots will be placed centrally on the cord, the space between them equalling the width of the finished macramé. Once all the other threads have been set on, undo the knots and the ends then hang down to become working threads.

Sometimes, depending on the project, a solid object such as the bar of a buckle or handle, or a curtain pull, can be used on which to mount the macramé directly in place of the foundation cord.

Working threads

The thread is cut into suitable lengths, then folded in half (unless otherwise stated) and set on to the foundation cord to form a pair of working threads. As a rough guide, working threads should be about four times the length of the finished article so each length should be cut to eight times that measurement. This can vary according to the thickness of the thread and the knots used. Never scrimp as joining in a new length may show.

Setting on knot (or lark's head)

Fold a length of thread in half. Pass the loop down behind the foundation cord. Take the two ends downwards through the loop and pull tight (Fig. 1).

Flat knot

This is made in two stages (see Fig. 2). It requires four threads. The two outside cords do all the work, knotting around the centre two which act as a core. As a result the outer threads will be used up much more quickly. It sometimes helps the beginner to pin the two centre threads about 13 cm (5 in) down the board. This keeps them taut while both hands are making the knot.

Take the left hand thread under the centre two and over the right hand thread. Take the right hand thread over the centre pair and through the loop made by the left hand thread. Pull tight. This completes the first stage.

Take the right hand thread under the centre pair and over the left hand thread.

Take the left hand thread over the centre pair and through the loop of the right hand threads. Pull up tightly. This second stage completes the flat knot.

Alternated flat knots (flat knot mesh)

Using threads in multiples of four and without pinning the core threads, make a row of flat knots. On the second row omit two threads at either end. Divide the remaining threads into groups of four and work a flat knot on each group (Fig. 3).

Work the third row as the first.

Continue in this way, alternating the groupings, so that the knots on any one row are positioned between the knots of the previous row.

Flat knot spiral (or banister bar)

By continuing to work only the first stage of the flat knot on a group of four threads the resulting braid will twist (Fig. 4). The result will be the same if only the second stage is used, but the direction of the twist will reverse.

Leaders

Once the work has started, any cord laid across the working threads and

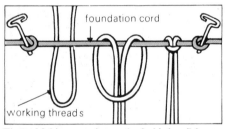
Fig. 1 Making a setting on (or lark's head) knot.

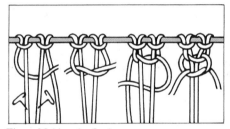
Fig. 2 Making the flat knot.

Fig. 3 Flat knot mesh.

Fig. 4 Flat knot spiral with change of direction.

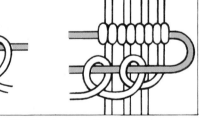
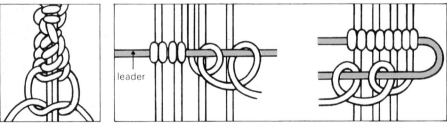
Fig. 5 Working horizontal cording in 2 directions.

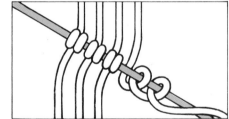
Fig. 6 Diagonal cording.

Fig. 7 Half hitch spiral with change of direction.

Fig. 8 Single knotted chain.

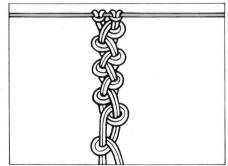
Fig. 9 Double knotted chain.

used as a core around which the knots are tied is known as a leader. As with the foundation cord, this can be a separate thread or one of the working threads.

Horizontal cording
A leader is laid across the working threads horizontally. Each working thread is taken in turn and knotted round the leader. The knot used is the half hitch.

When working from left to right, work the half hitch in a clockwise direction. A second half hitch with the same working thread secures the cording knot (Fig. 5).

When working from right to left, work the half hitches in an anti-clockwise direction.

Diagonal cording
This is worked exactly the same as horizontal cording, except that the leader is held at an angle, diagonally down across the working threads. As before, it can be worked from left or right (Fig. 6).

Half hitch spiral
Cording can be worked vertically and if the same half hitch, i.e. clockwise or anti-clockwise, is repeated over and over, the work will form a spiral. Changing the direction of the half hitch reverses the spiral (Fig. 7).

Single knotted chain
This is worked using two threads as shown in Fig. 8.

First the left hand thread is held taut to act as a core and the right hand thread is worked round it in a clockwise half hitch. Then the right hand thread is held taut and the left hand thread worked round it in an anti-clockwise half hitch. These two steps form one knotted chain.

Double knotted chain
This is worked exactly the same as single knotted chain but using four threads. Divide the threads into two pairs and work each pair together as one (Fig. 9).

Finishing off
Very often macramé ends with a fringe made from the working threads. The ends are often secured with a suitable knot such as cording and then all trimmed to an even length. The choice of knot, such as flat knots, could group the fringe threads into tassels.

Alternatively, the ends can be folded to the back of the work and either stitched or glued in place. This is also the method of finishing off the ends of any separate foundation cord or leaders.

Knot board sampler

This project will introduce the basic knots and when mounted makes an attractive sampler for a wall.

You will need
- Pulp board or thick cardboard 31 cm (12 in) square
- covering material 36 cm (14 in) square e.g. self-adhesive shelf paper
- large ball of medium weight parcel string (or 5s polished cotton)
- tracing paper
- paste glue
- awl
- macramé equipment as given on page 43

Instructions
All the techniques required for this project are given on this and the facing page.

Flat knot braid
Cut two lengths each 102 cm (40 in).

Fold so that the two inside threads measure 25 cm (10 in) and set on to a foundation cord.

Make fifteen flat knots.

Alternated flat knots
Cut eight lengths each 102 cm (40 in).

Double and set on to a foundation cord.

Starting with a row of four knots, work alternate flat knots for 18 rows.

Flat knot spiral (or banister bar)
Cut two lengths each 102 cm (40 in).

Fold so that the two inside threads measure 23 cm (9 in) and set on to a foundation cord.

Make a flat knot spiral by working the first half of a flat knot 36 times.

Double knotted chain
Cut two lengths each 102 cm (40 in).

Double and set on to a foundation cord. Work 10 double knotted chain.

Double alternated flat knots
Cut eight lengths each 114 cm (45 in).

Double and set on to a foundation cord.

First row. Divide the threads into four groups of four threads each and work two flat knots on each group.

Second row. Omit two threads at each end and make two flat knots on each of the three groups of four threads. Repeat these two rows three times more, then the first row once.

The knot board sampler **below** gives ample opportunity for the beginner to practise the basic know how of macramé as well as making a decorative panel and a useful reference when working on future projects.

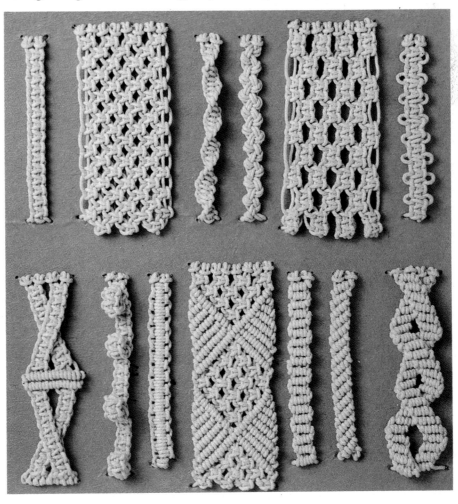

Flat knot braid with picots
Cut two lengths each 114 cm (45 in).

Fold so that the two inner threads measure 25 cm (10 in) and set on to a foundation cord.

Make a flat knot.

Make the next flat knot about 1 cm ($\frac{1}{3}$ in) down the core threads and then push it close up to the first knot (Fig. 10).

Continue until work measures 10 cm (4 in).

Crossed flat knot braid
Cut four lengths each 127 cm (50 in).

Fold so that the inner threads on both groups of four measure 33 cm (13 in) and set on to a foundation cord.

Divide the threads into two groups of four threads each and make eight flat knots on each group.

Cross the right hand group over the left hand group.

Cut a separate leader approximately 25 cm (10 in) long and pin half of it across all threads.

Work two rows of horizontal cording across all threads, using the second half of the leader for the second row.

Divide the threads into two groups of four threads each and make eight flat knots on each group.

Pin a separate leader across all the threads and work one row of horizontal cording.

Blackberry knot braid
Cut two lengths each 228 cm (90 in).

Fold so that the inner threads measure 92 cm (36 in) and set on to a foundation cord.

Make one flat knot.

Leave a space of about 1 cm ($\frac{1}{4}$ in) below the knot before making another five flat knots (Fig. 11).

Take the two centre threads up and through the space to the back of the work. Draw the five flat knots up into a ball. Work one flat knot underneath to secure.

Make four more flat knots, leave another space and continue in this way until the work measures 11 cm ($4\frac{1}{2}$ in).

Tatted bar
Cut two lengths each 102 cm (40 in).

Fold so that the inner threads each measure 20 cm (8 in) and set on to a foundation cord.

Using the right hand thread, work a clockwise half hitch over the two centre threads, then work a second one but in reverse, taking the thread to the back of the work.

Work in the same way with the left hand thread.

Continue alternating to right and left as in Fig. 12 until there are 14 knots on each side.

Diamond pattern
Cut eight lengths each 153 cm (60 in).

Double and set on to a foundation cord.

Divide the threads into four groups of four threads each and work a flat knot on each group.

Omit the two outer threads at each side and divide the remaining threads into three groups of four threads each. Work a flat knot on each group.

Omit the two outer threads at each side and divide the remaining threads into two groups of four threads each. Work a flat knot on each of the two groups.

Work a flat knot on the four centre threads.

Using the outer threads as leaders, work diagonal cording to right and left into the centre.

Using each inner thread to the left of the first row of cording in turn as leader, work seven rows of diagonal cording to the left as shown in Fig. 13.

Work seven rows of diagonal cording to the right to correspond.

Work three rows of alternated flat knots between the diagonal cording.

Repeat from the beginning, ending with a row of four flat knots.

Horizontal cording braid
Cut two lengths each 153 cm (60 in).

Double and set on to a foundation cord.

Using the right hand thread as a continuous leader, work in rows of horizontal cording to left and right until the work measures 10 cm (4 in).

Diagonal cording braid
Cut two lengths each 153 cm (60 in).

Double and set on to a foundation cord.

Using the right hand thread as leader, work diagonal cording to the left over all threads.

Repeat until the work measures 10 cm (4 in).

Interlocked horizontal cording
Cut four lengths each 153 cm (60 in).

Double and set on to a foundation cord.

Using the left hand thread as leader, cord horizontally to the right across each of the next three threads.

Repeat five times more.

On the same four threads and using the right hand thread as leader, cord horizontally to the left for six rows (Fig. 14).

Repeat from the beginning once more.

Work the right hand group of four threads in reverse, by cording to the left first (Fig. 15).

Complete by taking the left hand

Fig. 10 Flat knot braid with picots.

Fig. 11 Making a blackberry knot.

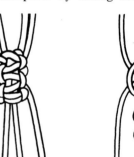

Fig. 12 Tatted bar.

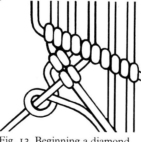

Fig. 13 Beginning a diamond pattern.

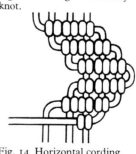

Fig. 14 Horizontal cording angled first to the right.

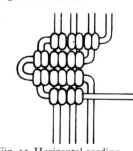

Fig. 15 Horizontal cording angled first to the left.

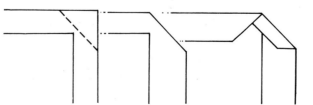

Fig. 16 Mitring the corner.

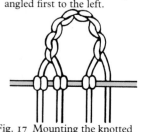

Fig. 17 Mounting the knotted chain loop.

braid of angled cording over and under the right hand braid to interlock.

To complete

Paste the board and the back of the material.

Lay the board on the material, glued sides together, mitre the four corners to 5 mm ($\frac{1}{4}$ in) of the corner as shown in Fig. 16. Bring the material over and stick it on to the back of the board. To prevent warping, keep the board under a heavy weight – books are ideal – for twenty-four hours.

Mark out the mounting board to left and right of the top of each sample, using the awl to make a hole at each mark.

With a needle, thread either end of each holding cord through to the back of the board using pliers if necessary. If desired, the holding cord can be replaced by a double length of button-hole thread so that its presence is minimized. Cut each end to 4 cm ($1\frac{1}{2}$ in) and glue down.

At the bottom of all the samples worked on four threads, sew all the ends through to the back of the board and glue as before.

On the others cut all ends except the outer threads (on flat knot mesh leave two threads at each side) to 4 cm ($1\frac{1}{2}$ in), turn to the back of the macramé and glue.

Take all remaining threads to the back of the covered board and finish off as before.

Book marker

The use of different coloured threads can produce interesting patterns which accentuate the stitches, as is shown by this book marker, worked in fine thread.

You will need

● One ball Twilley's Stalite no. 3 in pale colour (beige used here)
● one ball Twilley's Stalite no. 3 in dark colour (dark brown used here)
● macramé equipment as given on page 43

Instructions

All the techniques for this project are given on pages 44 and 45.

Cut eight lengths in beige each 127 cm (50 in).

Cut four lengths in dark brown each 127 cm (50 in).

Cut three lengths in beige each 25 cm (10 in) to use as foundation cord and leaders.

Lay two dark brown threads side by side on the board and find their centre.

Work four single chain in each direction from this centre point.

Work the other dark brown pair of threads and each of the four pairs of beige threads in the same way.

Pin a foundation cord to the board.

Form a dark brown single knotted chain into a loop and position it above

Instructions for the book marker are below, serviette ring and tea cosy panel overleaf.

the foundation cord. Cord each thread on to the foundation cord in turn, close against the chain loop (Fig. 17).

Cord on the other pairs of threads in the same way, first the four beige pairs then the dark brown pairs. (24 threads.)

Pin a leader on to the board and make a row of horizontal cording.

Divide the threads into pairs and make a four knot half hitched spiral on each pair.

Pin another leader on to the board and work a row of horizontal cording.

Divide the threads into six groups of four threads each and make a flat knot on each group. Continue in alternated flat knots for twenty-one rows more.

Divide the threads into pairs and make six single knotted chain on each pair.

Take the first group of four threads together as one and knot them round the next four threads as for the first stage of a multiple knotted chain. Bind the ends with extra thread in beige to form a tassel.

Work centre eight threads in the same way, binding in dark brown.

Work the third group of threads, taking the dark brown round the beige and binding with beige.

Trim the ends.

Tea cosy panel

This panel is worked here in two colours of strong thread. It could be used as a decoration for many other articles such as a cushion, a tote bag or a pyjama case using appropriate thread.

You will need

● One ball of 5s polished cotton in beige
● one ball of 5s polished cotton in dark brown
● purchased plain coloured tea cosy
● macramé equipment as given on page 43

Instructions

All the techniques required for this project are given on pages 44 and 45.

Cut twelve lengths of beige each 204 cm (80 in).

Cut twelve lengths of dark brown each 204 cm (80 in).

Cut seven lengths each 45 cm (18 in) for use as foundation cord and holding cords.

Pin foundation cord on the board.

Set on the threads as follows: two beige, four brown, two beige, two brown, four beige, two brown, two beige, four brown and two beige. (48 threads.)

Pin a leader across the board and work a row of horizontal cording across all the threads.

Pattern A

Using the centre four threads, make one and a half double knotted chain.

Using the left hand thread as leader, work diagonal cording to the right across the next seven threads, to end just below the centre of the double knotted chain.

Using the right hand thread as leader, work diagonal cording to the left across the next eight threads, to end in the same place.

Work two more rows of diagonal cording into the centre in the same way, immediately under the first two. On the outer two threads at each side make four knotted chain.

Counting from the left, use the seventh thread as leader and cord diagonally to the left over the next six threads.

Counting from the left, use the eighth thread as leader and work another row of diagonal cording over the next seven threads.

Work the right hand side to correspond.

Using the centre four threads, make one and a half double knotted chain.

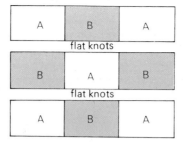

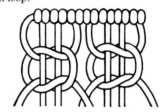

Fig. 18 Layout of panel.

Fig. 19 Angled foundation cord under knotted chain loop.

Fig. 20 Using a leader as 1st working thread.

Pattern B

Using the next sixteen threads and starting with a row of four knots, work seven rows of alternating flat knots, thus ending with a four knot row.

Work patterns A and B according to Fig. 18, separating the three sections by two rows of horizontal cording each over a separate leader with a row of flat knots between them. End with a single row of horizontal cording.

To complete

Sew the ends of the holding cords along the back of the work for about 5 cm (2 in) and trim.

Trim the working threads to 5 cm (2 in). Turn to the back of the work and, using latex glue, fix in place.

Position the macramé in the centre of the tea cosy front and using button-hole thread, sew in place.

Serviette ring

A pretty combination of stitches is backed with ribbon to show them to best effect. The ring fastens with a ball and loop and in a sturdier thread the design can be made into a belt.

You will need

● One ball Twilley's Stalite no. 3
● petersham ribbon 4 cm by 14 cm (1½ in by 5½ in) in a contrast colour to the thread
● macramé equipment as given on page 43

Instructions

All the techniques required for this project are given on pages 44 and 45.

Cut twelve lengths each 132 cm (52 in).

Find the centre of two lengths and pin, side by side, on the board.

Make three single knotted chain in either direction from this central point.

Form the chain into a loop and cord the ends on to the centre of a third length used as a foundation cord.

Angle the foundation cord downwards at about 45 degrees at each end and pin in this position to the board.

Using the centre four threads, make a flat knot.

Double and set on four of the remaining lengths on either side of the angled foundation cord (Fig. 19).

Taking in two new threads at either side on each row, work three rows more of alternated flat knots.

Place the last length centrally across the work and use as a leader to work a row of horizontal cording across all threads, including the ends of the foundation cord. Take the ends of the leader down each side as working threads (Fig. 20). (24 threads.)

Step 1. Divide the threads into six groups of four threads each and make three flat knots on each group.

Step 2. Omitting two threads at either side, divide the threads into five groups of four threads each and make two flat knots on each group.

Step 3. Divide the threads into six groups of four threads each and work a six knot flat knot spiral on each group.

Step 4. As step 2.
Step 5. As step 3, reversing twists.
Step 6. As step 2.

Repeat steps 1 to 6 then step 1 again.

Using the centre four threads, make seven flat knots, take the two threads up and through the centre of the first flat knot to make a blackberry ball and then secure with a flat knot.

Work two flat knots to right and left of the blackberry ball.

Make a row of six flat knots and then work in alternated flat knots for four further rows.

To complete

Lay the ribbon on the right side of the work and sew securely, using back stitch, along the edge just below the last row of knotting.

Trim the threads to 1 cm (½ in), turn the ribbon to the back and, making the ribbon slightly tighter than the macramé, slip stitch the ribbon along the sides and at the base of the triangle, turning in the raw edge.

Tatting

Tatting has a charming snowflake quality. It is a lace made in the fingers using a shuttle and as the equipment is small and takes up so little space, it is ideal for carrying around to fill in odd moments of leisure. However, tatting does need supple fingers and good hand coordination and whilst an eager child can often learn tatting from about the age of seven, mature and stiffer fingers sometimes find tatting difficult. The beautiful results, though, are well worth the perseverance.

Little is known of the origins of tatting. It is related to both netting and macramé, and seems to have been developed from these by early seamen, who used the tatting technique for making rope eyelets.

A simple form of tatting was practised in England during the 18th century, and its popularity can be judged by the many beautiful shuttles which have survived.

Materials and Equipment

A shuttle (sometimes two), a fine hook and thread are all that are needed to make the stitches. Some shuttles have a hook incorporated and sometimes a separate hook is supplied with the shuttle; otherwise a fine crochet hook will suffice. Some shuttles have a central spool which can be removed for winding.

A smooth, firm thread is essential; one that gives or stretches or is uneven in texture is not suitable. Crochet cotton is the most frequently used thread.

Sewing needles to finish off loose ends and scissors are the other basic equipment requirements, although sometimes a tape measure may be needed.

Fabric, thread and a purchased handkerchief are needed to make up the projects which the tatting decorates.

Know how

To prepare the shuttle, tie the thread to the centre and wind on sufficient thread to fill the shuttle without protruding beyond its edges. The thread should not unwind if the shuttle is accidentally dropped.

There is only one knot or stitch used in tatting, usually known as a double stitch. It consists of two half knots or half stitches. Practise each half stitch separately before pairing them to make the basic double stitch. This is then built up into the delicate rings and chains from which tatting designs are produced.

Single stitch (or first half stitch)

Hold the shuttle in the right hand with about 51 cm (20 in) of thread unwound.

Grasp the end of the thread with the thumb and first finger of the left hand and form a ring with the thread between the left hand and the shuttle by passing the thread over the remaining outstretched fingers of the left hand, then underneath and back to the thumb and forefinger, placing the thumb over the crossing point of the threads (Fig. 1). The thread round the left hand fingers is called the ring thread, the rest is the shuttle thread. Unwind more thread from the shuttle as it is required.

Lay the shuttle thread in a loop over the top of the left hand as shown in Fig. 2.

Pass the shuttle from right to left through the ring and up through the loop (Fig. 3). At this point the shuttle thread is looped around the ring thread (Fig. 4).

The next step is most important. The loop has to be transferred from the shuttle thread to the ring thread. This is done by pulling the shuttle sharply to the right whilst lowering the middle finger of the left hand to relax the thread. The ring thread is now looped round the shuttle thread (Fig. 5).

Raise the middle finger of the left hand to slide the knot until it is close to the thumb (Fig. 6). Hold it firmly in place with the thumb and first finger. The single stitch (or first half stitch) is now completed.

Repeat from Fig. 2 to practise a series of them, pulling each one close up to the last and holding it firmly in place as before.

When the ring thread becomes used up, unwind more from the shuttle and enlarge the ring by stretching the fingers of the left hand. The stitches should slide easily along the shuttle thread. If they do not, the transfer of the loop from shuttle thread to ring thread has not been made correctly. Tatting will not unravel but any mistakes can be unpicked with the hook.

Double stitch
(or second half stitch)

First work a single stitch (or first half stitch), then pass the shuttle from the top downwards through the ring from left to right and over the shuttle thread (Fig. 7).

Transfer the loop from the shuttle thread to the ring thread as before and slide the second half close up to the first half. This completes a double stitch (Fig. 8).

Again, practise a series, making sure that all the stitches slide easily along the shuttle thread.

Picot

This is a decorative loop formed between double stitches.

When making the first half stitch of the double stitch to follow the picot, instead of pulling it close to the previous double stitch, position it about 6 mm ($\frac{1}{4}$ in) away and complete the double stitch in the usual way (Fig. 9). Then slide the double stitch close up to the previous one so that the thread between the two loops up to form the picot.

Ring

To close a ring, once the required number of double stitches has been worked release the ring thread from the left hand, hold the beginning of the row of stitches between the thumb and forefinger of the left hand whilst gently pulling the shuttle thread. If the ring will not draw in then the transfer of the loop from the shuttle thread to the ring thread has been omitted or incorrectly worked at some point.

Joining

Rings are usually formed into patterns by holding them in position by joining adjacent picots.

Work a ring of four double stitches, a picot, four double stitches, a picot, four double stitches, a picot, four double stitches, close the ring.

Hold the completed ring between the thumb and first finger of the left hand and pass the shuttle thread round the remaining outstretched fingers to form a new ring thread. Start the next ring close up to the first with four double stitches.

Join to the last picot of the first ring by inserting the hook through that picot from front to back. Draw through the ring thread to make a large enough loop to take the shuttle. Pass the shuttle through from back to front (Fig. 10) then raise the middle finger of the left hand to tighten and position this loop close up against the previous double stitch. It must slide on the shuttle thread and is counted as a first half stitch. Now work a second half stitch to secure the join and complete the ring with three double stitches, a picot, four double stitches, a picot,

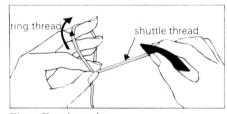

Fig. 1 Forming a ring.

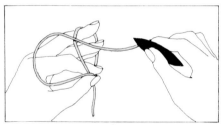

Fig. 2 Looping the shuttle thread.

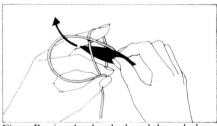

Fig. 3 Passing the shuttle thread through the ring.

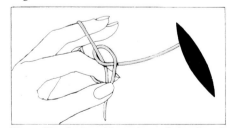

Fig. 4 Shuttle thread looped round ring thread.

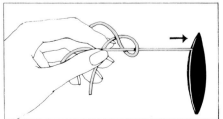

Fig. 5 Ring thread looped round shuttle thread.

four double stitches, close the ring.

Chain

A chain is made using two separate threads. Usually the second thread can be used straight from the ball although some designs will require it to be wound on to a second shuttle. Two different colours can be used.

Tie both threads together, hold the knot with the thumb and first finger of the left hand and wrap the ball thread (or second shuttle thread) over the left hand and around the little finger as shown in Fig. 11. This takes the place of the ring thread and double stitches

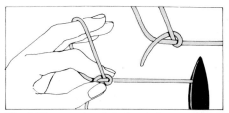
Fig. 6 The completed single stitch.

Fig. 7 Shuttle thread through ring and over loop.

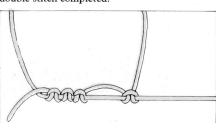
Fig. 8 Transferring loop to ring thread and double stitch completed.

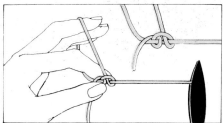
Fig. 9 Forming a picot.

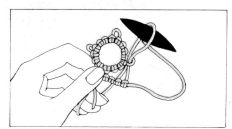
Fig. 10 Joining rings.

are worked over it in the usual way to produce a chain.

Combining rings and chains

If, after working a chain, the pattern directions then require a ring, remove the ball thread from the left hand and use the shuttle thread on its own.

If, after working a ring, the pattern then requires a chain, wind the ball thread on to the left hand and use both threads.

Begin each ring or chain as closely as possible to the preceding ring or chain unless the pattern directions state otherwise (Fig. 12).

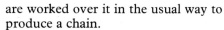

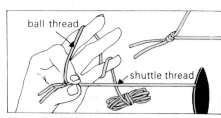
Fig. 11 Beginning a chain.

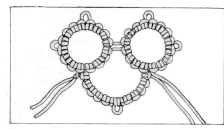
Fig. 12 Positioning of stitches.

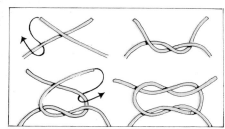
Fig. 13 A reef knot.

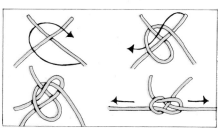
Fig. 14 A weaver's knot.

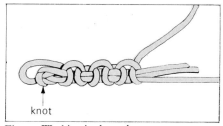
Fig. 15 Working in the ends.

Reversing. Work often has to be turned when changing from ring to chain or vice versa.

Simply take the ring or chain just completed and therefore arching upwards and turn it upside down so that it points downwards. This is usually given in instructions as 'reverse work'.

Joining threads

At some stage during work it is likely the shuttle will need refilling. When there is not a spare ball, avoid cutting the ball thread whilst it is being used for chains. To supply the empty shuttle, wind sufficient thread on to a card or reel before beginning.

Join a new shuttle thread at the beginning of a ring by overlapping old and new threads so that both completely encircle the left hand. Work the first few double stitches with both threads then drop the old thread and continue with the new. Only trim the ends after the ring has been securely closed. This method of overlapping can also be used to join a new ball thread for a chain.

If there is not sufficient length left for an overlapped join, tie the old and new ends together with either a reef knot (Fig. 13) or a weaver's knot (Fig. 14) at the beginning of a ring or a chain and run these ends along the shuttle thread so that they lie inside a series of double stitches (Fig. 15). Use the hook to pull the short ends through each half stitch before it is tightened in position.

To avoid joining threads at the beginning of work, shuttle and ball thread need not be cut apart.

Finishing off

Tie shuttle and ball threads together with a final reef knot or weaver's knot. The ends should be left long enough to thread into a needle.

Use either one end to overcast the other to the back of the tatting or stab stitch each end through the heads of several double stitches.

Laundering

Wash in the usual way in a good soap powder.

A small article of white tatting, if heavily soiled, can be boiled.

To make the best of decorative tatting pin it outstretched while still damp on an ironing board or similar surface and leave it until completely dry. When pinning, pull out all the picots and ensure that the overall shape is accurate.

Tatting intended for regular wear and, therefore, washing, need only be pressed under a damp cloth.

Abbreviations

The most usual tatting abbreviations are:

ss	single stitch
ds	double stitch
p	picot
r	ring
ch	chain
rw	reverse work
sep	separated
sp	space

Below The child's dress (also inset **above**), handkerchief and bridal veil have tatted trimmings, the tablecloth is made entirely of tatting.

Girl's dress trimmed with tatting

The dress will fit an average seven to eight year old but the simple shape can easily be enlarged.

You will need

- **Tatting.** 1 ball Twilley's Lyscordet
- tatting shuttle
- **Dress.** 2.60 m (3 yd) cotton lawn
- sewing thread
- 1 m (1 yd) bias binding
- 2 wrist lengths plus overlaps of elastic
- squared paper for pattern

Measurements

Tatting. Width 2 cm ($\frac{3}{4}$ in)

Dress. To fit 66 to 68 cm (26 to 27 in) chest

length 75 cm (29 in), adjustable

Each square on the pattern (Fig. 16) represents 5 cm (2 in). Hems and a 1.5 cm ($\frac{5}{8}$ in) seam allowance are included

Instructions
Dress

Stitch yoke fronts to yoke back at shoulder. Repeat with yoke linings.

Make neck ties by folding each one in half lengthways, right sides together. Seam 6 mm ($\frac{1}{4}$ in) from the raw edges, leaving one end open. Turn to the right side.

Attach the open end of one neck tie to one yoke front by placing it on the right side 15 mm ($\frac{5}{8}$ in) from the top with raw edges together. Tack in place.

Repeat with other neck tie and front.

With right sides together, stitch yoke to lining at front opening and neck edge. Clip neck seam. Turn fabric to right side and press. The yoke front pieces are designed to meet without overlap.

Tack the raw edges at sides and lower edges of yoke and lining together.

Stitch skirt front to skirt back at the sides.

Gather the top of the skirt to fit the yoke. With right sides together, stitch skirt to yoke.

Stitch the sleeve seams.

Gather the top of each sleeve to fit sleeve opening. With right sides together, stitch in each sleeve.

Make a 1 cm ($\frac{3}{8}$ in) hem on the sleeves.

Stitch bias binding inside each sleeve 2 cm ($\frac{3}{4}$ in) from the cuff edge as a casing for the elastic. Insert elastic.

Make a 6 cm ($2\frac{1}{2}$ in) hem – or depth required – on skirt.

Tatting

All the techniques required for this project are given on pages 50 and 51. Once the shuttle has been fully wound do not break off the thread from the ball.

Letters A, B and C are for identification only.

R of 4 ds, p, 4 ds, p, 4 ds, p, 4 ds, close, rw.

Ch of 3 ds, p, 3 ds, p, 3 ds, join by shuttle thread to last picot of r by inserting hook into p, catch shuttle thread and draw out into a loop, pass the shuttle through the loop and adjust the knot, rw.

*Ch A of 2 ds, 4 p sep by 2 ds, 3 ds, join by shuttle thread to last p of previous ch, rw.

Ch B of 3 ds, p, 3 ds, p, 3 ds, join by shuttle thread to last p of ch A, rw.

Ch C of 3 ds, p, 3 ds, p, 3 ds, join by shuttle thread to last p of ch B, rw.

Repeat from * for length required.

To complete

Using sewing thread to match the tatting, attach the trimming to the dress as illustrated using small stitches through the central picots.

Detail of wedding veil trim.

Two tier bridal veil

Shown here on a bridal veil, this lovely daisy-chain edging would also be ideal for the collar and cuffs on a silk blouse.

You will need
- 2 balls of crochet cotton no. 40
- tatting shuttle
- 2.50 m ($2\frac{3}{4}$ yd) of 180 cm (70–72 in) wide bridal veiling
- sewing needle
- white sewing thread

Measurements
Width of tatting 1.5 cm ($\frac{5}{8}$ in)

length of head veil 75 cm (29 in)

length of main veil 175 cm (70 in)

Fig. 16 Dress pattern cutting layout.

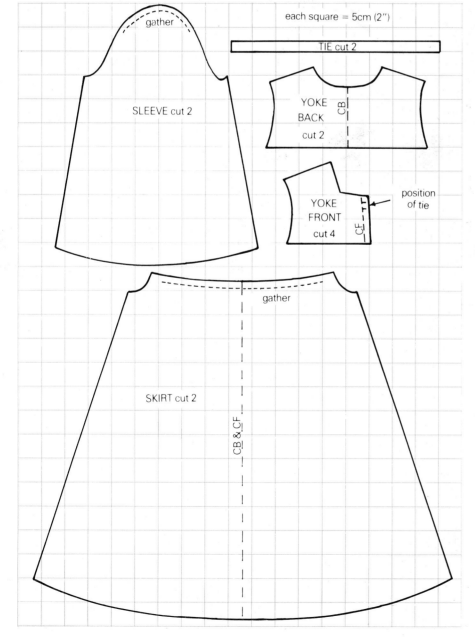

each square = 5cm (2")

gather

TIE cut 2

SLEEVE cut 2

YOKE BACK cut 2   CB

YOKE FRONT cut 4   CF   position of tie

gather

SKIRT cut 2

CB & CF

Instructions
Edging

All the techniques required for this project are given on pages 50 and 51.

Fill the shuttle from one ball of thread and use the other to work the chains.

*R of 5 ds, p, 5 ds, close, rw.

Ch of 5 ds, p, 5 ds, rw.

Large r of 3 ds, join to picot of previous r, 2 ds, 8 p sep by 2 ds, 3 ds, close, rw.

Ch of 5 ds, p, 5 ds, rw.

R of 5 ds, join to last p of large r, 5 ds, close.

Repeat from * for the length required to fit the side and bottom edges of each veil.

To complete

Cut the veiling to the lengths given and shape the bottom corners of each veil into a curve.

Press the tatting under a damp cloth.

Sew a length of tatting neatly to each veil using hemming stitches.

Gather the top of each veil as required to fit the head-dress which can then be attached to the gathers with oversewing stitches.

Detail of the handkerchief corner.

Handkerchief edging

A variation of the daisy-chain edging gives a delightful finish to a handkerchief. The motif of a purchased handkerchief here adds an interesting detail.

You will need
- 1 ball of crochet cotton no. 60
- tatting shuttle

Measurements

Width of tatting approximately 1.5 cm ($\frac{5}{8}$ in)

Instructions
Edging

All the techniques required for this project are given on pages 50 and 51.

Large r of 7 ds, 7 p sep by 2 ds, 5 ds, close.

*Small r of 4 ds, join to last p of large r, 1 ds, p, 5 ds, close, rw.

Ch of 7 ds, p, 7 ds, rw.

Large r of 7 ds, join to picot of previous small r, 2 ds, 6 p sep by 2 ds, 5 ds, close.**

Repeat from * to ** until corner is reached.

To work a corner

Large r of 5 ds, join to last p of previous large r, 2 ds, 6 p sep by 2 ds, 5 ds, close.

Repeat from * to ** to next corner and so on all around edge, joining the final small r to the first large r at the beginning.

Finish by tying the final ch to the first r.

To complete

Press the tatting under a damp cloth.

Attach it to the handkerchief at the picots on the chains, using small hemming stitches.

Detail of some of the chain wheel motifs.

Coffee tablecloth

The heavy richness of the chain wheel motifs requires a great deal of concentration but once made up into this beautiful hexagonal cloth they are most impressive.

You will need
- 5 balls of crochet cotton no. 10
- tatting shuttle

Measurements

Each motif is 8.5 cm ($3\frac{1}{4}$ in) across cloth approximately 56 cm (22 in) across

Instructions
First motif

All the techniques required for this project are given on pages 50 and 51.

Letters A, B, C and D are for identification only (see Fig. 17).

R A of 7 ds, p, 4 ds, p, 9 ds, close.

R B of 7 ds, p, 7 ds, close, rw.

Ch A of 7 ds, p, 11 ds, small p (leave a 3 mm ($\frac{1}{8}$ in) space between stitches), 1 ds, small p, 9 ds, join to picot of ring B by inserting hook into p, catch shuttle thread and draw out into a loop, pass the shuttle through the loop and adjust the knot.

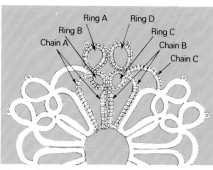

Fig. 17 Identifying rings and chains.

Fig. 18 Joining points.

*Ch B of 9 ds, join to last small p of ch A, 1 ds, small p, 11 ds, p, 7 ds, rw.

R C of 7 ds, join to junction of chains with r B, 7 ds, close.

R D of 9 ds, join to last p of ring A, 4 ds, p, 7 ds, close.

Ch C of 14 ds.

Work rings A and B as before.

Ch A of 7 ds, join to last p of ch B, 11 ds, join to small p of ch B, 1 ds, small p, 9 ds, join by shuttle thread as before to picot of ring B.**

Repeat from * to ** 4 times more, then repeat ch B joining it to ch A at beginning of the motif.

Repeat rings C and D and ch C.

Cut and tie ends to beginning of motif.

Second motif

Work as given for first motif as far as r C.

R D of 9 ds, join to last p of r A, 4 ds, join to corresponding p of any r A on first motif, 7 ds, close.

Ch C of 14 ds.

R A of 7 ds, join to corresponding p on r D of first motif, 4 ds, p, 9 ds, close.

Continue as given for first motif.

To complete

Make 37 motifs altogether, joining all corresponding rings in the same way as the second motif was joined to the first (see Fig. 18) to make the hexagonal shape of the cloth.

There are 4 motifs in the 1st and 7th rows, 5 in the 2nd and 6th rows, 6 in the 3rd and 5th rows and 7 in the middle row.

Finish off ends.

Press under a damp cloth.

Collage

Collage, which comes from the French word 'coller' meaning to stick, has its origins around 1912. At this time the famous artists Picasso and Braque began sticking pieces of newsprint on to their oil paintings as part of the picture. This idea has gradually developed so that nowadays a range of objects is incorporated into pictures and sculptures.

The projects described in this section, however, are mainly made with pieces of fabric and thread.

As a craft, collage has many advantages. Because it is a relatively new idea, it has no conventions and individuals are free to express themselves in their own way. It is not even necessary to be good at drawing because the aim is not to imitate drawings and paintings, but to assemble materials to create a pleasing and harmonious effect.

Materials and Equipment

Very little equipment is needed, probably nothing which is not already in the home. Collecting pieces of fabric, oddments of lace, beads from old necklaces, knitting yarns and ribbon is fun and they will all come in useful to add interest to the collage.

Collage fabrics can be almost anything, with the following tips in mind.

Some fabrics naturally suggest types of scenery: rough hessians, tweeds and bouclés are useful for walls, rocks and tree bark; silks and rayons look like water; tiny floral prints suggest summer fields; nets can represent clouds or smoke.

Some materials with a pile, such as corduroy, look light or dark according to which way they are hung.

Overlaying with net softens the contours, tones down bright colours and lends distance in a landscape. Lurex materials can be a little too glittery, but under chiffon, organdie or other semi-transparent material, they give a subtle sheen to frost or to moonlit water.

Some fabrics fray badly but this apparent drawback can be put to good use for a thatched roof or a field of stubble.

Background fabrics must be strong and furnishing fabrics are usually excellent. Do not use a fabric that stretches. If the background fabric is lightweight, strengthen it by tacking it over a firmer fabric and treat the two pieces as one. If the background will not show once the picture is finished, old sheeting will do.

Glue should be clear and quick drying. White latex glue spreads easily but darkens in time, so keep it for heavy fabrics like leather, felt or furnishing fabrics and for mounting pictures.

Iron-on interfacing will stop the fabric from fraying and help to keep its shape.

Transparent nail varnish on the underside edge of velvet helps to prevent fraying.

Matchsticks or cocktail sticks are used to spread small amounts of glue.

Stiff card or hardboard is used for mounting, unless it is intended as a wall hanging.

General items include scissors, a washable working surface, paper, tracing paper, pen or pencil, tape measure, needles and sewing cotton. Strong linen thread or buttonhole twist, a knife and clothes pegs.

Know how

Planning a picture

Draw the outlines of the design on to paper to the finished size. Decide which parts will be cut whole and which will be added later. It is useful to experiment first with paper shapes and coloured cut-outs from magazines are useful for this.

Once the basic parts of the picture are decided, either use the magazine cut-outs or trace the shapes on to thin paper to make templates.

Assembling – first method

Cut a piece of stiff card or cardboard to the size of the picture. If the card-

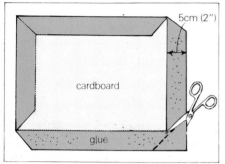

Fig. 1 Assembling picture, 1st method.

board is brown, slip a piece of white paper between it and the fabric.

Cut a piece of background fabric 4–5 cm (1½–2 in) bigger all round than the card.

Place the card centrally on the wrong side of the fabric. Glue the wrong side of the fabric where it overlaps the card. Cut the corners and fold over on to the card, as shown in Fig. 1.

Cut a second piece of white card slightly smaller than the first. Stick this over the back of the fabric-covered card to hide the fabric edges and to add strength. Weight it down with books while the glue sets.

In the meantime, use the templates to cut out the pieces from the chosen fabrics. It is at this stage that difficult materials are backed with iron-on interfacing to prevent fraying and stiffen the fabric. It also provides a barrier to protect delicate materials from direct contact with glue.

Second method

If any sewing is to be used, and for large framed pictures, use the traditional lacing method of mounting the fabric. After the picture is finished, fold the spare material over the back

of the mounting board and lace it backwards and forwards from side to side and from top to bottom with strong linen thread or buttonhole twist at 3 cm (1 in) intervals.

Next neaten and oversew the corners. Mounted this way, pictures remain well stretched.

Glueing

Use a clear, quick-drying glue sparingly, keeping the tube upright in a glass while working to prevent spilling out on the working surface and perhaps marking the front of the picture. Spread it on to the back of each piece using a matchstick or cocktail stick.

Net is best attached with a few widely spaced tiny stitches which are quite invisible if the thread used matches the background colour.

Prevent velvet from fraying by spreading a little nail varnish underneath the edges of the shape and allowing it to dry, before glueing it.

After a few pieces have been stuck down, prop the collage up and view it from the far end of the room to obtain a true idea of how work is progressing.

When all the pieces have been added, leave to dry thoroughly for a day.

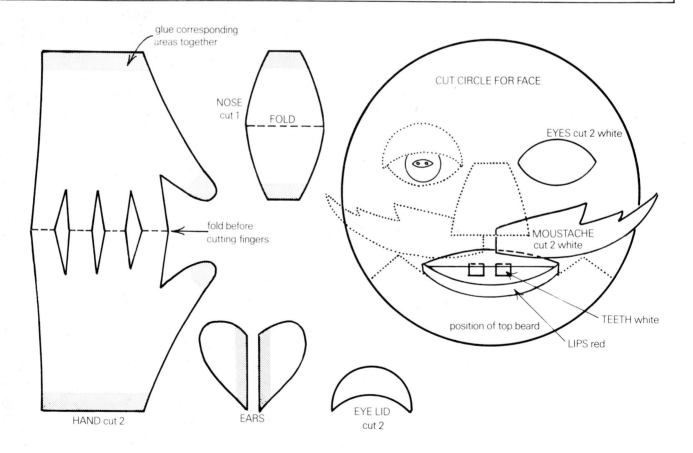

Fig. 2 1st cutting plan for Father Christmas.

Christmas hanging

Here Father Christmas is seen in the
snow against the dark green of a
forest but he could just as well be
placed against a night sky twinkling
with sequined stars or cotton wool
snow flakes.

You will need
● One piece of white felt 30 cm (12
in) square
● one piece of red felt 30 cm (12 in)
square
● one piece of flesh pink felt 15 cm (6
in) square
● two small buttons
● one piece of background fabric 48
cm by 30 cm (19 in by 12 in)
● oddments of black felt
● a scrap of bouclé wool
● 1.30 m (1½ yd) red lace edging or
ribbon
● one small net bag from supermarket
bag of oranges or nuts
● dowel rod 36 cm (14 in) long
● 91 cm (1 yd) coloured string or cord
● two small safety pins
● collage equipment as given on page
55

Measurements
46 cm by 29 cm (18 in by 11½ in)

Instructions
All the techniques required for this
project are given on page 56. From
the flesh pink felt cut out a circle for
the face and then the shapes for the
hands, eyelids, nose and ears as given
in Fig. 2.

Fold the nose and glue the ends together. Stick the nose in position on
the face leaving the bottom half un-
glued.

From the white felt, cut out two
pieces for the moustache, two eyes and
two teeth as given in Fig. 2.

Sew one small button in the centre
of each white eye piece. Glue the eyes
to the face.

Next from white felt cut two strips
10 cm by 5.5 cm (4 in by 2¼ in) for
the tassels and 1 strip 29 cm by 6 cm
(11½ in. by 2½ in) for the snow. Cut
one of the long edges of the snow piece
in a curve. Also from white felt and
enlarging the shapes given in Fig. 3,
cut two pieces for the beard, two cuffs
and the hood trim.

From the black felt remnants cut
out two feet and a shape for the inside
of the mouth as given in Fig. 3 and two
small circles for the pupils of the eyes.

Father Christmas with a sack full of toys.

each square=5cm (2″) sq.

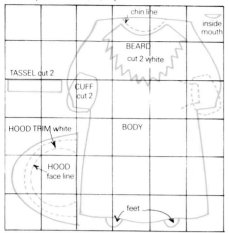

Fig. 3 2nd cutting plan for Father Christmas.

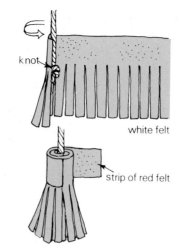

Fig. 4 Making the tassel.

Glue the small black eye circles in the middle of the buttons.

Glue the top edges of the eyelids and position them over the eyes so that they just overlap the button.

Glue the ears to underneath the face, top of the ears level with the centre of the eyes.

From the red felt, cut out two pieces for the lips (Fig. 2), two tassel strips, the hood and the coat as given in Fig. 3.

Glue the lips, teeth and black mouth piece and position them on the face with the teeth tucked under the top lip.

Glue the moustache pieces and position them under the nose.

Cut two small pieces of white bouclé wool, or white felt, for the eyebrows and stick them in place. Lay the red coat and hood pieces together, edge to edge.

Position the face over the coat and hood, glueing at top and bottom. Glue the white hood trim round the face, taking it under the ears. Stick one beard piece just below the chin line as shown in Fig. 3, the other on top and against the lower lip. Glue the wrists and thumbs of the hands and fold together, leaving the hands hollow.

Take the two white cuff pieces and glue them in position, see Fig. 3, slotting in the wrists at the same time.

Make a hem at the top of the background fabric for the rod and turn under small hems on the side and lower edges.

After positioning the snow on the background fabric, trim with the red lace. Position Father Christmas just above the snow, then stick on the feet.

Tie the string or cord to the rod so that equal lengths hang free on either side. Knot the ends.

Decorate the knotted ends with tassels, see Fig. 4. Fill the net sack with brightly wrapped presents.

Trim the net, leaving enough at either end of the top to push through the hands. Secure these ends with a small safety pin hidden inside each hand.

Silhouette calendar

Silhouette pictures were named after a very clever and scissor-happy French politician who lived in the 18th century, Etienne de Silhouette. The fashion grew and became extremely popular in Victorian England.

Originally these black on white pictures were painted or cut out in paper. However, it is fascinating to use fabrics instead of paper, because the tones of black vary with different materials and semi-transparent effects are made with lace and net.

Books of fairy stories or nursery rhymes usually have distinctive illustrations which can easily be adapted.

You will need
● Remnants of velvet, felt, black interfacing, poplin, net and lace
● slub wool or teased-out yarn
● soft embroidery cotton, knitting or darning wool
● braid and/or velvet ribbon
● white material such as cotton 36 cm by 51 cm (14 in by 20 in)
● two pieces of firm white card each 31 cm by 46 cm (12 in by 18 in)
● a calendar
● collage equipment as given on page 55

Measurements
31 cm by 46 cm (12 in by 18 in)

An unusual silhouette picture in which details are picked out by using different shades of black fabric.

each square=5cm (2") sq.

Fig. 5 Cutting plan for silhouette.

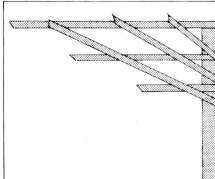

Fig. 6 Making the trellis.

Instructions

All the techniques required for this project are given on page 56.

Glue the white background material to cover one piece of card, or stretch background material over first piece of card and glue spare fabric to the back.

Glue two small pieces of black velvet ribbon at right angles to the top edge of the calendar.

Glue the second piece of white card to the back of the background, trapping the ends of the ribbon holding the calendar between the two cards, and adding a loop at the top to hang it by.

Weight with books for an hour until the glue sets.

From the interfacing cut one strip about 2 cm by 39 cm ($\frac{3}{4}$ in by $15\frac{1}{2}$ in) and stick it on the right hand side of the picture, about 2 cm ($\frac{3}{4}$ in) in from the edge. Cut six more strips of about 1 cm ($\frac{3}{8}$ in) wide as shown in Fig. 6 and trim ends diagonally.

Make up the trellis, beginning about 3.5 cm ($1\frac{1}{2}$ in) from the top. Glue three vertical pieces of soft embroidery thread or wool to the upright trellis post. Decorate the trellis with climbing plants of lace and bouclé yarn. Cut a piece of felt about 2.5 cm by 21 cm (1 in by 8 in) for the wall at the bottom. Glue it in place, 1.5 cm ($\frac{1}{2}$ in) in from the bottom and right hand edges.

Cut two flower pot shapes in felt and some pieces of lace and net for the flowers. Glue in place, as shown in photograph.

Cut out round the outline of the whole of each figure (see Fig. 5) from interfacing then cut the clothes and hats separately from pieces of velvet, felt, poplin, net and lace.

Glue the interfacing in position on the white background and then add the clothes.

Make the chairs, table and flowers from remnants of lace and wool. Glue in position.

Add plain black netting to represent a shadow at the feet of the couple.

Finally, frame the picture with four lengths of braid or velvet ribbon (or both), two 31 cm (12 in) long and two 46 cm (18 in) long, mitring them at the corners. To avoid the cut edges fraying, lightly glue or paint with transparent nail varnish.

When the varnish is dry, glue to the background.

Fig. 7 Cutting plan for seascape.   each square=5cm (2″) sq.

Seascape

The special feature of this picture is the phosphorescent sparkle of the moonlit sea and ship, brought about by using blue, green and silver lurex material with the rest of the fabrics. The leaping fish, too, have been cut from the glittering remains of an old party dress, which when used on its reverse side has a soft enough effect for the moon.

You will need
● Remnants of brocade in blue and green, light and dark, for the waves, in bright colours for the fish and moon; lurex in blue and green, light and dark, in silver and blue; green net; white lace; dark blue velvet about 53 cm (21 in) square; iron-on interfacing
● coloured sequins for the fishes' eyes and one red and one green for the ship's lights
● stiff white card, one piece 57 cm (22½ in) square and four strips each 57 cm by 3 cm (22½ in by 1¼ in)
● 1.10 m (1¼ yd) cord or invisible fishing line
● collage equipment as given on page 55

Left A midnight seascape set against its real life counterpart. **Right** Carefully chosen greens and browns suggest a country scene in autumn.

Measurements

57 cm (22½ in) square

Instructions

All the techniques required for this project are given on page 56.

Enlarge the design given in Fig. 7 on to squared or graph paper and number each wave.

Make a separate tracing of each wave, with an extra 1.5 cm (⅝ in) at either end and on the lower edge. Cut out the shapes from the tracing paper, numbering each pattern piece to correspond with the drawings.

Cut out the waves in the chosen fabrics.

Make a paper pattern of the ship by tracing it from the drawing, with an extra 1.5 cm (⅝ in) on the lower edge of the ship's hull.

Cut out the fabric ship pieces.

Make paper patterns of the fish and the seagulls and cut out the fabric pieces.

To prevent fraying, back all these pieces with iron-on interfacing.

Make two holes evenly in the large piece of card about 2 cm (¾ in) from the top and about 36 cm (14 in) apart and insert the hanging wire.

Apply glue to the back of the velvet very lightly except where it will be hidden such as all round the edges and under other fabrics, and position it centrally on the background.

Cut scraps of white lace for the foam on the crest of the waves. Stick them to the underside edge of the top of the appropriate waves.

Assemble the waves, fishes and ship against the background. If the effect is not satisfying, try different materials or shapes for the waves. Once the desired effect is achieved stick the pieces to the velvet, beginning with the ship and gradually working towards the foreground, overlapping each layer.

Add the seagulls and the moon.

Stick down the sequins for the ship's lights and the fishes' eyes.

Mitre the corners of the strips of card and glue them firmly in position to frame the picture. To do this, place one strip in position along the top of the picture and another down the side. At the corner where they overlap, draw a pencil line joining the outer point of the corner to the inner. Cut the uppermost strip along this line, then use it as a guide to cut the strip beneath. Repeat for the other corners. Hold in place with clips or clothes pegs while the glue sets.

Alternatively, edge the picture with braid.

Landscape

This peaceful landscape with its distant farmstead, oast houses and foreground tree glowing with autumn colours in an evening sky is an example of how a picture can be tailor made for a particular room.

In this case, white painted cottage walls make a perfect background for the peachy, cream-coloured sky, especially chosen to match the paintwork on doors and ceilings. The flowered cotton print of a field is a remnant of the curtain material used in the room. The dark green upholstery of the chairs and sofa is picked up in the distant trees and the creeper, and its scatter cushions in autumnal tones in the leaves on the foreground tree.

You will need
● Furnishing fabric in cream or a thinner material backed with old sheeting or curtain lining for the background and net in orange, cream and yellow each 56 cm by 66 cm (22 in by 26 in)
● remnants of curtain material, tweed and corduroy in stripes, floral or plain in autumnal colours; felt in white, light grey and dark grey
● lengths of bouclé wool in dark green and dark brown
● hardboard 51 cm by 61 cm (20 in by 24 in)
● picture frame with pins and hooks for mounting
● collage equipment as given on page 55

Measurements

51 cm by 61 cm (20 in by 24 in)

Instructions

All the techniques required for this project are given on page 56.

Tack the curtain lining and cotton background fabrics together.

Cut small pieces of white lace for the clouds. Stick in position in the top left hand area of the background fabric, remembering that there are 5 cm (2 in) extra all round for mounting.

Cut strips of orange and yellow net the full width of the background fabric but in varying depths and fix in place only at the edges.

Cover the whole of the sky area with a piece of cream net. Tack all edges together round the sides and top of the sky area, close to the edge.

Cut shapes for the most distant hills going right across the picture and a castle on a hill from greyish or dark blue fabrics, to give distance.

Slip them underneath the lower edge of the cream net and tack through all layers, including the background fabric.

Cut out and arrange some shapes for the fields at the bottom, making templates first. Fray the top edge of some of the shapes to represent stubble. Floral prints will represent fields of flowers. Each shape should overlap the one behind. The fields in the picture illustrated curve downwards in the middle of the scene to give the idea of a valley, but experiment with different effects.

Cut a shape for behind and beyond the group of farm buildings and oast houses to represent trees. Herringbone tweed, which has been used here, is very effective for a suggestion of trees.

Assemble the group of buildings on the shape, cutting the farm buildings from scraps of felt and furnishing fabrics. Glue the pieces in place then stick the whole section on to the main picture.

To make the foreground tree, start by tearing out its general shape in newspaper. When it looks more or less right against the rest of the picture in terms of weight, size and position, cut it out in firm mid brown fabric.

Cut out lots of leaves all in the same shape but of slightly different sizes. Use lots of different fabrics in gold, red, brown and green. A few leaves in brown net will look like leaves at the back of the tree.

Pin some of the leaves over the tree shape and then refine the tree by cutting away parts of it to let the sky through here and there. When happy with the effect, glue the whole tree to the background. Add more leaves. Giving thought to the direction of the leaves can indicate movement as if a gentle breeze were blowing.

Finally add pieces of dark green wool to the tree trunk to resemble climbing ivy and some dark brown wool horizontally at the bottom of the picture to suggest tree roots.

Place the picture over the hardboard, folding the spare material to the back. Stretch and lace the back using strong linen carpet thread or buttonhole twist.

If the picture does not have a reasonably flat surface because of thick wool, beads and folded fabric, use a box frame or run a small strip of wood round the rebate between the glass and the rebate. Details on how to make a suitable box frame are given on page 8.

Tie dyeing and tritik

Tie dyeing is a fascinating method of dyeing fabrics in which the design is pre-arranged but somewhat random. By tying the fabric the dye is prevented from reaching certain parts and only reaches the gaps between the ties, so creating the pattern. These ties are called resists.

Tritik is a refinement of tie dyeing which is not so random in design. Instead of tying, the pattern is worked in stitches which are then gathered before the fabric is dyed. This is easier to control than tie dyeing and therefore the finished effect is more easily predetermined.

The craft dates back to very early cultures as can be seen by ancient artifacts unearthed from Peru, India, Japan, China, Africa and South America. However, its origins cannot be traced to any one area.

Tie dyeing today is practised in south east Asia and in parts of Africa where it is sometimes enhanced with heavy embroidery.

Materials and Equipment

Some of the things needed for this craft are ordinary household items. These include a kettle or saucepan, an iron, a bucket or bowl (plastic will do for cold water dyes), a tablespoon and measuring jug, a wooden spoon, soft 'B' pencils and paper to work out the designs, tapemeasure or ruler, scissors, a stitch unpicker, elastic bands or string, needles and thread, pebbles or buttons to bind into the dyeing, cooking salt and soda to fix cold dyes, soap liquids, soapflakes or mild soap powder (but *not* biological powder), a protective overall and rubber gloves.

Special purchases include fabric which should always be white and of natural, not manmade, fibre (100% cotton is easiest and cheapest although linen, silk, wool or a combination of any of these work well). Avoid fibres that have been specially treated, for example crease resistant or drip dry, as the chemicals used in these processes may make them dye resistant. Never use a combination of natural and manmade fibres such as polycotton as the polyester warp or weft will not dye and the result will be pale.

Nylon, Terylene or any other strong thread such as waxed button thread or thread used by tailors must be used for tritik sewing as ordinary thread snaps too easily.

Cold water dyes are easier and safer to use than hot dyes and produce good colours, which are faster than hot dyes.

Purchased 'cold dye fix' can be used instead of washing soda.

Know how

Preparation

Always wash the fabric or garment to be dyed thoroughly both to clean it and to pre-shrink it. Washing also helps remove any dressing.

Any permanent sewing which will show when the article is finished, such as the rolled hem on a headscarf, should be done at this stage. Use thread of the same fibre as the fabric, for example 100% cotton thread for cotton, silk thread for silk. When the article is dyed this will dye to match.

Tying

Each tie involves making a resist – an area where the dye cannot penetrate. The simplest example is the sort of knot made in the corner of a handkerchief as a memory aid (see Fig. 1).

The material is folded, gathered, or in some way bunched up and the resulting bundle secured tightly by binding. The binding is done with thread, elastic bands or string wrapped round and round and fastened securely. The fabric is then dyed, dried and undone or dyed and further binding added without undoing. At the first dye the binding will ensure that certain areas remain white. Binding can be used in a second and subsequent dyeing both to preserve the white and to preserve the first and second colours.

Folding. The material is folded and then tied at regular intervals for a linear pattern. The folds can be made in any direction and can be spaced regularly or at random.

Gathering. A method similar to folding, but in which only a section of the material is gathered up with the fingers and then tied.

Objects. If a pebble or a button is tied into the fabric (see Fig. 2) the resulting pattern will be a white ring surrounding the area in which the object was tied. Thus a large pebble will give a large ring and lots of marbles will give a series of circles and rings. The depth of the tie will also affect the design of the ring.

Tying in a piece of wood or cork will vary the shape and texture of the dyed areas, but these objects will make the fabric float and must be weighed down.

Marbling. This involves crumpling the fabric into a ball and binding it round and round in all directions as shown in Fig. 3. As a result, the material in the centre of the ball is left white and an overall random pattern is obtained.

Other resists. Dye can be prevented from reaching chosen sections by tying them into plastic bags or clipping them with clothes pegs or clips. Do not use metal as it will rust and mark the fabric.

Tie bindings so that the right side of the fabric is outside and in closest contact with the dye. Tie really tightly to prevent the dye seeping behind the thread.

The amount, as well as the method, of binding can be varied in order to produce different patterns.

Tritik

Using stitches to create an area of resist is called tritik and gives more control over the end product. All the projects in this section use the tritik method. The designs can still be abstract as with the tying method but shapes can vary more to include ovals, diamonds and other geometric shapes or flowers, animals, letters or numbers. Mark out the design with a soft 'B' pencil and use a paper pattern or template if necessary.

Tritik uses the simple running stitch or oversewing and varying the size of the stitches alters the effect.

Running stitches. Using a double thread for strength, start with a large knot and work running stitches along the outline of the design (Fig. 4). Use a really sharp needle to avoid holes in the finished work. Sometimes gathering as work progresses is possible but, where this would mask other planned sewing guide lines, use a long thread and do not gather until later.

When the line of stitching is complete, tie a knot in the double thread.

Gathering. Cut off the knot, unpick one stitch in one of the threads, gather and then tie the two ends together securely as shown in Fig. 5. Alternatively, the ends can be re-threaded into the needle and a few back stitches worked. Cut off the remaining thread.

Oversewing. Use either a pencilled line as a guide (Fig. 6) or iron a crease in the fabric and oversew the edge (Fig. 7). This method gives particularly clear resists.

The stitches are worked tightly and finished securely with small stitches or a knot.

To bind for a second colour or to strengthen the first pattern, take the gathered bunch and bind it round with thread. To bind a large piece of gathered fabric hold the spool of thread in the hand and unwind it as the binding progresses, keeping the tension tight.

Shapes. Any simple shape drawn in outline on fabric can be sewn and gathered.

Symmetrical shapes such as diamonds or butterflies are worked by folding the fabric and drawing half

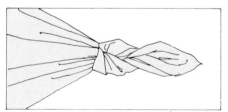
Fig. 1 A knot resist.

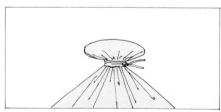
Fig. 4 Running stitches around a design.

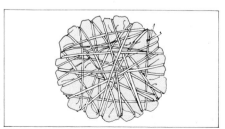
Fig. 2 Tying in a button.

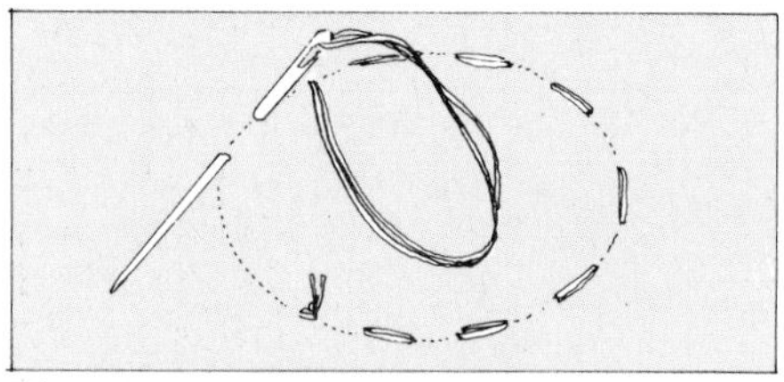

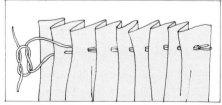
Fig. 5 Tying the end of the gathering threads.

Fig. 3 Marbling.

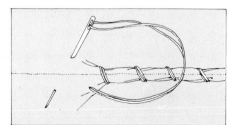
Fig. 6 Oversewing a pencilled line.

the shape so that the central line of the shape is against the fold. The sewing is worked through both thicknesses.

Sewn spirals give evenly marked rounds of colour (see Fig. 8). Pencil in the spiral then start at the centre, pulling the stitches as they are worked. When it is all pulled up, wind the spare thread back up the resulting peak and tie off with the first knot as shown in Fig. 9.

Dyeing

Wetting out. Soak the material thoroughly in clear water before dyeing it. Squeeze out the excess water but do not spin or dry it. This is called 'wetting out' and is a further means of preventing dye from penetrating the tied areas as the clean water soaked behind the resists helps the material to resist the dye.

Fabrics. Note that fabrics do not always take the dye in the same way. For example, silk and cotton put in the same dye bath will probably not match when dyed.

Dyeing. Follow the maker's instructions carefully when making up the dyes, using a plastic bucket or bowl for cold water dyes and a saucepan for hot water dyes.

Be careful with all dyes that the powder is completely dissolved but do not use boiling water with cold water dyes as this may 'kill' the dye and render it inactive. All the projects in

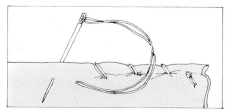

Fig. 7 Oversewing an ironed crease.

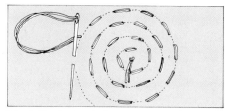

Fig. 8 Sewing a spiral.

Fig. 9 Tying a spiral.

this chapter have been made with cold water dyes.

Once dye (hot or cold) is mixed it has a limited time in which it is active whether fabric is in it or not, so immerse the fabric as soon as possible.

There is no need to keep the material moving as instructions often direct. The movement is to ensure that the dye reaches every part of the fabric evenly but this is obviously not necessary for tie dyeing. However, keep the fabric below the surface of the dye to avoid unintentionally undyed areas. This can be done with spoons, one end on the bundle, the other propped against the side of the dye bath.

Colours. When using more than one dye on a fabric follow a sequence of light to bright to dark.

Colour rules are broadly the same as with paint: red and yellow make orange, yellow and blue make green, blue and red make purple. This rule applies when mixing two dyes as well as when overlapping on the fabric. For example, for a finished result of yellow, green and blue, dye the pattern yellow, then unbind to reveal the white and bind up any of the yellow part which is to stay yellow. Use blue for the second dyeing. The result will be yellow retained, green where blue and yellow have overlapped and blue where the white was.

Finishing off. Rinse the dyed fabric thoroughly. Spin or part dry it.

Undo all the binding and sewing. This is when the result is seen for the first time and if there is not enough pattern, now is the time to add tying and dye a second or third time.

Take great care not to damage the fabric while untying. It is best to work in daylight. Untying is sometimes easier done under water or, alternatively, left until the fabric is completely dry. If scissors are used be careful not to cut the fabric. Undo all the stitching with a stitch unpicker, easing gathers open.

Wash and rinse until all the loose dye is out and the water quite clear. This takes some time but means that the article can be washed with other items later.

Finally, dry and iron the article.

Remember that individual variations are inevitable. Exactly the same effect cannot be achieved twice.

A rather pleasant and individual finish to work can be made by signing or initialling the work with tritik or by using fabric paint.

T-shirt

This is a simple idea for a child to wear. The pattern is made from a combination of light and dark shades of the same colour.

You will need
● A purchased T-shirt or simple top in white cotton
● two dyes, a light shade and a dark shade
● tie dyeing and tritik equipment as given on page 63

Nine years old and full of mischief.

Instructions
All the techniques required for this project are given on pages 64 and 65.

Wash, dry and iron the top.

There are two main patterns: the child's initial on the front and on the back the child's age. Pencil these on, positioning them in the centre.

Oversew the pencilled lines with stitches at least 1 cm ($\frac{1}{2}$ in) long and about 1 cm ($\frac{1}{2}$ in) apart. It may help to place card inside the T-shirt to prevent sewing the front and back together. Gather up the oversewing.

Round each armhole sew one line of running stitches through both thicknesses, 2 cm (1 in) from the edge. Sew two lines of running stitches, the first 2 cm (1 in), the second 3 cm ($1\frac{1}{2}$ in) from the neck edge. Finally, sew four lines of running stitches 2 cm, 3 cm, 4 cm and 5cm (1 in, $1\frac{1}{2}$ in, 2 in and $2\frac{1}{2}$ in) respectively from the lower edge. Pull up tightly to gather.

If desired, sew a spiral inside the curved parts of the numbers 2, 3, 5, 6, 8 and 9 and the letters A, B, C, D, G,

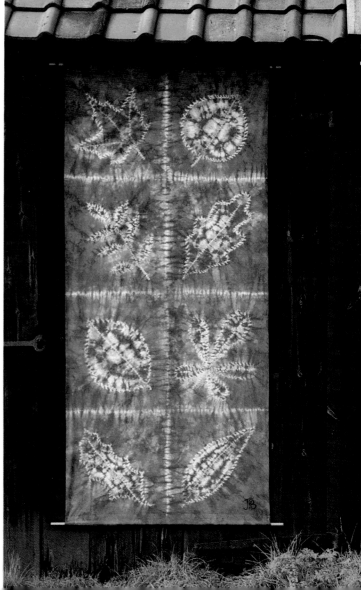

Top Back and front views of the T-shirts, while the tablecloth comes under fire. **Bottom left** The stole worn high-fashion style. **Bottom right** The wall hanging.

J, O, P, Q, R, S and U. In the T-shirts illustrated the 8 and 9 have spiral sewing but the S has not.

Wet out the T-shirt then make up the light shade of dye. Dye the T-shirt according to the manufacturer's instructions given with the particular dye which is being used.

Rinse and dry.

For the second dye, bind with elastic bands or string round the two bunches made by the gathered letter and number.

Repeat round the neck, armhole and bottom of the T-shirt a little away from the gathering.

Make up a new dye bath with the dark shade. Repeat the dyeing and rinsing.

Undo the binding and stitching. Rinse until the water runs clear. Dry and iron.

Stole

This stole is dyed in an abstract pattern of green and violet. The tritik designs are geometric. They are made along the length of the fabric using vertical divisions as a guide for the even spacing of the repeated designs.

You will need
● White fabric in silk, fine cotton or muslin: 2 m by 50 cm (6 ft by 18 in)
● two dyes of blending colours
● tie dyeing and tritik equipment as given on page 63

Instructions
All the techniques required for this project are given on pages 64 and 65.
Wash, dry and iron the fabric.

For fine silk or cotton, first make a rolled hem. Thicker fabric can be left and frayed later.

Make five creases along the length of the stole as shown in Fig. 10 as follows:

Fold the fabric in half wrong sides together and iron along the centre fold. Open out, fold each edge to the centre fold and iron the folds. Open out again and fold each edge to the second fold line nearest it, iron and open out. The creases should measure as follows: two approximately 6 cm (2½ in) from the edge, two approximately 12 cm (5 in) in and one in the middle.

Make 15 creases vertically across the

stole as follows:

Fold in half and iron the fold, fold each half in two and iron these two folds, then fold each section in half again and iron. Finally, fold the new sections again and iron.

Work the tritik design using running stitches.

Sew one line of zig zags to make eight diamonds on the centre fold using the lengthways centre crease and the widthways creases as a guide and making the end diamonds smaller.

Sew 16 half ovals against the second folds, down each length.

Sewing against the third folds work a row of straight running stitches (see Fig. 10).

Gather the diamonds and the outside lines tightly and the ovals loosely. Knot and cut off the spare threads.

Prepare a dye bath using the first colour (green) according to the manufacturer's instructions.

Dye the fabric. Rinse thoroughly and dry.

For the second dyeing, pull up the ovals more tightly, bind each diamond separately and bunch up the whole stole and bind round between the diamonds and the ovals and again between the outside edge and the straight running stitches.

Prepare the second dye bath using the second (violet) dye.

Dye, undo carefully and rinse well.

Iron silk while it is still damp. To fray the edges, gently pull out the lengthways threads on the long edges until 5 mm (¼ in) is frayed. Ease out some of the widthway threads similarly from the short sides.

Tablecloth

This design is intended as a tablecloth but can be adapted for a floor cushion or a headsquare. It has a floral pattern in three colours (yellow, orange and purple) and a purchased fringe.

You will need
● White cotton (shown here is sateen curtain lining) 1.20 m square (48 in square)
● 5 m (5½ yd) white cotton fringing
● three dyes of blending colours
● tie dyeing and tritik equipment as given on page 63

Instructions
All the techniques required for this project are given on pages 64 and 65.

Wash cotton and fringing, dry and iron the cloth.

Make a single narrow hem round the cloth or oversew the edges with a machine zig zag stitch. For frayed edges, do a little of the fraying at this stage and the rest after the dyeing.

Mark two tritik guide lines all round from the edge using an iron or pencil, one line 10 cm (4 in) from the edge and another 20 cm (8 in) from the edge. To iron in the guide lines, fold the fabric wrong sides together before ironing the creases.

Pencil or iron in the diagonal, vertical and horizontal lines shown in Fig. 11. Open out the cloth.

The diagonal lines are the centre lines of each petal. Fold the cloth along the diagonal line AB as shown in Fig. 12, wrong sides together.

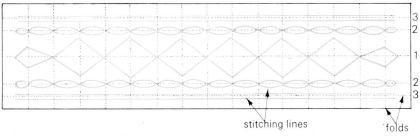

Fig. 10 The folds and stitching for the stole.

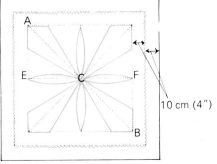

Fig. 11 The folds and stitching for the cloth.

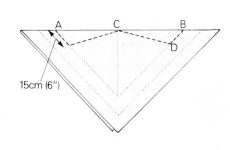

Fig. 12 Stitching the first 2 main petals.

Use a double thread long enough to work the line without gathering and keeping the work flat on a hard surface, sew through both thicknesses of material. Start at A and make large running stitches along the inner square line for 15 cm (6 in) to D, then sew to the centre of the diagonal fold at C. Cut and knot the thread.

Complete the other half of this diagonal fold to correspond. Cut and knot the thread.

Open out the material and refold on the other diagonal. Work as before to complete the four main petals.

Fold the cloth horizontally along the line EF (see Fig. 13) and work a curved line of running stitches as shown, knotting the thread at C and F.

Open and refold on the remaining vertical line. Work as before to complete the four smaller petals.

Oversew along the outer square formed by the lines 10 cm (4 in) in from the edge. Do this in four separate lines. Do not pull up for the first dyeing.

Pull up the threads tightly to gather the petals at their centre. Tie and knot the threads together.

Prepare the first (yellow) dye.
Dye the cloth and fringe.
Rinse thoroughly and dry.

For the second dyeing, pull up the square of oversewing, knotting the threads at each corner. Reinforce the gathering of the petals by binding round each of the eight petals. Then use a large elastic band to make them into one large bunch (see Fig. 14).

Prepare the second (orange) dye.
Dye the cloth and fringe.
Rinse thoroughly and dry.

For the third dyeing, put extra binding round the eight petals. Take off the large elastic band and rebunch to give the marbled effect and bind round and round with strong thread. Bind between the cloth edge and the oversewn square.

Prepare the third (purple) dye.
Dye the cloth and fringe.
Rinse thoroughly.

Undo all the binding and sewing, dry and iron. Stretch the fringe as it dries or it may shrink.

Sew on the fringe, rounding off the corners of the cloth as you do so.

For a frayed edge, complete the fraying now.

Wall hanging

This design is intended as a wallhanging but it could be a door curtain. It is a more advanced tritik worked in four colours (shown here are pink, red, brown and charcoal) but is still not difficult. The design shows eight leaf motifs. The choice of colours could suggest a seasonal mood – the bright greens and yellows of spring or the browns, reds and rusts of autumn.

You will need
- 2.10 m by 90 cm (7 ft by 36 in) white dress weight fabric in cotton, heavy muslin or calico
- four dyes of blending colours
- two dowelling rods each 1 m (3 ft 3 in) long
- black and white thread
- tie dyeing and tritik equipment as given on page 63

Instructions
All the techniques required for this project are given on pages 64 and 65.

Wash, dry and iron the fabric.

Make a hem of 5 cm (2 in) at each end leaving the ends open for the dowelling.

Divide the fabric into eight with pencilled or ironed lines. Fold in half and half again lengthways. Then open and refold in half widthways.

Draw a leaf shape in each rectangle as shown in Fig. 15.

Using black thread and long running stitches each about 1 cm (½ in), sew along the dividing lines.

Using black thread, sew the leaf veins with a single row of smaller running stitches.

Using a separate black thread, sew each stem with three rows of the smaller running stitches.

Do not pull up any of these stitches.

Using white thread, oversew round each leaf with short stitches. Pull up tightly as work progresses,

Prepare the first (pink) dye.
Dye the fabric. Rinse thoroughly and dry.

Pull up all the black stitching (veins, stems and the dividing lines). Pull the fabric inside the leaves forward and bind the larger parts a little.

Prepare the second (red) dye.
Dye the fabric. Rinse thoroughly and dry.

Bind the dividing lines lightly, starting with the horizontal ones. Keep the leaf bunches free and reinforce their binding. Marble bind the rest of the fabric with black thread.

Prepare the third (brown) dye.
Dye the fabric. Rinse thoroughly and dry.

Bind the whole hanging with black cotton. It should now be in eight lumpy bunches and quite small so that half a tin of dye will suffice for the fourth and final dye. It is this binding which completes the marbled effect.

Dye the fabric with the fourth colour (charcoal).

Undo, cutting the binding off and easing the sewing open. Rinse thoroughly, dry and iron.

To complete
Slip the two dowel rods through the hems, one at each end.

Attach a cord to either end of the top rod. The lower rod acts as a weight.

Fig. 13 Stitching the first 2 smaller petals.

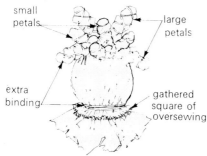

Fig. 14 Tying for the 2nd dyeing.

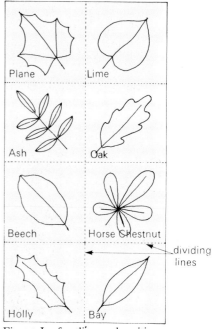

Fig. 15 Leaf outlines and positions.

Appliqué

Appliqué is the process of stitching pieces of fabric to a background cloth to make a design. The ever increasing range of exciting fabrics at our disposal gives endless scope for experimentation in colour, texture and imagination. Anyone interested in sewing will already have a good rag bag and the other basic requirements, so that objects can be made at comparatively little cost.

The sewing machine has brought a new dimension to the art of decorating fabric with a needle. It can be bold or very delicate and is a technique with its own advantages and limitations, the greatest advantage being speed.

Hand work, though, may be more relaxing. It is certainly more portable and can be picked up in odd moments. The projects given here are for both hand and machine decorated articles, but any of them could be done by either method.

Materials and Equipment

Two pairs of scissors – one for cutting out shapes and a fine pointed pair for notching edges and snipping threads.

Needles in a packet of assorted sizes should cover all requirements. Choose a needle that is comfortable for the stitch, using the larger needles for embroidery stitches.

Pins, very fine, will hold the pieces in position while sewing.

A thimble will speed the work along.

An embroidery hoop makes large scale work easier although it is possible to do a lot of work, if not all, in the hand. An ideal size is 20 cm (8 in).

Regular pure cotton sewing thread is the most comfortable to use but cotton and synthetic mixture threads are also suitable. For slip stitching, a matching colour to the appliqué piece would normally be used but there are no rules. Transparent thread is useful when it is difficult to match a colour and a contrast is not wanted. For machine stitching, a machine embroidery cotton (either no. 50 or no. 30) is most suitable because it is very fine and lustrous. But if this is not available, use sewing thread or silk. Embroidery threads and fine wools are used for adding decorative stitches.

Tracing paper is used for designing.

A non-slip paper, such as shelf paper or wall lining paper, is best for backing machine appliqué work.

A hard, sharp pencil is needed for marking out designs.

A sewing machine should ideally have a swing needle if it is to be used to apply the pieces.

Fabric of almost any description is usually worth keeping for future appliqué projects. For machine appliqué, it is wise to use firm fabric backgrounds and for the appliqué pieces, finely woven, plain weave fabrics. The choice is wider for hand appliqué. Nevertheless, pure synthetic fabrics are slippery and difficult for the beginner and natural fibre fabrics are always the most manageable. Thin fabrics can be used provided there are neatly cut turnings which will show through and become part of the design. Alternatively, they can be backed with interfacing. The choice of fabric can depend on the project – for example, very fine fabrics for transparent curtains, heavy ones for cushion covers, wall hangings, etc. For articles which do not need frequent cleaning, felt is a good choice as it comes in a brilliant colour range.

Know how

Design

Subjects must be simplified to the limitations of the craft. An easy way to do this is to place a piece of tracing or greaseproof paper over the drawing so that detail is eliminated and the structure of the design becomes clearer and more easily divided into individual shapes.

Transferring the design

Draw the design out twice. Draw a vertical grain line on each shape of the first tracing and cut the shapes as templates for cutting out the appliqué pieces. Use the second tracing as a guide to the accurate positioning of the pieces on the background fabric.

From the second tracing cut out the outline shapes of the design neatly without damaging the background (Fig. 1). Lay the tracing in position on the background fabric and use it as a guide to the accurate positioning of the appliqué pieces by placing them in the gaps (Fig. 2).

Alternatively, if the appliqué pieces are touching and the design will be lost by cutting, pin the top edge of the tracing to the work and slide the appliqué pieces underneath to the correct position. Finally, the second tracing can be perforated from the right side with the machine needle (unthreaded). Place the tracing in position on the background fabric. Rub talcum powder through the holes with a soft cloth, cut and pin on the appliqué shapes and then shake off the powder.

Hand appliqué

Cutting the pieces

Cut pieces of plain fabric with the grain to correspond to that of the background fabric. The design of patterned fabrics will probably dictate the direction of the grain although it is still better, from a purely technical point of view, to match them with the background.

When cutting the appliqué pieces, allow an extra 5 mm ($\frac{1}{4}$ in) all round the tracing paper templates for turnings. However, if the fabrics do not fray (felt, leather, etc.), cut them to the exact size of the finished pieces. If two shapes touch in the design, cut one with a 5 mm ($\frac{1}{4}$ in) allowance on the edge which touches. When the pieces are positioned the allowance goes underneath, so that one line of stitching can be used instead of two.

Preparing the pieces

Iron all the pieces.

Allowances can be turned under by hand or pressed, it is a matter of personal choice. There are two ways of applying pieces which have their edges turned under. In either case, secure the pieces to the background fabric with pins.

Method one. Secure the shapes on the background. The edges will be turned in as the work progresses. Some people use a stitch ripper to turn the fabric in, sliding it under the folded edge and pinning as they go.

Method two. Turn in the edges and tack before securing the piece on the background. Do not use knots so that the tacking thread will be easy to remove. Do not use dark or bright coloured tacking cotton on pale fabrics as this may leave marks.

With either method any corners must be mitred and any curved edges clipped to allow the turnings to lie flat.

To mitre very sharp corners of 45 degrees or less, turn the point over first, then turn in each of the sides as shown in Fig. 3 and tack with very small stitches.

On a wider angled corner, turn in the left hand side, then turn in the right hand side as shown in Fig. 4 and tack with very small stitches. Only trim the turnings if the fabric is thick.

Applying the pieces

The stitches used to apply the pieces to the background fabric can be simple and unobtrusive or decorative enough to become a special feature.

If very large shapes are underlapped, tack within the allowance on the under piece as added support. This will be hidden when the second piece is overlapped.

Slip stitching. This should be at 90 degrees to the edge (Fig. 5) and evenly spaced. The distance will depend on the shape and effect required. On fine fabrics and tight curves keep stitches close together, about 2 mm ($\frac{1}{16}$ in) apart.

Running stitch. This looks best if the stitches are close together (Fig. 6). Experiment with different thicknesses of thread for the best effect.

Double knot stitch. This gives a pretty, raised edging to either turned in or raw edges. Bring the needle out through the background fabric close to the edge of the appliqué piece. *Take a small stitch to the right into the appliqué piece inserting the needle at right angles to the edge of the shape

and bringing it out through the background fabric. Pass the needle from top to bottom through the surface stitch just made without picking up the fabric and keeping the needle to the left of the thread. Keeping the thread below the needle, pass the needle under the first stitch again to the right of the last stitch made (Fig. 7). Repeat from *.

Decoration

Areas of the design can be enhanced with embroidery threads or fine wool. Couched embroidery is explained in

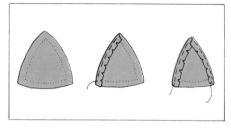

Fig. 1 Cutting outline from 2nd tracing.

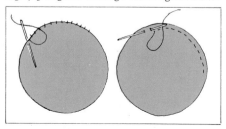

Fig. 2 Positioning 2nd tracing on background fabric.

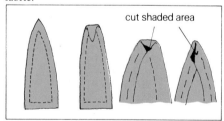

cut shaded area

Fig. 3 4 stages of mitring a sharp corner.

Fig. 4 3 stages of mitring a wide angled corner.

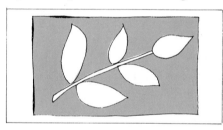

Fig. 5 Slip stitching and Fig. 6 Running stitch.

the Metal Thread Embroidery chapter (page 134). Here we give a few other suitable embroidery stitches which can be used not only for decoration but sometimes actually to apply the pieces.

Fly stitch. This stitch is best worked over a faintly pencilled vertical guideline. Bring the needle up to the left of the line. Insert it at the same level to the right of the line so that the line is in the centre of the thread. Do not pull the thread tight. Bring the needle up through the vertical line a little way down. Make a small down-

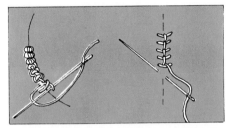

Fig. 7 Double knot stitch and Fig. 8 Fly stitch.

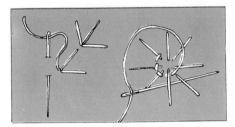

Fig. 9 Fern stitch and Fig. 10 Spider stitch.

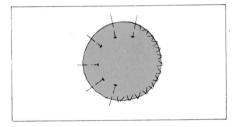

Fig. 11 Positioning pins and zig-zag stitch.

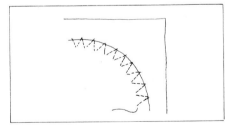

Fig. 12 Multiple zig-zag.

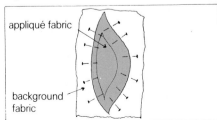

Fig. 13 Pinning appliqué piece, fabric and paper (underneath).

wards stitch on the line, taking the thread over the top of the original stitch to make a V shape (Fig. 8).

Fern stitch. This stitch is made up of three straight stitches of equal length radiating from one point. The points can follow a straight line or a curve. Bring the needle up and make a straight stitch above the point, returning the needle to the starting point. Make a second straight stitch of equal length to the right of the first and return the needle to the starting point. Make a third straight stitch to the left. Bring the needle out below the first stitch leaving a gap the length of the stitch away from the original starting point. Make three straight stitches in the same way (Fig. 9).

Spider stitch. This stitch fills a circular shape when completed. Bring the needle up in the centre of the circle. Work eight straight stitches in the form of a star radiating from the central point. Finish by bringing the needle up in the centre. Pass the needle under two threads and bring it back over one. Continue working back stitch in this way over all the threads (Fig. 10). Take the needle to the back of the fabric to finish off.

Pressing
Press the work face down on a folded blanket to prevent the embroidery being flattened.

Machine appliqué

The appliqué pieces are cut the exact size of the shapes and the rules for matching grains are the same as for hand appliqué. However, the method of applying the pieces to the background varies, depending on the stitch used. With a swing-needle sewing machine, any stitch can be attempted, without a swing-needle the straight stitching method will be used. Mark out the design by one of the methods described earlier.

Method 1: Zig-zag stitching
Position the pieces and pin near, and at right angles to, the edge placing the pins about 2 cm (1 in) apart (Fig. 11).

If the fabric is at all flexible or distorts easily when pulled on the bias, place a piece of backing paper slightly larger than the shape under the background fabric before pinning.

Sew the edge with an ordinary or a multiple zig-zag stitch, using width 3 to 4, depending on the weight of the fabric (Fig. 12). With either stitch, the stitches should be close together to

ensure that untidy shreds of fabric do not come out between them. The action of the needle of multiple zig-zag may dislodge threads at the edge of the fabric during working, in which case run a finger nail along the edge of the shape to lift any such ends and trim them with sharp scissors.

Use the finest possible cotton, preferably machine embroidery cotton no. 50 in either a perfectly matching colour or a transparent thread on top and a near match in the bobbin. In this case press the work on the wrong side or under a cloth as transparent thread melts under a hot iron.

Method 2: Satin stitching
A close satin stitch can never be used directly on to a raw edge as the close stitching stretches the fabric.

Individual shapes. Cut out the pieces of fabric to be applied very roughly to the right shape but a few centimetres (1–1½ inches) larger all round. Using a paper template, mark the exact outline of the shape with a hard, sharp pencil. Lay the pieces in position on the right side of the background fabric. Cut a piece of backing paper about 4 cm (1½ in) larger all round than the shape. Slide it under the background fabric until it is below the appliqué piece. Pin through all thicknesses including the paper (Fig. 13). Machine from the right side along the pencilled lines with a shorter than normal stitch in a matching colour. The stitch must not be too short, however, or the paper will be cut through. If it does tear, remove it and start again.

Repeated shapes. If the same motif is to be repeated at regular intervals, draw the motif the required number of times on separate bits of paper with at least a 4 cm (1½ in) allowance around the edges. Transfer the design to the back of the piece of paper by tracing over the lines. If paper is not transparent hold it against a window to trace the lines. Mark the wrong side with a cross to prevent a reverse image appearing on the right side of the work. Place the tracings in position on the wrong side of the fabric with the wrong side of the motif upwards. Temporarily secure each with three or four pins. With the work still face downwards on the table, slide the roughly cut appliqué pieces into position under the work, matching grains. Repin each piece through all thicknesses as already described and stitch along the design lines marked in pencil on the back of the paper. If

continued

there are shapes in different colours so close together that there is risk of extra fabric round shapes getting caught in one another's stitching, cut away the edges of the first colour before pinning the second colour in position. When all the shapes are stitched, turn the fabric to the right side. Trim the excess fabric round the appliqué pieces close to the stitching. From the right side, pin the background to the paper about 2–3 cm (1 in approximately) at the edge of the shape and all round it. This supports the work during the satin stitching.

Use machine embroidery cotton for the satin stitching as it is softer, finer and more lustrous than sewing cotton and gives a smoother satin stitch. Try out the stitch length and tension on some spare fabric supported by paper first. Although the work must move freely through the machine the fabric should not show between the stitches. Modern machines have a very fine degree of adjustment so that a perfect stitch can be obtained for any thickness of thread. With older or badly adjusted machines, it sometimes helps to use very fine thread double on top with a slightly longer stitch length.

With such a short length it is an easy stitch to guide. Exert a very firm downward pressure beside and just in front

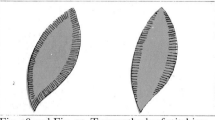

Fig. 14 Reversing to start: Fig. 15 Satin stitching.

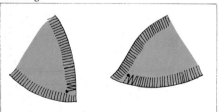

Fig. 16 End on left hand swing and Fig. 17 Turn through 90°.

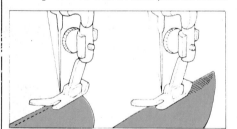

Fig. 18 and Fig. 19 Two methods of stitching corners.

of the presser foot with the first and second fingers of both hands. Run the machine at top speed taking care though to keep fingers clear of the needle.

To begin, position the needle 0.5 cm ($\frac{1}{4}$ in) in front of the starting point and reverse to it in straight stitching (Fig. 14). Then, with the presser foot down, lift the needle and set the required swing. Set forward stitch length and satin stitch, thus hiding the line of straight stitching (Fig. 15).

To finish, end on the left hand swing with the needle still in the fabric (Fig. 16). Lift the presser foot and turn clockwise through 90 degrees (Fig. 17). Being very careful that there is no drag from the work on the needle, move the stitch width lever to nought and do a few straight stitches alongside the end of the satin stitching.

Corners. There are two methods of dealing with corners. The first uses uniform width stitching throughout (Fig. 18) and is strong and easy to do.

In the second method the satin stitch is tapered to nearly nothing at the corners (Fig. 19). This is only secure because there are already straight stitches all round the shape. Work the satin stitch, guiding the work with the left hand only, while opening and closing the stitch width lever with the right. It is well worth the trouble of mastering this technique because the effect is much more subtle and interesting but it requires practice.

Remove the pins and tear away the paper.

Method 3: Straight stitching

With a machine which only does straight stitching, the shapes with turnings are prepared as for hand appliqué. Stitch very close to the edge. Unless the fabric is very thin and flexible it will not be necessary to use a backing paper, but take care that the work is well supported in front of the machine with no pull on it as it approaches the needle.

Layering

When one or more shapes are applied on top of one another, first apply the smallest shape to the next size and it in turn to the largest. In this way the machine stitching never goes through more than two thicknesses of fabric. This ensures that the draping qualities of the fabric are unimpaired and makes the handling much easier.

Pressing

Press machine appliqué as given for hand appliqué.

Bed linen

Appliqué has been used here to add an individual touch to purchased bed linen. Working it by machine makes it strong enough to withstand frequent washing.

You will need
Medium weight cotton or poly cotton:
● 30 cm (12 in) in each of colours A (white) and B (navy)
● 30 cm (12 in) in finely woven, plain weave patterned fabric
● light weight hand embroidery thread (coton perlé no. 8, coton à broder or buttonhole twist) in B
● no. 50 sewing cotton in each of A and B and a toning colour (turquoise)
● purchased sheet and pillowcase in poly cotton mixture
● appliqué equipment as given on page 69

Instructions
All the techniques required for this project are given on pages 70–72.

Draw the design to scale from Fig. 20 on strips of medium weight paper 10 cm (4 in) wide, joined together to make the required length. Make five repeats for the pillow case, 17 for a single sheet and approximately 34 for a double. The design does not continue to the side edges of the sheet as only the decorated part will be seen when the bed is made up.

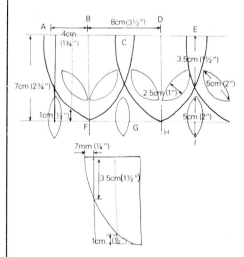

Fig. 20 Design for bed linen.

Top left The matching pillowcase and sheet have been worked with machine appliqué and embroidery. **Top right** The bright flower design on the skirt is made up of ribbons and appliquéd circles. **Middle right** Double knot stitch and couched threads are added to the hand appliqué stitches for the oven glove motif. **Below right** Details on the number hanging are made with embroidery stitches.

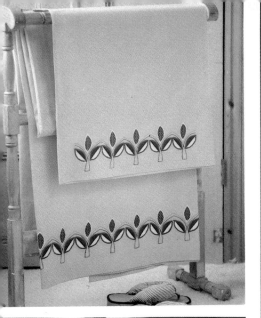

Position the paper on the wrong side of the sheet or pillowcase, above the stitched hem, and pin at intervals of not more than 5 cm (2 in) placing the pins at right angles to and over the B line.

Hand wind the embroidery thread on the machine bobbin and use matching sewing thread on top. Test stitch on a scrap of fabric and alter the lower tension if necessary.

With the paper facing upwards machine along the curved line, keeping the needle in the fabric when turning the corners. Pass the ends of the embroidery thread through to the back and tie securely.

Transfer the positions of the petal shapes to the right side by passing a pin through each point from the back and making a pencil dot where it emerges.

Cut a strip or strips in each of A and B 2·5 cm (1 in) wide and long enough for all the petals, allowing for a gap of 0.5 cm (¼ in) between the petals.

Stitch the strips together leaving a 0.75 cm (⅓ in) seam allowance. Press seams open.

Make a template of the petal shapes. Draw round it on the fabric with a hard sharp pencil, positioning the points on the seam and leaving 0.5 cm (¼ in) between petals. Separate the petals by cutting through the middle of the gaps.

Pin the pieces in position, aligning the pencilled points of the petals with the pencil dots on the background fabric.

Thread the machine with the toning colour and machine round the design lines of all the petals. Start at the side of the design rather than at the tip of the petal so that the stitches overlap (Fig. 21).

Trim the ends on both sides of the work and cut away the excess fabric.

Work a close satin stitch round the petals with uniform width stitching. Cut out the remaining petal shapes from the patterned fabric, leaving extra fabric all round.

Pin them in position.

Using A sewing cotton, start straight stitching at the point of a petal and machine down the centre before proceeding round the edge (Fig. 22).

Trim and finish with satin stitch in A of uniform width.

Put in the toning line using the curved line as a guide.

Tie the ends at the back and trim any fabric strands which may have come through the satin stitch.

Remove the backing paper and steam press on the wrong side.

Skirt

A plain coloured fabric and a simple style are needed as a background to this bold, machine appliquéd design. Instructions are given for making up the skirt but the design could be done on a purchased skirt of similar style. The design has two complete repeats, one at the front and one at the back.

You will need
● A simple four gore skirt pattern without shaping on the side seams

plain closely woven, medium weight fabric (e.g. linen, cotton, polyester/cotton):
● skirt length
● 30 cm (12 in) in each of A (white), B (dark beige), C (light beige), D (yellow), E (gold), F (green), G (rust)
● 12 m (13 yd) narrow nylon ribbon in H (tan). (For every 4 cm (1½ in) added to the length of the skirt given here, 1.5 m (1⅔ yd) extra ribbon will be needed. The circles and the leaves may also need to be enlarged proportionately. Deduct similar amount for smaller sizes.)
● machine embroidery cotton no. 50 or fine sewing cotton in richer shades of A, C, E, H and I (navy)
● 20 cm (8 in) zip fastening
● waistband stiffening
● hooks and eyes
● appliqué equipment as given on page 69

Measurements
To fit 71 cm (28 in) waist length, 76 cm (30 in)

Instructions

All the techniques required for this project are given on pages 70–72.

If making a skirt, cut out the skirt and waistband.

Join the skirt pieces, leaving the centre back seam open.

Find the centre and quarters of each of the four gores, remembering to allow for seam allowances on the two outer gores. Press lightly or mark with tailor's chalk.

Measure from the top edge and cut each ribbon to the required length (Fig. 23).

Place the correct length of ribbon along the creases or chalk lines. The top of the ribbon is aligned with the top of the skirt and the bottom edge left raw. On a purchased skirt, slightly overlap the ends of the ribbons with the waist band. Remember that straight grain ribbon is being placed on the bias of the skirt fabric and care must be taken not to distort the bias.

Use plenty of pins placed at right angles to the ribbon.

Using a straight stitch and starting at the top of the ribbon, machine down one edge taking out the pins just before the needle reaches them. Stitch the second edge of the ribbon in the same direction.

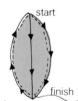

Figs. 21 and 22 Straight stitching on plain and patterned petals.

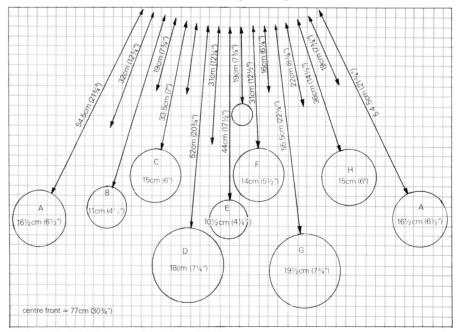

Fig. 23 Length of ribbons and position of circles.

Stitch ribbons over the three seams.

Finally, pin and stitch the ribbons which will lead to the small circles half way between the stitched ribbons.

Cut out templates for the circles and leaves.

Using the templates, cut out circles of fabric in the chosen colours leaving an extra 2 cm (1 in) all round.

Cut out paper circles a good 4 cm (2 in) larger than the templates.

Place the small circles over the medium sized ones and slide a paper circle behind both. Stitch first with a short straight stitch. Trim away fabric up to stitched line, then re-pin paper on right side round the edges. Finish with a uniform width satin stitch, concealing raw edge. Steam press on the wrong side.

Stitch the medium shapes to the large ones and press in the same way.

Apply these multiple circles to the skirt using the widest satin stitch, matching the grain with the ribbons, just covering the raw end of each.

Stitch the small circles in position, then the leaf shapes, using the tapering method of satin stitching on the latter.

Stitch and neaten the last seam, leaving an opening for the zip.

Press two lengths of ribbon in half to encase the folded edges of the zip opening. Open out the ribbon and place the centre along the edge of the opening on the right side. Straight stitch near the outer edges of the ribbon. Fold the ribbon to the back of the skirt and slip stitch in place.

Stitch the last length of ribbon over the remaining seam turning in the top of the length and placing it over the

Fig. 24 Sewing the pocket on main fabric.

Fig. 25 Joining main fabric and lining.

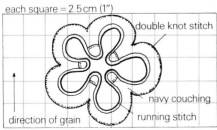

Fig. 26 3 piece design for oven glove.

raw edges of the bottom of the two pieces of ribbon encasing the zip opening.

Using sewing thread in B, stitch the zip in by hand to the skirt fabric.

Finish the waistband and stitch the ribbon over the lower edge.

Turn up the hem.

Oven glove

The bright design on this oven glove is made with just three shapes and enhanced with contrasting embroidery stitches.

You will need
● Cotton fabric:
● 110 cm by 18 cm (44 in by 7 in) in colour A (red) and B (orange)
● small pieces in C (navy), D (orange) and E (white)
● 2 oz wadding or a piece of old blanket 108 cm by 16 cm (43 in by 6 in)
● embroidery thread in C, D and E (yellow)
● sewing cotton in A and C
● appliqué equipment as given on page 69

Measurements
Glove: 80 cm by 16 cm (32 in by 6 in)
motif: 13.5 cm (5¼ in) square

Instructions
All the techniques required for this project are given on pages 70–72, except for couching which is given on page 134.

Draw out the design given in Fig. 26 to its full size.

Use this drawing to cut out templates for the three shapes.

Cut out the circle in E and the middle size shape in B, both with 0.5 cm (¼ in) all round for turnings. Cut the outer shape in C to the same size as the template.

Couch a line of colour C embroidery thread round the middle sized shape.

Clip and turn in the edges of the circle. Attach it to the largest shape with close running stitches worked in colour B in embroidery thread.

Clip the edges of the middle sized shape at frequent intervals, turn under the edges and tack. Slip stitch this piece to the other two.

Attach the whole shape to the main fabric, using widely spaced slip stitches in a matching sewing cotton. Stitch

over the raw edge of the outer shape with double knot stitch using colour E embroidery thread. It can either go on the pockets where it will not come in contact with pans or on the outside of the glove to provide added protection against the heat.

Make a matching appliqué for the other pocket.

Place the wadding centrally on the wrong side of the main fabric.

Turn in the spare fabric on the short edges and pin it to the wadding. Tack through all thicknesses.

Fold 15 cm (6 in) of wadding and fabric at either end to the right side. Stitch a 1 cm (½ in) seam along the top and bottom edges as shown in Fig. 24.

Trim the wadding close to the stitching.

Make the lining in the same way omitting the wadding and fold over only 14.5 cm (5¾ in).

Place the lining and glove right sides together and stitch between A and B as shown in Fig. 25.

Turn the two lengths of fabric right sides out first, then the pockets.

Tuck the pocket linings into the outer pockets.

Join the edges of the pockets with oversewing or buttonhole stitch.

Child's number hanging

This brightly coloured hanging affords plenty of scope for hand appliqué. Felt is a natural choice for a design of this complexity.

You will need
● Medium weight dress fabric or light weight furnishing fabric 100 cm by 147 cm (40 in by 58 in).
● slightly textured pure cotton in 10 different colours each the size shown in Fig. 27 plus 1 cm (½ in) allowance all round.
● 25 cm (10 in) square of felt (without edging perforations) in nine different colours.
● embroidery thread (coton perlé or coton à broder) in five different colours
● sewing cottons in colours to match the felts and the rectangles
● couching thread (soft embroidery thread or fine four ply wool) in four colours
● sewing cotton to match the couching threads
● two 132 cm (52 in) dowelling rods
● appliqué equipment as given on page 69

Measurements

90 cm by 132 cm (36 in by 52 in)

Instructions

All the techniques required for this project are given on pages 70–72, except for couching which is given on page 134.

Draw the design of each rectangle full size on paper (Fig. 27).

Cut out the outlines of all the shapes from the drawing without damaging the surrounding paper. Lay the stencil over the appropriate rectangles of fabric.

Use Fig. 28 to cut templates for the felt shapes. Where pieces overlap, cut the underneath piece slightly larger. Write on each shape what colour it will be.

Once all the pieces are cut, group together all those of one colour on the appropriate square of felt. Laying all the patterns on at once ensures the most economic cutting.

Slip stitch all the numbers in place on the appropriate fabric rectangle.

Make up the rectangles as follows:

1. Slip stitch small petals to large petals.

Slip stitch large petals and stalk to background.

Couch flower centre to background.

Fly stitch leaves to background.

2. Fern stitch shapes to apple.

Slip stitch apple and stalks to background.

3. Couch lower edge of hulls to background.

Slip stitch rest of hulls and masts to background.

Couch sails to background then slip stitch between couching.

4. Fern stitch shapes to circles.

Slip stitch circles to background.

5. Spider stitch eyes to bodies.

Couch bodies with fins underlapped to background.

Straight stitch tails to background, underlapping bodies.

Slip stitch fins to background.

Straight stitch over fins.

6. In a diamond shape, straight stitch eyes to heads.

Fly stitch tails to background.

Couch bodies to background, underlapping tails.

Slip stitch bibs to background, underlapping bodies.

Slip stitch heads to background, underlapping bodies and bibs.

Straight stitch claws, whiskers, noses and mouths.

7. Couch van bodies to background.

Slip stitch remaining edges to background.

In square shapes, straight stitch windows in place.

Fern stitch roofs to background.

Straight stitch wheels to background.

Straight stitch radiators to bonnets.

8. Spider stitch eyes to heads.

Slip stitch top edges of bodies to background.

Slip stitch heads and tails to background, underlapping bodies.

Slip stitch legs and beaks to background.

Fern stitch wings to background, overlapping bodies.

Straight stitch tail.

9. Fern stitch three shapes together.

Slip stitch outer shape to background.

10. Spider stitch second square to third.

In square shapes, straight stitch centre square to second and third squares.

Slip stitch third square to fourth.

Slip stitch fourth square to background.

To complete

Turn under allowance round each rectangle. Pin and slip stitch to the background fabric.

Turn in the side edges and hem.

Make a 2.5 cm (1 in) hem at the top and bottom edges to take the dowel rods for hanging.

Make two loops with red embroidery thread either by plaiting the thread or crocheting it. The loop should roughly be large enough to fit twice round the dowel rod.

Tie sewing cotton to the loop and thread the other end in a needle. Insert the needle through the upper hem and out through the fabric at the top of the hanging.

Insert the dowel rod and place the loop round it.

Pull hard on the thread so that it draws part of the loop through the top of the fabric.

Remove the sewing thread. Work another loop to correspond at the other end.

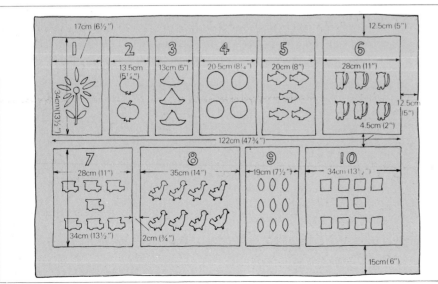

Fig. 27 Position of designs and rectangles.

Fig. 28 Pattern for templates.

Patchwork quilting

Patchwork is a craft which evolved from domestic economy when fabric was at a premium and every available scrap had to be used and reused. Either snippets left over from other projects or good sections of otherwise worn garments would be sewn together to make a new fabric for garments or household items.

In time it became an art form to join the pieces to form a pattern. Nowadays it is just as likely that the fabrics have been bought specially to make a piece of patchwork with a clearly defined colour scheme. Quilting adds warmth and a luxurious look to the fabric, sometimes helping to emphasize the patchwork patterning.

Materials and Equipment
A sewing machine is optional because the pieces can be sewn by hand.

A steam iron is preferable as it flattens the seams better but an ordinary iron and a damp cloth will suffice.

Other sewing aids include scissors (ideally three pairs – cutting out shears, paper scissors and nail scissors for cutting thread), a selection of hand sewing needles, dressmaking pins, tape measure and a selection of sewing thread.

General items needed are a ruler, pencils (lead for marking light fabric, chalk pencil for marking dark fabric), graph paper, card and glue or paste.

A good selection of fabric is, of course, essential. It is a good idea to wash fabrics before cutting in case they shrink or lose dye and, therefore, colour.

There are two types of wadding. Cotton wadding can be used on items that will be dry cleaned only, or that have a really good network of quilting stitches on them. Synthetic wadding of either Courtelle or Terylene comes in various thicknesses. The thin 60 g (2 oz) type is best and can be washed.

Know how

The basic techniques involved in working a simple piece of patchwork quilting can best be demonstrated using one of the most straightforward American patchwork designs, the nine patch block. Simply constructed out of nine equal squares, a number of these blocks are then stitched together and quilted.

Patchwork

Making the template
First decide how large the block is to be, then draw it full scale on graph paper (Fig. 1). For example, in our 21 cm (8¼ in) block each individual square will measure 7 cm (2¾ in).

As all the squares are identical, make only one template by cutting one out and sticking it down on a piece of card.

The template is used to mark the cutting line on to the fabric so first add a seam allowance all round the paper square.

A 6 mm (¼ in) seam allowance is useful for two reasons. Firstly, when sewing the pieces together by machine, the edge of the machine foot when matched to the edge of the fabric will usually give a 6 mm (¼ in) seam exactly. And secondly, when several small pieces are sewn together it gives a satisfactory seam which will not fray out whilst giving a minimum of bulk.

Measure 6 mm (¼ in) out all round the square and cut out the card to this measurement.

Mark a grain line on the template.
Cutting the fabric
Use this template to mark the fabric. When placing it on the fabric keep the grain of the fabric running the same way as the grain line. This will stop the edges from stretching and keep the grain of the patchwork uniform.

For a nine patch block mark out five squares in dark fabric and four in light.

Cut the fabric in single layers. At this stage it is important to be accurate. If the fabric is cut inaccurately, it will also be sewn inaccurately.
Making a block
When joining the pieces together, take in the full seam allowance. Sewing can be either by machine or by hand. Although hand sewing, for preference or necessity, is more traditional, machine sewing is quicker and stronger.

Pin the seams together with the right sides of the fabric facing.

When **machine sewing**, match the raw edges to the edge of the machine foot and with most machines this finishes the seam at 6 mm (¼ in) (Fig. 2). Make a few back stitches at the beginning and end of each seam.

When **hand sewing**, make sure the pins are exactly 6 mm (¼ in) from the edge and follow this line exactly, making small running stitches (Fig. 3).

If you intend to quilt by machine (see below), the seams should be pressed open. For hand quilting, the seams are pressed to one side. Always press towards the darker fabric so that the seams do not show through. Press each seam before joining on the next piece.

To complete the nine patch block, sew the squares together in rows of three (Fig. 4). On rows one and three alternate two dark squares and one light, on row two alternate two light squares with one dark.

After making the three rows sew them together. Match the squares carefully by placing the pins at right angles to the seam to be sewn, slipping them exactly through both seam lines of the squares already joined (Fig. 5).
Joining the blocks
Once made, the blocks can be pieced together in many different colour combinations. Experiment with the colour pattern on graph paper by outlining the same number of squares across and down that will be used in the final project, although preferably a scaled-down version.

Trace off a few copies and try out different colour combinations.

Once the combination is decided, join the blocks together, taking care to match seams.

Press the seams open for machine quilting, in one direction for hand quilting but alternating the direction from block to block.

Fasten off all ends.

Quilting

After the piecing is completed, the patchwork is quilted by hand or machine. Although it is against all tradition, the sewing machine works very successfully in terms of both strength and speed.
Preparation
Cut a piece of plain fabric about 2.5 cm (1 in) larger than the patchwork all round.

Lay the wadding on this fabric, smoothed out, and cut to the same size. It may be necessary to join the wadding at some point. With *cotton* wadding overlap the edges slightly, with *synthetic* wadding place it edge to edge, and in both cases oversew very loosely using large stitches.

Lay the patchwork on top of the wadding, smoothing it down gently.

Tack all three layers together thoroughly, beginning in the centre and working a star shape and then all round the edges (see Fig. 6).
Machine quilting
Sew along the seam lines, sinking the stitches into the actual seam as shown in Fig. 7. Hold both hands firmly either side of the machine foot to keep the fabric taut. The stitching goes through all three layers.

Not all seam lines need to be quilted but obviously it should be done at regular intervals. The quilting can be all in one direction or both lengthways and crossways.
Hand quilting
Hand held. Begin quilting by threading the needle and tying a small knot in the end.

Start at the back of the quilt and bring the needle up through the three layers to the point where the quilting is to begin. Tug a little at the thread so that the knot slips through the backing fabric to become hidden inside.

Work a running stitch kept as even as possible on both the back and front of the work. Pick up four stitches on the needle at a time, then draw the thread through. Make sure that each stitch goes right through to the back.

Finish off by tying another knot near the surface of the top fabric but without cutting the thread. Take the thread back through the top fabric and feed the needle along inside the layers for about 2.5 cm (1 in). Draw it out through the top surface again, tug the knot through the fabric so that it disappears and cut off the thread.

It is usual to work hand quilting about 6 mm (¼ in) away from the seam lines so that the stitching shows (Fig. 8). Alternatively, work out a design and mark in the lines to be quilted with a chalk pencil.

Frame or hoop held. The patchwork can be stretched taut while quilting either on a frame or in a hoop. The hoop, like an embroidery frame, stretches only a small area at a time.

Finishing off

The threads
At the end of every row of stitching,

the threads must be fastened off. Pull them through to the back of the work, thread both ends into a large-eyed needle and make a back stitch.

Feed the needle along inside for about 2.5 cm (1 in) under the back layer of fabric. Return through the backing fabric and cut the thread close to the fabric.

The edges

Trim off the excess wadding and backing fabric before finishing off the edges. The top fabric can then be turned to the back of the work and stitched in place.

Alternatively, bind the edges with a bias strip. Cut bias strips as shown in Fig. 9 and join as shown in Fig. 10 to form a continuous length to the measurement required. Press the joins out flat. Then place one raw edge of the binding along the edge of the patchwork, right sides together. First tack, then sew the binding along the seam line, working through all thicknesses (Fig. 11). Turn any corners by snipping in to the seam allowance of the binding. Join the beginning and end of the binding diagonally. Turn the binding to the back of the work, fold for a narrow hem and sew in place by hand, using small hemming stitches.

Laundering

Cleaning depends on the wadding and materials used. Synthetic wadding with fabrics which have been washed before cutting can be washed. Cotton wadding, provided there is a substantial amount of quilting throughout (i.e. never more than about 10 cm (4 in) square left unquilted), can also be washed.

Always wash by hand, using the bath for large items. Fully dissolve washing powder in enough warm water to cover the article. Immerse it in the water and gently agitate without lifting it from the water. Pull out the plug and allow the water to drain away. Rinse by running water and then draining it out in the same manner. Rinse at least three times and finally squeeze out the excess water.

Something as large as a quilt will become very heavy and it would be advisable to have help in taking it out of the bath. If it will fit easily into the machine, give it a short spin. If not, squeeze out as much water as possible by hand.

Choose a fine day, not too windy, and hang out the article. Hang a quilt over a washing line padded with towels or sheets to prevent it marking the quilt. Alternatively, lay the quilt flat on a lawn over a sheet. Always avoid direct sunlight.

When dry, run a steam iron lightly over the top surface, barely touching it, to remove creases or wrinkles.

Patchwork with cotton wadding throughout and not closely quilted can be dry cleaned as can all the other versions if it seems too much of a task to hand wash. But be sure to go to a specialist cleaner who will take good care of your painstaking work.

All the projects are really double projects – firstly a patchwork motif which can be used in any project as required; and secondly a specific project in which the motif has been used.

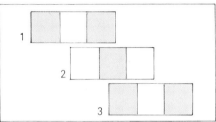

Fig. 4 Construction of the nine patch block.

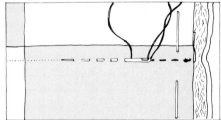

Fig. 8 Quilting by hand.

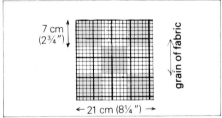

Fig. 1 Nine patch block.

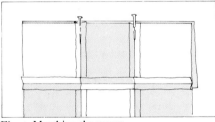

Fig. 5 Matching the seams.

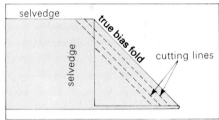

Fig. 9 Cutting a bias strip.

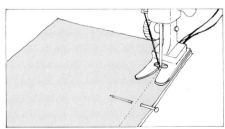

Fig. 2 Machine sewing the seams.

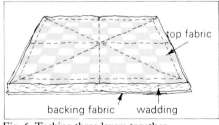

Fig. 6 Tacking three layers together.

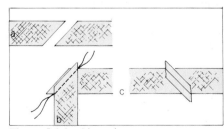

Fig. 10 Joining bias strips.

Fig. 3 Hand sewing the seams.

Fig. 7 Sink stitching.

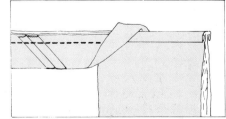

Fig. 11 Binding the edge.

Maple leaf block

The maple leaf (or tea leaf) block is a variation on the nine patch block. This time, though, five of the squares are divided in various ways to create the leaf design (Fig. 12).

You will need
- Four templates: A) square, B) large triangle, C) small triangle and D) a thin strip for the stem (Fig. 13).
- dark fabric
- light fabric

Instructions
All the techniques required for this project are given on pages 78 and 79.

Making the templates
Draw the design full scale on graph paper and make the templates.

Cutting the fabric
Cut the templates as follows:

    A: three dark, one light
    B: four dark, five light
    C: one light
    D: one dark

Making a block
Join the pieces.

To join two equal triangles, match the corners and stitch along the longest side, taking in the full seam allowance.

To join C to D, place right sides together, matching the edges exactly and seam 6 mm ($\frac{1}{4}$ in) from the edge as shown in Fig. 14.

Press all the seams.

Joining the blocks
There are many ways the maple leaf can be pieced together. For example, Fig. 15 is the same as the quilt in the photograph below but with the leaf motif reversed. In Fig. 16 the alternating blocks have been made up with both direction and colour scheme reversed.

Experiment on graph paper.

Quilting
Prepare for quilting as given on page 78.

Quilt round each of the nine squares or along whichever seam lines are preferred.

Finish off the threads.

Wall hanging

You will need
- 2.50 m (2 yd 20 in) black fabric 90 cm (36 in) wide
- 1.15 m ($1\frac{1}{4}$ yd) white fabric 90 cm (36 in) wide
- black sewing thread
- 15 mm ($\frac{1}{2}$ in) dowelling 81 cm (32 in) long
- 128 cm by 80 cm (50 in by 32 in) of wadding

Measurements
Block. 23 cm (9 in)
Hanging. 122 cm by 76 cm (48 in by 30 in)
Border. 4 cm ($1\frac{1}{2}$ in) wide

To make up
Make 15 blocks the same and join them in three rows of five blocks each, all facing in the same direction (see illustration below).

Cut strips in black 5 cm (2 in) wide. Using a 6 mm ($\frac{1}{4}$ in) seam, stitch border to patchwork, mitring corners.

Cut a piece 6.5 cm ($2\frac{1}{2}$ in) by the

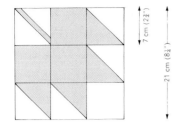

Fig. 12 Maple leaf block.

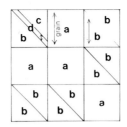

Fig. 13 Cutting the templates.

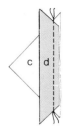

Fig. 14 Joining the stem section.

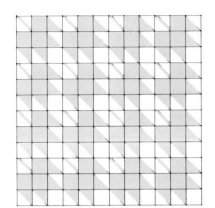

Fig. 15 Maple leaf layout.

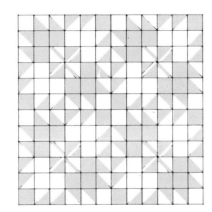

Fig. 16 Maple leaf layout variation.

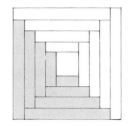

Fig. 17 Log cabin block.

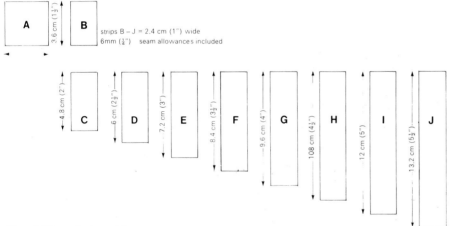

Fig. 18 Pieces for log cabin.

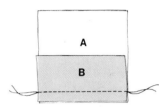

Fig. 19 Joining first 2 pieces.

width of the patchwork and attach it in a loop across the top end of the backing fabric to hold the dowelling for hanging.

Make a second border the same to use to bind the raw edges.

Prepare and quilt the patchwork.

Sew the second made-up border, right sides facing, to the border on the front. Take the usual 6 mm ($\frac{1}{4}$ in) seam allowances. Sew around all the edges, then turn this border to the back. Poke out the corners with scissors, then hem stitch the back border to the backing.

Left The maple leaf shape is picked out in black against a white background. The log cabin cushions are shown in various combinations of plain and patterned strips, made up in blocks of four, nine and sixteen.

Log cabin

The fabric must be chosen carefully for this particular block. On one side there is a range of dark shades and on the other a range of light to create the traditional three dimensional effect (see Fig. 17).

You will need
- 10 templates: A) square, B)–J) rectangles (Fig. 18)
- central colour fabric
- light shade(s) fabric
- dark shade(s) fabric

Instructions
All the techniques required for this project are given on pages 78 and 79.

Making the templates
Draw out the design on graph paper and make the templates.

You will need one square for the centre and a number of rectangles all the same width to surround the square.

For example, for a square of 2.5 cm (1 in), plus seam allowance, cut a square 4 cm ($1\frac{1}{2}$ in) across. The rectangles would be 1.5 cm ($\frac{1}{2}$ in) wide when finished, therefore cut them 2.5 cm (1 in) wide. The length of the rectangles will vary by 1.5 cm ($\frac{1}{2}$ in) to accommodate the preceding one. This would result in a block measuring 12.5 cm (5 in) square, the dimensions for which are given in full in Fig. 18. These measurements include the seam allowance.

Cutting the fabric
Cut the templates as follows:
A: one light
B: one dark
C–I: one dark and one light
J: one light

Making a block
Begin by joining B to one side of A (Fig. 19). Press the seam.

Next sew the dark coloured C to the lower edge of the newly formed rectangle and press.

Add the light coloured C to the newly formed square and press.

Continue in this manner, working clockwise and keeping the dark fabrics to one side and the light to the other until the block is completed (Fig. 20).

To enlarge the square continue to sew strips on to the block, each time cutting a pair of strips, one dark and one light, 1.5 cm ($\frac{1}{2}$ in) longer than the previous pair.

Alternatively, the size of the central square and rectangles can be scaled up to lessen sewing time.

Joining the blocks

Once the required number of blocks has been made there are many ways of piecing them together. Figs. 21–23 show three traditional ways but there are many alternatives. Log cabin is a particularly marvellous traditional block with endless permutations because of its three dimensional quality. Experiment on graph paper with colour and positioning.

Quilting

Prepare for quilting as given on page 78.

Quilt in every other seam thus forming a square (Fig. 24), or only round each block. Finish off the threads.

Cushion

You will need

- 46 cm ($\frac{1}{2}$ yd) fabric for centre square and cushion back in black, 90 cm (36 in) wide
- 22 cm ($\frac{1}{4}$ yd) in each of eight shades of fabric 90 cm (36 in) wide
- piece of wadding 40 cm (16 in) square
- backing fabric 40 cm (16 in) square
- 30 cm (12 in) zip
- black sewing thread

Fig. 20 Planning the log cabin pieces.

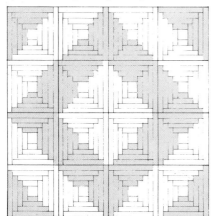

Fig. 23 'Barn raising' variation.

Measurements

Block. 12.5 cm (5 in)
Cushion. 38 cm (15 in) square

To make up

Make nine blocks and join them in three rows of three blocks each, all positioned with the dark strips facing the same way (see the cushion at the front of the photograph on page 80).

Prepare and quilt.

Because quilting 'takes up' the fabric slightly, measure the cushion size again before cutting out a cushion back. Make it the same size as the cushion front including the seam allowance all round plus an additional 6 mm ($\frac{1}{4}$ in) allowance on one edge for the zip.

Turn in 1.5 cm ($\frac{5}{8}$ in) on this edge and press. Place the zip face down on the right side of the patchwork. Sew in place close to the zip teeth either using a zipper foot or by hand using back stitch.

Turn the zip over, bringing it face upwards. Position the folded edge of the cushion back on to the right side of the zip so that it extends 3 mm ($\frac{1}{8}$ in) beyond the teeth and tack in place. Stitch round the zip (Fig. 25).

Place cushion front and back right sides together. Begin sewing at one end of the zip, continue round the other three sides of the cushion and back along the remaining short edge to the other end of the zip. Turn right sides out and press.

The cushion could, alternatively, be made up of a sixteen block square or a four block square.

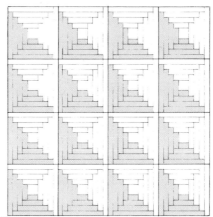

Fig. 21 Log cabin layout.

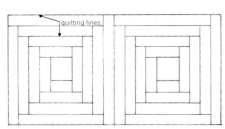

Fig. 24 Quilting lines.

Windmill

Four triangles joined to form a square within a mitred frame make up this windmill block (Fig. 26). Because of the geometric design the colours can be made to pick out the detail within each block or the shapes which emerge once the blocks have been joined.

You will need

- Two templates: A) triangle, B) rectangle
- same weight fabric in four colours

Instructions

Making the templates

Draw out the design on graph paper and make the templates. The finished size of the block is 20.5 cm (8 in) square.

Cutting the fabric

Cut the templates as follows:
A: one in each of the four colours
B: two in each of the four colours

Making a block

Join the pieces.

Each sail of the windmill is worked in one colour as shown in Fig. 27. Using the appropriate colours, join two B pieces at their straight edges, then sew them to the base of the A triangle to form an extended triangle. Finally, join the four triangles together (see Fig. 28).

Press all the seams.

Joining the blocks

All the blocks can be worked in the same four colours or in several com-

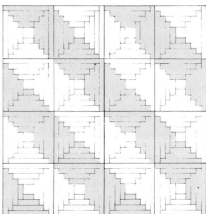

Fig. 22 'Straight furrow' variation.

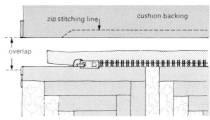

Fig. 25 Sewing in the zip.

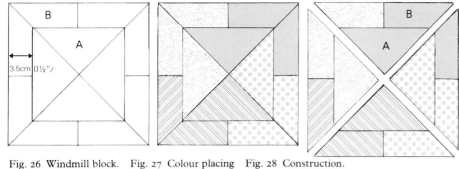

Fig. 26 Windmill block.   Fig. 27 Colour placing   Fig. 28 Construction.

binations evenly distributed or with one particular combination grouped together and surrounded by a different colour combination. As always, the permutations are almost limitless.

Experiment on graph paper.

Quilting

Prepare for quilting.

Quilt all the seams, vertical, horizontal and diagonal.

The windmill quilt with two alternating colour combinations in the central panel and a third round the outside.

Quilt

You will need

● 50 cm ($\frac{1}{2}$ yd) fabric in each of eight colours for central 24 blocks
● 1.50 m (1$\frac{3}{4}$ yd) fabric in each of four colours for surrounding 36 blocks
● sewing thread
● wadding 208 cm by 127 cm (82 in by 50 in)
● backing fabric 208 cm by 127 cm (82 in by 50 in)

Measurements

Block. 20.5 cm (8 in) square
Quilt. 205 cm by 123 cm (80 in by 48 in)

To make up

Make twelve blocks in one of the colourways for the central panel and twelve blocks in the second colourway. Join them in two sections so that there are three rows of four blocks in each, and the colourways are alternated with the darkest colour in the same position.

Make thirty-six blocks in the third colourway and join them to the two central sections – a single row down each side and a double row across the bottom of one central section and across the top of the other. This means that the quilt is split in half horizontally for ease when quilting.

Prepare and quilt.

Join the two sections together and cover the joining seam with a bias strip of backing fabric.

Finish the edges as desired.

Plaited border

This attractive border is made from only one template. It looks particularly well with the windmill quilt (see page 83) but could also be used on other items to a proportionate scale.

You will need
● One four-sided template (see Fig. 29).

Instructions
All the techniques required for this project are given on pages 78 and 79.

Making the template
Rule out a graph as shown in Fig. 29. A to A is the width of the border required. C is half way between, and B to C is one sixth of A to A. The distance between the vertical lines is one sixth of A to A.

Draw in the plaited border as shown in Fig. 29 and then cut the template.

Cutting the fabric
The border is worked in four colours used in the same sequence throughout each pattern repeat. Cut one piece in each of the four colours for each repeat required.

Making the block
Join the first two pieces as shown in Fig. 30. Sew the third piece along the combined length of the first two and so on in the sequence shown in Fig. 31, always working in the same direction.

The colours used in the plaited border reflect those used in the windmill design.

Quilt border

You will need
● 1.20 m ($1\frac{1}{3}$ yd) in each of four colours of fabric 90 cm (36 in) wide
● 2.10 m ($2\frac{1}{4}$ yd) wadding
● 2.10 m ($2\frac{1}{4}$ yd) backing fabric
● 1 m ($1\frac{1}{4}$ yd) extra of one of the four colours for binding
● sewing thread

Measurements
15 cm (6 in) wide
to fit in four sections round Windmill Quilt (see page 83)

To make up
Cut 72 pieces in each of the four colours.

Make into four blocks each 102.5 cm (40 in) long and two blocks each 153 cm (60 in) long.

Before quilting, join one long block and two side blocks to each of the two sections of the quilt. Fold the border to give a straight edge where the short side joins the long edge.

Quilting
Prepare the border for quilting.

Quilt along all the seams.

Finish off threads.

Join the two sections together as given for the Windmill Quilt (see page 83).

Fasten off ends.

Cut several lengths of bias strips 5 cm (2 in) wide in one of the four colours and bind the edges.

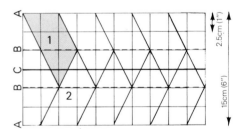

Fig. 29 Constructing the plaited border.

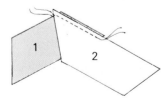

Fig. 30 Joining 1st two pieces.

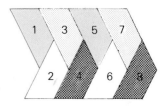

Fig. 31 Piecing the plaited border.

Felt making

Felt making is a very ancient and simple method of making a fabric. Excavations have discovered pieces of felt dating back to 3000 B.C. and it is still widely made today by nomadic tribes in Iran. They make rugs to sleep on, to line their tents and for their camels' backs. It is also made in Turkey, Afghanistan and some parts of Russia.

It is a very inexpensive way of making fabric as wool can be collected from fences and hedges on country walks. The necessary equipment is all in the kitchen except for one item, the carders, but even these are not necessary to try a small piece as an experiment.

A piece of felt is only as hard wearing and compact as the amount of wool used and pressure applied. It is fun to make and the material can be put to a variety of uses.

Materials and Equipment

Unmanufactured wool comes in locks which can be separated into pieces of wool called staples. Different fleeces have staples of different thickness and length. All wool will felt because it is made up of fibres covered in scales and under the right conditions these scales will slide together to form a fabric. However, the finer the wool and shorter the staple, the easier it is to felt as finer fabrics have more scales. Coarser wools will take longer to matt together. Suggested wools for felt making come from the following sheep: Suffolk, Dorset Down and Romney Marsh. Fleeces are categorized by price by the British Wool Board, elsewhere the wool is available by weight. One fleece would make all the projects in this section.

Rubber gloves are necessary because the water is very hot.

A sheet of polythene to make the felt in.

Hand carders are a bed of flexible needles mounted in pieces of rectangular wood with handles. Their job is to prepare the wool for felt making or spinning. They are essential for a large piece of felt, but small experimental pieces of felt can be prepared without them.

A dish for holding the hot water.

Embroidery yarns can be chunky knitting wool, tapestry wool or rug yarns. A thick yarn will show up best against the felt.

Crochet hook size 4.50 makes the lengths of decorative chain.

Iron-on woven and non-woven interfacing are used to keep the shape of the felt for garments.

Lining is sometimes required to provide a smooth inside surface.

Paper is used to make templates for pattern shapes.

General items include scissors, pens, pencils, notebook, a large-eyed needle, dressmakers' pins, tape measure, ruler and washing up liquid or detergent.

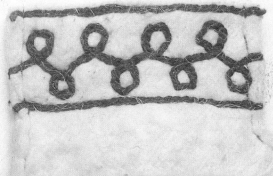

Know how

Carding

This is the process of straightening out and loosening the fibres of the wool and is the same for either felt making or spinning. Each person will have an individual result from carding because different amounts of wool will be used and different pressures applied. It is important, therefore, to work a sample for each project and to keep accurate notes of the amount of wool used for each carding and the number of layers put together for the felt making. In this way a personal record builds up about one's own techniques.

Wash and dry the wool locks.

Take a couple of locks of wool and tease them (Fig. 1) by holding them gently with both hands and lightly separating the fibres. This loosens the wool and makes it easier to card. It will also remove large bits of vegetation.

Keep the movements exaggerated for the first few attempts with wrist and elbow flexible and the pressure light. There should be no sound of grating metal. Take care not to embed the wool into the needles as it is difficult to remove and too much pressure will damage the carders.

Left-handed people should read left for right and right for left.

Rest one carder, needle side up, on the right knee with the handle across the left knee.

Lightly place the wool across the carder down the centre as shown in Fig. 2. Place the left hand on the wool, near the handle of the carder, to prevent it being dragged off.

Hold the second carder, needle side down, in the right hand over the first.

Position the top edge against the bottom edge of the left hand carder. Take the right hand carder in a circular movement through the air, away from the other carder (Fig. 3) and back to overlap with it slightly (Fig. 4).

Draw the right hand carder across and then away from the left hand carder in the same circular movement, to return with about a quarter of each carder overlapping (Fig. 5).

Continue in this way, gradually working across the lower carder until the whole bed of each carder comes into contact (Fig. 6). Draw the right hand carder across the left.

There should now be equal amounts of wool on each carder (Fig. 7).

Hold the carders with the handles upwards and the beds of needles facing each other (Fig. 8). Place the top edge of the left hand carder along the bottom edge of the right hand carder. Bring the left hand carder down and the right hand carder up, gently brushing against one another to transfer all the wool to the right hand carder. The left hand carder should be empty.

Repeat the entire carding process. The first time straightened the fibres on the surface, subsequent processes will get at the fibres underneath. After the second time there will not be equal amounts of wool on each carder and when it comes to transferring the wool, the right hand carder goes to the top. Usually it is only necessary to repeat the carding three times.

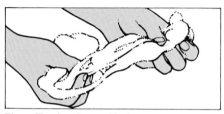
Fig. 1 Teasing the wool locks.

Fig. 2 Placing wool on carder.

Figs. 3 and 4 Carding movements as seen by feltworker.

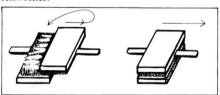
Figs. 5 and 6 Overlapping and finally bringing both carders together.

Fig. 7 Equal division of wool.

Finally, transfer all the wool on to either carder.

Form a V shape with the carders touching along the bottom edge as shown in Fig. 9. With the empty carder, lift off the wool. It should be in a flat, rectangular shape.

Repeat the entire process until enough wool has been prepared for the project. A few sample pieces are needed to experiment with to find how many will make the correct thickness.

To work without carders, tease out all the fibres as best as possible, so that they are smooth and evenly spaced.

Felt making

Carded or teased wool will felt when put under heat, friction and pressure

Fig. 8 Transferring wool.

Fig. 9 Lifting off wool.

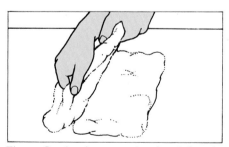
Fig. 10 Overlapping rectangles of carded wool.

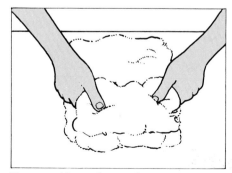
Fig. 11 2nd layer of rectangles.

Painting

Using white acrylic, oil paint, poster paint or white emulsion, give the head an undercoat.

While this is drying, mix a good amount of a peach colour by using plenty of white, some yellow and a dash of red. When the undercoat is dry, paint the peach colour over the whole head and neck.

Paint on the features. Paint the whites of the eyes first, then use black or brown for the eybrows, eyes and lines round the eyes. Use a darker peach (add a little more red and yellow) to make a shadow under the eyebrows and in the ears. Use red for the nose and mouth. Finish the mouth with a line of white round the outside.

The foam rubber head
Carving

In this method, instead of adding pieces as for the modelled head, pieces are cut away from a block of foam until the required shape is achieved.

The shape of the block used will differ according to the type of puppet being made but the sequence of cutting away is the same. The techniques described here relate particularly to the horse's head of the second project.

The size of the head should relate to the size of the operator's hand. Thus a large hand (e.g. an average man's hand) would need a foam block 10 cm by 20 cm by 30 cm (4 in by 8 in by 12 in). A smaller hand (e.g. an average woman's hand) would need a block about 10 cm by 15 cm by 25 cm (4 in by 6½ in by 10 in).

Using a felt tip pen, draw the horse's profile on to each of the two longest sides of the foam block (Fig. 7). With a sharp knife, slice off a wedge of foam

above the horse's nose (Fig. 8) and set aside.

Cut the shape out roughly with the knife, working only across the head (Fig. 9).

With the front of the head facing, draw on guidelines in felt tip pen to help cut the muzzle shape roughly (Fig. 10). Cut lengthways across the guidelines.

Turn the foam round so that the back of the head is facing and repeat this process as shown in Fig. 11.

Cut away the underside of the upper jaw, only to a point level with the start of the forehead (Fig. 12).

Round off the corners of the head by snipping away with sharp scissors. Start by snipping away larger pieces and, as the shape develops, snip away much smaller pieces until the surface is smooth and rounded.

Carving the head is not an easy task but, by constantly referring to the finished shape, a good head shape should be produced.

Do not be over enthusiastic, however. The underside of the muzzle should be no smaller than the width of the operator's hand plus 2 cm (1 in).

A pear-shaped hollow is now made into the underside of the muzzle to take the fingers and back of the hand for operating the puppet. Turn the head upside down and draw on a pear shape, the narrowest part to start directly under the tip of the horse's nose and the largest part to finish two thirds of the way down the length of the head. Leave at least 1 cm (½ in) of foam around the edge of the hollow (Fig. 13). Use a knife to cut out this hollow so that the fingers and back of the hand fit snugly into it.

To make the lower mouth piece,

take the wedge of foam first cut from the block. Draw and cut this out in the same way as the head, firstly cutting across and secondly down the length. Fig. 14 shows the finished shape. It should be the same width as the muzzle and approximately one third of the total length of the head. Hollow a shallow scoop on the inside of the jaw for the thumb to rest in.

Making the features

Draw the eyes and nostrils on the foam block with a felt tip pen. Pinch the foam within these circles between the fingers and pull it into a peak. With scissors, snip round and remove the peak. The foam will fall back to form a hollow.

To make the nose and ears of a human character, draw and cut a nose shape from a wedge of discarded foam, leaving the back of the nose flat. It should be thick at the base, becoming thinner and narrower to the top. Cut the two ears from a sheet of foam rubber. Use a pair of scissors to do this and round off the sharp edges.

Other features are cut out of felt and added later.

Covering the head

Using stretch fabric, cover the main head piece. In the case of the horse's head, use the fabric in three sections, to meet along the lines of the bridle as shown by the double unbroken lines in Fig. 15. Cut pieces of fabric large enough to cover each section and fit each piece over the head. Stretch the fabric tightly to fit, pinning it at the same time.

Cut away any excess fabric and glue the edge down with contact adhesive along the bridle lines and under the base of the head. In some cases, as on the horse's head, it may be necessary to make pleats, as indicated by the dotted lines in Fig. 15, for the fabric to fit properly at the eyes and nostrils. Sew the pleats with matching sewing thread, then pass the needle and thread through the centre of one eye hollow, through the middle of the foam and out through the other eye hollow. Repeat this in the opposite direction and draw the thread tight so that the stretch fabric fits into the hollows of the eyes. Work in the same way for the nostrils. Cover the lower mouth piece in the same way, using only one piece of fabric.

Attaching the mouth piece

Felt is used to cover the untidy edges of the stretch fabric and to fix the two sections together.

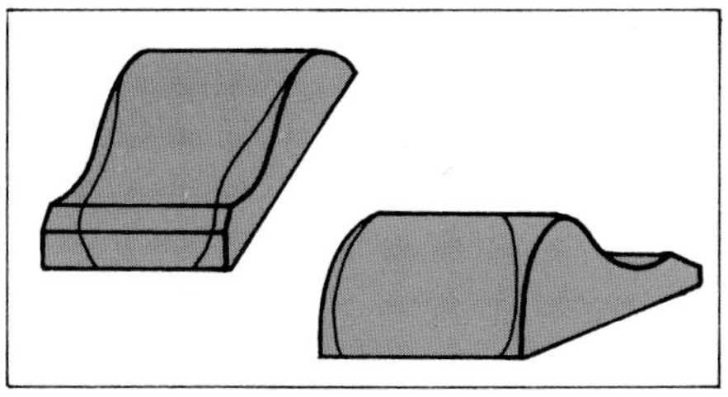

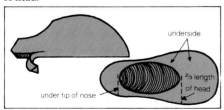

Fig. 10 Cutting muzzle shape and Fig. 11 back of head.

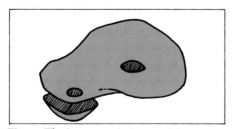

Fig. 14 The lower mouth shape and features.

Fig. 12 Cutting underneath jaw and Fig. 13 pear-shaped hollow.

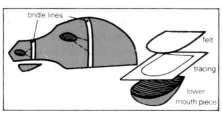

Fig. 15 3 sections of fabric and Fig. 16 tracing mouth piece.

continued

In the case of the horse's head, first sew two strips of braid over the bridle lines on the top of the head, allowing 1.5 cm ($\frac{3}{4}$ in) at each end of the braid to turn under the head.

Trace the shapes of the upper and lower inside mouth pieces and cut these shapes out of felt (Fig. 16). Pin the felt in place to cover the edges of the stretch fabric and tucking the loose ends of the bridle braid underneath the felt of the upper mouth. Stitch all round both pieces except the straight back edges.

Pin the lower mouth piece in place beneath the muzzle and sew the straight back edges together, taking the line of stitching just over the edge of the felt and on to the head fabric in order to hinge the two pieces more securely. This makes an upper and a lower pocket between the foam and the felt to take the fingers and thumb respectively.

The body
Making the body
The bodies of all the puppets described here are made of fabric. Paper patterns can be made by enlarging the pattern shapes given with the individual project to the size that suits. Sew by machine or hand; for hand stitching use overstitch as the puppets must be strong enough to use without coming apart at the seams.

Operating
The various ways of holding and operating the puppets in this book are given at the end of each project. The skill of operating comes first with using the correct hold and then with practice – and a lot of patience. By 'playing' with the puppet, that is moving it about freely and finding what it can do, the operator will improve his or her ability.

The stage
The puppet stage is known as the 'playboard'. It should successfully hide the operator and focus the audience's attention on the puppets. One very immediate playboard can be found in the home by simply kneeling behind an easy chair or sofa and working the puppet over the back.

Another simple playboard can be made by fixing a sheet or large curtain between two supports such as the frame of an open door and at a height that will hide the operator. The puppet can then be worked at arm's length, above the sheet.

Clown

The clown is a glove puppet operated with one hand. His head is made by the modelling method.

You will need
- 1 kilo (2.2 lb) modelling clay
- heavy cotton, velvet or furnishing fabric approximately 60 cm by 45 cm (24 in by 18 in)
- dark blue felt, 20 cm (8 in) square
- bright green felt, 30 cm by 15 cm (12 in by 6 in)
- 2.25 m ($2\frac{1}{2}$ yd) bias binding, 5 cm (2 in) wide
- puppetry equipment as given on page 91

Instructions
All the puppetry techniques required for this project are given on pages 92 to 94.
Head
Use the modelling clay to make the head, nose, ears and neck, then make a papier-mâché model.

Give the head an undercoat of white paint and, when dry, a top coat of peach coloured paint. For a white faced clown, simply apply a second layer of white instead of the peach.

When dry, paint on the clown's make-up, either copying the make-up of the puppet illustrated or making an original design.
Body
Enlarge the hand and body patterns given in Fig. 17 to the required size, draw on to brown paper and cut out.

Pin the body pattern to the fabric and cut two pieces to the required size.

Fit the pieces with right sides together. Sew about 1 cm ($\frac{1}{2}$ in) from the edge where indicated in Fig. 17, leaving the wrists open. Do not turn right sides out.

Pin the hand pattern to the felt and cut four.

Pin two pieces of felt together and sew right round 0.5 cm ($\frac{1}{4}$ in) from the

edge, leaving the wrists open (Fig. 17). Turn both hands right sides out.

Insert the hands into the armholes, fingers pointing inwards as shown in Fig. 18. Pin and stitch as indicated. Turn the body right side out.

Turn under the neck and hem about 1 cm (½ in) and slip stitch in place.

To complete

Glue the head into the neck opening taking care to position the head so the face is at centre front.

Add any details such as hair and neck ruff and any other details desired – bow tie, large coloured buttons or fringes, for instance.

To make the ruff, gather a strip of bias binding along one edge to fit round the neck and sew in place.

To make the hair, cut small strips of felt and snip along one edge to make a fringe. Glue these strips in layers round the back of the head, sticking them

A strange duet, sung by the horse on the **right** and Dai the Choir on the **left** ably conducted by the clown puppet in the **centre**.

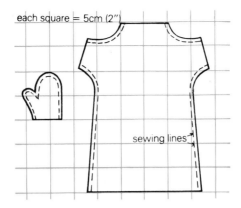

each square = 5cm (2″)

sewing lines

Fig. 17 Hand and body pattern for clown puppet.

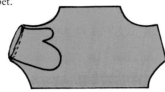

Fig. 18 Inserting hand inside armhole.

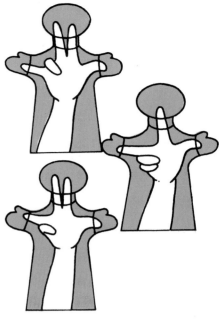

Fig. 19 3 ways of operating the clown.

along the uncut edge and starting at the neck and working upwards to just above the ears.

Operating

There are three alternative ways of holding the clown puppet (Fig. 19).

Horse

This is a hand puppet operated with two hands. The head is of the foam rubber type and his rump is made of foam sheeting.

You will need
● Block of foam rubber 10 cm (4 in) thick, 20 cm (8 in) wide and 30 cm (12 in) long
● sheet of foam rubber 2 cm (¾ in) thick, 20 cm by 30 cm (8 in by 12 in)
● stretch polyester fabric in a plain colour to cover the horse's head, 120 cm by 35 cm (47 in by 14 in)
● patterned fabric 80 cm by 100 cm (31½ in by 39½ in)
● interfacing 60 cm by 25 cm (23½ in by 10 in)
● 63 cm (25 in) of braid, 2 cm (¾ in) wide
● two pieces of felt, one 35 cm (13¾ in) square for eyes, nose, mouth and mantle edging, the other 20 cm by 35 cm (8 in by 13¾ in) in the same colour as the head, for tail and ears
● small quantity of black and white felt
● puppetry equipment as given on page 91

Instructions
All the puppetry techniques required for this project are given on pages 92 to 94.
Head
Make a horse's head as given in the Know How (see pages 93 and 94).
Neck
Enlarge pattern piece A of Fig. 20 for the neck. Check that the inside edge of this shape is the same measurement as the line that runs around the base of the head, as indicated by the dotted line in Fig. 21. Lengthen or shorten as necessary at the central dotted line. Draw on brown paper and cut out.

Cut two neck shapes, one from interfacing and the other from the same fabric as the head but cut 0.5 cm (¼ in) larger all round.

Pin the interfacing to the wrong side of the fabric. Turn the inside curves and side edges of the fabric over the interfacing and sew.

Pin the neck around the base of the head as indicated by the dotted line in Fig. 21 and sew, turning the ends of the upper strip of bridle into the neck at the same time. The end pieces of the neck meet and overlap below the mouth and are then sewn together.

Sew a strip of braid to either side of the head along the neck join, connecting the two previous strips.
Rump
Enlarge pattern piece B (Fig. 20), draw on paper and cut out two of this shape from the foam rubber sheeting.

Mark the notches either side of the dotted line on to each piece of foam. Glue the pieces together along the notched edge, matching the notches.

Round off the X edge of the shape. Cut a hole in the centre, between the notches, large enough to poke a forefinger through.
The mantle
Enlarge pattern piece C (Fig. 20), adjusting the neckline to the same measurement as the neck and allowing 4 cm (2 in) extra for seams. Draw on paper.

Cut two of this shape from the patterned fabric.

Pin right sides together and stitch the front and back seams, leaving a space between the two notches on the back seam. Turn to the right side and press.

Pin the rump inside the mantle matching the notched tail openings and with the Y end facing the front. Tack lightly in place, sewing right through the foam.

Turn under the neck edge of the mantle, pin 2 cm (1 in) from the edge of the neck and sew.
Tail
Using felt the colour of the head, make a finger pouch with a rounded top and large enough for the forefinger to fit inside up to the second joint. Leave the bottom edge of the pouch open and turn inside out so that the seam allowances are on the inside.

Sew the opening of the pouch into the tail opening of the mantle so that the pouch itself stands up like a short tail.

In the same colour felt, cut several pieces as shown in Fig. 22. Glue or sew the strips in layers around the tail pouch, pointed ends to the tip of the tail, attaching each strip along the full depth of the pouch. Sew a band of felt around the base of the tail to secure it to the mantle.
To complete
Enlarge pattern piece D (Fig. 20) and draw on paper.

Cut two in the same felt as for the tail.

Pin the ears to the head in the position illustrated and sew in place.

From the same felt as the mouth, cut all shapes to fit into the eye and nostril hollows and sew in place.

Cut two small discs from black felt and four small triangles from white felt for the eyes. Glue the discs into the centre of the eye sockets with a white triangle on each side.

From felt, cut a decorative trimming to edge the mantle and two rosettes to decorate the bridle.

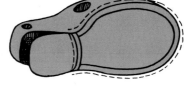

Fig. 21 Base of head with mouth piece in position.

Fig. 22 Tail piece.

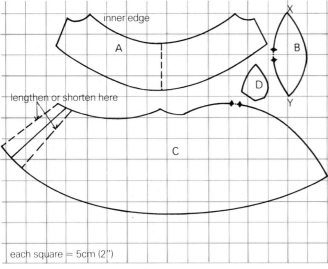
Fig. 20 Pattern pieces for the horse.

Fig. 23 Operating with 2 hands.

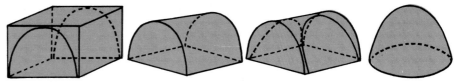

Fig. 24 Cutting the crown shape from a block of foam.

Operating

This horse is operated with two hands – one works the head, the other the tail. The fingers of the hand fit into the hollow carved under the head and the thumb fits between the felt mouth piece and the foam rubber of the chin (Fig. 23). With practice, the horse can gallop, turn and flick his tail, neighing as he does so!

Dai the choir

Here is a real character to make. He has a carved foam rubber head, foam rubber sheeting for body and hands and arms operated by the rods attached to them. He is a hand and rod puppet.

You will need

● Block of foam rubber 10 cm (4 in) thick, 40 cm by 30 cm (16 in by 12 in)
● sheet of foam rubber 2 cm ($\frac{3}{4}$ in) thick, 50 cm by 60 cm (20 in by 24 in)
● serge or any other heavy fabric 120 cm by 60 cm (48 in by 24 in) for the coat
● white fabric 35 cm (14 in) square for the shirt
● stretch polyester fabric 160 cm by 35 cm (63 in by 14 in) for face and hands
● felt, two pieces each 20 cm by 30 cm (8 in by 12 in) in black and blue and three pieces each 20 cm (8 in) square in rust, white and yellow
● two wire coat hangers
● two small black spherical buttons
● puppetry equipment as given on page 91

Fig. 25 Cutting thumb hollow and back section from chin piece.   Fig. 26 Nose shape.   Fig. 27 Pinning fabric at back of head.

Fig. 28 Pinning chin to crown.   Fig. 29 Sewing strip to make back of neck.

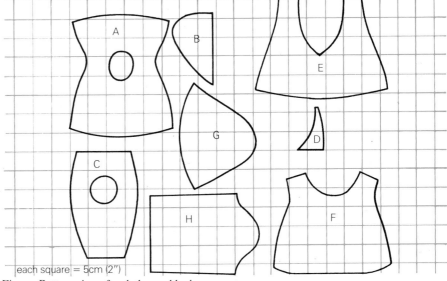

Fig. 30 Pattern pieces for clothes and body.

each square = 5cm (2″)

Instructions

All the puppetry techniques required for this project are given on pages 92 to 94.

Head

Cut three pieces from the block of foam, one 20 cm by 14 cm by 10 cm (8 in by 5$\frac{1}{2}$ in by 4 in) for the chin and two pieces each 20 cm by 16 cm by 10 cm (8 in by 6$\frac{1}{4}$ in by 4 in) for the crown. Glue the crown pieces together to form one block 20 cm by 16 cm by 20 cm (8 in by 6$\frac{1}{4}$ in by 8 in).

Draw a crown shape in felt pen on to the front and back of the larger block as in Fig. 24. Using a sharp knife, cut away the foam outside the pen line, working from front to back. Draw the same shape on the two sides and cut away the foam, working across.

Using sharp scissors, round off the corners and snip away at the foam to obtain a smooth shape with a base of approximately 14 cm (5$\frac{1}{2}$ in) wide by 18 cm (7 in) deep and 13 cm (5 in) high.

Cut a hollow into the base of the crown close to the front edge and the same width as the distance from finger tips to knuckles.

Draw a chin shape on to the smaller block and cut out in the same way as the crown to have a base approximately 14 cm (5$\frac{1}{2}$ in) wide by 12 cm (4$\frac{3}{4}$ in) deep and 7 cm (2$\frac{3}{4}$ in) high.

Cut a section away from the back of the chin as shown in Fig. 25 and cut a hollow into the remaining upper surface for the thumb (see Fig. 25).

Draw and cut a nose shape from foam, leaving the back of the nose flat (Fig. 26), to measure 8 cm (3 in) high, 5 cm (2 in) wide and 2.5 cm (1 in) deep at the base, becoming thinner and narrower to the top.

Cut two ears about 4 cm (1$\frac{1}{2}$ in) wide and 5.5 cm (2$\frac{1}{4}$ in) high from a sheet of foam rubber, using a pair of scissors and rounding off the edges.

Cover the crown with polyester fabric, stretching it across the front and over the top. There will be several folds at the back of the head. Pin the fabric down at the start of the folds then cut it away leaving a V shape uncovered (Fig. 27).

Glue the fabric down around the V and the underside of the crown. Cover the V shape with a second piece of fabric and sew it to the first piece.

Cover the chin in the same way using one piece of fabric and leaving the back uncovered.

Cover the nose with one piece of fabric and glue the edges to the back of the nose. Sew the nose in position on the crown, approximately 1.5 cm ($\frac{1}{2}$ in) up from the base.

Cut two ear shaped pieces of fabric

Fig. 31 Forming the body from foam.

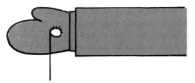

Fig. 32 Sewing the rod in place.

Fig. 33 Making the bow tie.

Fig. 34 Daffodil pieces.

Fig. 35 Operating the head and rod.

and sew them together around the outside edge to cover each ear then sew the ears in place.

Pin the chin in place under the crown and make a tracing from your puppet of the two shaded areas shown in Fig. 28. Cut these pieces from the rust coloured felt and pin them into place. Stitch the curved edge of each, covering the glued edge of the face fabric.

Sew the straight sides of the two felt pieces together and the chin and crown together at the sides to form a hinge and continue stitching the chin and crown together towards the front for about 3 cm (1¼ in) on each side.

Cut a strip of the face fabric to fit around the back of the head and deeper than the chin by 2 cm (¾ in) plus seam allowance. Join it to the chin at either side. Pin and sew in place to make the back of the neck (Fig. 29).

Body

Enlarge pattern pieces A and B (Fig. 30) and draw on brown paper.

Cut one from A and two from B out of foam sheeting.

Glue the sides of A over the curve of the two B pieces to form the body (Fig. 31).

Cut two mitt shapes out of foam sheeting approximately 12 cm (4¾ in) across and 13 cm (5 in) high and round off the edges.

Cut two long strips of foam 5 cm (2 in) wide and 30 cm (12 in) long for the arms, again rounding off the edges.

Cover each hand in the same way as the ears, with two mitt shaped pieces sewn together around the outer edge.

Cut a slit 1.5 cm (½ in) deep into the thickness of one end of each of the arms. Glue the hands into these slits.

To complete

Enlarge and cut pattern shape C (Fig. 30) out of the white fabric to make the shirt. Fit the fabric over the body so that the neck holes match and glue down around the outside edge.

Pin the head in place over the neck hole and sew the edge of the back of the neck to the shirt around the hole.

Trace the shape of the gap under the chin shown by the shaded area in Fig. 29 and cut this shape out of white fabric. Pin into place and sew around the outside edge where it joins chin and body.

Using pattern D (Fig. 30), cut two collar shapes out of white felt and sew these around the top edge of the previous piece, under the chin, to conceal the join between the face and shirt.

Enlarge pattern pieces E, F, G and H (Fig. 30) and draw on brown paper. Cut one each of E and F and two each of G and H in the coat fabric.

Fit the side pieces (G) to the sides of the body and glue them down where they will overlap with E and F.

Turn under 0.5 cm (¼ in) on the neck lines of E and F and stitch.

Pin F on the back of the body and turn under the edges which overlap with the side pieces. Pin E on the front with the V shaped neckline ending approximately 3 cm (1¼ in) above the lower edge of the body. Turn under the outer edges where they overlap the side pieces and the shoulder edges on the shoulder line, overlapping the back section. Slip stitch the shoulder and side seams. Sew a strip of interfacing on the wrong side of the lower edge of the coat front to keep its shape. Hem the bottom edge of the coat.

Cut two strips of white felt, each about 5 cm (2 in) wide and long enough to wrap around the base of the hand, to make cuffs and cover the wrist joins. Sew the cuffs in place on the hands.

Turn under 0.5 cm (¼ in) on the shoulder and cuff edges of the sleeves and stitch. With right sides together, sew a 0.5 cm (¼ in) seam down the length of each sleeve then turn to the right side.

Slide a foam arm into each sleeve, the top of the arm reaching almost to the top of the edge of the sleeve and the cuffs showing just below the sleeve. Glue the arm to the inside of the sleeve along the seam.

Pin the shoulder opening of each sleeve to the side of the body so that the hands are angled forward slightly and the shoulders backwards. Stitch.

Straighten out the wire coat hangers to make the hand rods. Using a pair of pliers, bend the wire into a small loop at one end and trim away the 'tail' of wire protruding from the loop. Cut each rod down to a length of 50 cm (20 in). Sew one side of the rod's loop to the palm of the hand about 1 cm (½ in) away from the cuff (Fig. 32).

Sew on the two buttons for eyes.

Cut two curly eyebrow shapes from black felt and glue above the eyes.

Cut out a quantity of long strips with curved ends from the black felt and glue these around the back of the head in layers, working from ear to ear, for the hair. Snip some black felt into small pieces, spread glue on the head just in front of each ear in the shape of a sideburn and press the small pieces of felt on to the glue.

Cut two small ovals from black felt for nostrils and glue on the underside of the nose.

Cut the lapels from blue felt. The inside edge of these should match the line of the V shaped opening on the front of the coat. Glue the lapels along the edge of the front opening.

From the same blue felt cut out two pieces to make the bow tie (Fig. 33). Fold the two ends of the large curved strip to the centre and sew down, wrap the smaller strip around the centre and sew the ends together. Sew the bow tie to the felt collar.

Make the daffodil in two pieces cut from yellow felt (Fig. 34), cutting the outside edge of the fan shape with pinking shears. Sew the two sides together to make the trumpet then sew the narrow end of it into the centre of the petals. Sew the daffodil to the coat.

Operating

Two people may be needed to operate this puppet fully – one to work the mouth and another to work the hand rods. A solo operator will be able to work only one hand at the same time as the mouth. Fig. 35 shows how to hold the puppet.

Batik

Batik is the ancient art of wax resist dyeing, a process developed thousands of years ago when it was found that water and wax do not mix. The name is Indonesian in origin meaning wax writing.

Batik uses wax as a dye resist, i.e. an area not penetrated by the dye. The wax creates a barrier between each colour, thus protecting one colour from the next. The design is built up in a progression of colours, tones and shades either painted on with a brush or immersed in a dye bath. The most common characteristic of batik dyeing is the 'crackle', caused by the wax cracking, either accidentally or by design, and the dye seeping in to make tiny veins. This form of dyeing fabric is very effective for soft furnishings such as curtains, cushions, blinds, room dividers and lampshades. Wall hangings show off batik to advantage particularly if it can be arranged for light to shine through from behind.

It is used extensively for dyeing dress fabrics especially thin, delicate textures, and is also found on accessories such as belts, bags and scarves.

Materials and Equipment

Fabrics should be of a finely woven type such as muslin, batiste, lawn or a light weight cotton. Pure silk is particularly effective but it is more expensive. The smooth surface of these fabrics accepts the dye readily and the colours remain vibrant. For the beginner it is best to experiment with a light weight bleached cotton. No synthetics or materials which have been chemically treated should be used.

Paper and pencil are used for designing, and a soft 2 or 3 B pencil is best for transferring the design to the fabric.

Brushes in a selection of sizes from 5 mm to 10 cm ($\frac{1}{4}$ in to 4 in) are used for waxing and painting. To help the wax to penetrate the cloth the waxing brushes must be stiffer than the brushes used to paint on the dye.

Rubber gloves are essential to protect the hands when making up the dyes, in using the dye baths and during the fixing process.

Wax generally used for batik is a combination of beeswax and paraffin wax called Batik Mixture. This is simple to use because it is ready mixed in the correct proportions. For more selective waxing it may be necessary to use either the beeswax or the paraffin wax only. Beeswax is expensive but if the aim is to avoid having any crackle in some part of the design then it is well worth using as it is much more pliant. Paraffin wax is more brittle so it cracks easily to give fine lines where needed.

A double saucepan makes an ideal wax pot.

A thermometer of the cooking type with a clip to fix it to the edge of a pan can be used for both the preparation of the dye bath, if it is a hot water dye, and heating the wax.

The tjanting tools, penlike with long wells or with miniature tubs from which the melted wax flows through the spout, vary in size to leave a thick or fine transparent line.

A pad of absorbent tissue held under the tool will catch any drips.

A frame is used to stretch the fabric. It can be an old picture frame, art canvas stretchers or an adjustable frame with notches cut into one side of each of the four strips of wood. The fabric is held in place either with drawing pins or masking tape.

Dyes usually come in liquid or powder form. Water is added and a 'fix' has to be mixed into the dye bath. Salt or washing soda are the most common mordants used for fixing the dyes.

The dye bath depends on the quantity of fabric to be dyed so that a bucket, a wide basin or just a bowl may be the most suitable.

An electric iron is used to remove the wax from the fabric.

Newspaper is placed above and below the fabric to absorb the melting wax whilst ironing.

A household culinary steamer is used to fix the dyes permanently and to brighten the colours.

Carpet felt (the sort used as underlay) is used in the steaming process, to enclose the batik.

A roll of paper towel is always useful to mop up any excess dye.

Clear plastic or glass with a light behind makes an improvized light box for seeing through thick fabrics when transferring designs.

Dressmakers' carbon is an alternative to a light box.

Know how

Preparing the fabric

Fabrics have to be carefully prepared before they are dyed to remove any dressing which contains starch and bleach so that nothing inhibits dye penetration.

Wash the fabric in hot water and pure soap, powder or flakes, or use Lissapol D or Soda Ash, 5 ml (one teaspoonful) to half a litre (one pint) of water. Colgon added to the water will loosen the fibres so they are more receptive to the dye.

A coloured fabric should be immersed in boiling water to remove any excess colour.

Designing

Cut a piece of paper to the same size as the piece of material. Draw the design and ink over the outline.

If the fabric is thin enough to see the design easily, it can be transferred on to the fabric by placing the fabric over the design and tracing over the outlines with a 2B or 3B pencil, or simply place the design under the frame and wax the lines freehand. If it is impossible to see through the fabric, either place the fabric and paper on to a sheet of clear plastic or glass with a light behind, or use dressmakers' carbon paper. Designs can range from realistic flowers and birds to abstract shapes.

Before waxing stretch the fabric on to the frame with either drawing pins or masking tape. The fabric must be taut enough to withstand the pressure of the brush or tjanting tool.

Waxing

Heat the wax in the pot until it has thoroughly melted, but not so hot that it smokes. The temperature should ideally be 56°C to 65°C (120°F to 140°F). Beeswax requires more heating than paraffin wax or Batik Mixture. The wax must be kept hot but never too hot. Use a hot plate or a very low flame – an asbestos mat between the saucepan and the heat is ideal for maintaining a low but constant temperature. Use a thermometer clipped to the side of the saucepan to judge the correct temperature.

Cover the floor and table tops between the wax pot and the fabric with newspaper to catch any drops.

Apply the wax to the fabric either with a brush or tjanting tool. If using a brush, choose the size most suited to the shape to be waxed and take care to remove any surplus wax on the side of the pot before the brush is taken from the pan. With a tjanting tool, keep the spout of the tool close to the fabric. Hold a pad of absorbent tissue in the left hand (or right if left-handed) to catch any drips when lifting the brush or tool from the wax pot over to the fabric, or when moving from one part of the design to the other.

The fabric should become transparent when the hot wax seeps into it. If it looks milky then the wax is not hot enough and will not have gone right through the fabric.

Leave the wax to harden before removing from the frame.

Dyeing

Cold water dyes are the best for batik dyeing to avoid melting the wax, which must be hard if it is to resist the dye. But hot water dyeing can be used, even if the dye has to be boiled in its preparation, provided it is allowed to cool to below 37°C (100°F) before a waxed fabric is immersed in it. All the projects here were done with cold water dyes.

Wet the fabric after it has been waxed and before it is put in the dye bath to help distribute the dye more evenly.

Instructions given with each type of dye, of which there are several on the market, must be read carefully and followed. Keep small samples of fabric with each dye and a note of the make of dye and the colour or its number for future reference. Keep notes too about any jar of dye stored for re-use. Dye must be tested before re-use because its strength may have deteriorated. The dye cannot be used after a few hours if washing soda has been added, so only make up a small quantity, just enough for the immediate use.

Stir the fabric occasionally in the dye bath to make sure the dye penetrates the fabric evenly and leave for the time specified in the instructions.

If a small piece of fabric is to be dyed after an area of no crackle has been waxed, a wide shallow dish, such as the ones used by photographers, will make it easier to avoid unwanted dye seeping into those areas of the design.

Remove from the dye bath by dripping back any excess dye into the bath before laying the fabric flat on to a good layer of newspapers. Blot off any pools of dye that may have collected with paper towel.

Hang up the fabric to drip dry, suspended by one edge only. When it is completely dry, fix it back on to the frame ready for the next waxing.

Second and subsequent waxings and dyeings

Each colour has to be added in turn starting with the palest shade and working through to the darkest. Between each colour apply wax to the area that is to be protected from the next dye. Remelt the wax for each new application.

'Crackle' can be introduced when the final waxing has been completed and hardened. To do this, crumple the fabric gently in the hands until fine cracks appear in the waxed areas. Be careful not to overdo the cracking, otherwise small lumps of wax may flake off completely.

After the final dye bath, hang up the fabric to dry once more.

Ironing

Place as many sheets of newspaper as required underneath and on top of the fabric, more will be needed according to the amount of wax used. Use a hot iron and replace the sheets of newspaper as they absorb the wax. Repeat until all the wax has been removed from the fabric.

If the fabric feels slightly stiff it will soften at the next stage.

Steaming

Set a steamer over a pan of hot water. Lay the batiked fabric on to clean sheets of newspaper large enough to be rolled into a tube. Twist the tube round so that it will fit into the steamer and secure with string as shown in Fig. 1.

Place a round of carpet felt over the holes at the base of the steamer and another piece of felt over the top of the pan.

Steam for about half an hour then untie. This fixes the dye, softens the fabric and brightens the colours.

Wash the fabric in hot water to remove any excess dye. One or two rinses may be necessary.

Finish off by ironing both sides of the cloth.

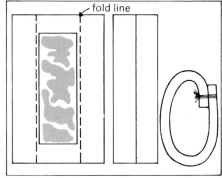

Fig. 1 Wrapping batik before steaming.

Headscarf

This fine muslin scarf has been batiked and dyed in two shades of one colour. Its simple design makes a suitable start for the beginner. The dimensions of the square can be adapted to suit many other projects.

You will need
- Fine white muslin, voile, batiste or a thin handkerchief lawn, 76 cm (30 in) square
- two small tins of dye in light and dark shades of the chosen colour
- needle and a fine white thread
- batik equipment as given on page 99

Instructions
All the techniques required for this project are given on page 100.

Enlarge the design given in Fig. 2 on to a square of paper the same size as the headscarf. Neaten the raw edges of the fabric with a rolled hem.

Wash, dry and iron the fabric.

Trace the outlines on to the fabric.

Stretch the fabric on to the frame and heat the wax.

Use either a fine brush or a tjanting tool to outline the design with wax.

Remove the fabric from the frame.

each square = 5cm (2")

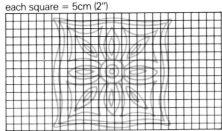

Fig. 2 Headscarf design.

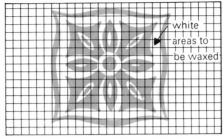

white areas to be waxed

Fig. 3 Areas to be waxed for 2nd dye bath.

Make up a dye bath with the paler of the two tones, following the instructions on the packet.

Add sufficient cold water to cover the fabric and immerse it for one hour, stirring occasionally.

Remove the fabric from the dye bath and blot off. Hang up to dry, by one edge only.

When dry, replace on the frame.

Remelt and heat the wax. Wax the areas shown in Fig. 3.

Remove the fabric from the frame.

When the wax has hardened, crumple the waxed areas gently to produce a 'crackle'.

Make up the second dye bath in the same way as the first using the darker colour.

Dye the fabric following the instructions. This will give a plain dark colouring to all the areas not waxed, at the same time as penetrating the cracked lines on the white and the first dyed, paler coloured areas, to give fine dark lines.

When the second dyeing is completed, dry off the fabric and remove the wax.

Steam, wash and iron whilst slightly damp.

Lampshade

The light shining through this batiked lampshade shows up fabric and pattern to best advantage. The design can be used on a table lamp, pendant light or standard lamp. Made up of circles, it is achieved by two dye baths, one waxing and painting with direct fabric dyes.

Below left Note the fine 'crackle' over the white and pale purple areas of the headscarf.
Below right Batik on a lampshade adds an individual touch to a room.

Batik

You will need

● For a shade measuring 25 cm (10 in) diameter at base and 22.5 cm (9 in) at top, 25 cm (10 in) deep: white, pure 'Jap' silk, or Swiss lawn 35 cm by 93 cm (14 in by 36½ in)
● firm lampshade backing (self adhesive or iron-on with PVC or card on the inside) 25 cm by 84 cm (10 in by 33 in)
● two lampshade rings, one 23 cm (9 in) diameter and one including a light bulb fitting 25 cm (10 in) diameter
● 1.6 m (2 yd) lampshade tape
● two cold water dyes, one pastel pink and one dark green
● four direct paint-on dyes in pale and dark blue, mauve and dark pink
● braid to match darkest colour
● clear adhesive
● two plain metal pastry rings, one two sizes smaller than the other
● pair of small tongs
● clothes pegs
● batik equipment as given on page 99

Instructions

All the techniques required for this project are given on page 100.

Cut the lampshade backing to fit allowing 1 cm (½ in) for the overlap as shown in Fig. 4.

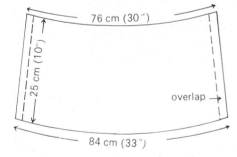

Fig. 4 Template for lampshade backing.

Cut the fabric to the same shape as the backing plus a good 5 cm (2 in) on all sides.

Wash and rinse the fabric.

Prepare the pale pink dye bath.

Immerse the fabric in the dye bath while it is still damp and hang it up to dry. When it is dry, iron it.

Stretch the fabric on to the frame. Melt the wax.

Pick up the larger of the two pastry rings, using the tongs. Dip the cutting edge into the hot wax long enough for the ring to become well heated and coated with wax. Remove the ring from the wax, tapping it on the side of the pan to remove any excess. Press the ring on to the fabric so that the imprint

gives the outline of a complete circle.

Repeat so that the circles are scattered in a random pattern over the whole length of the fabric.

Follow the same process with the smaller of the rings but overlap with some of the large circles or place a small circle within a large circle. Check that each circle's outline is complete, otherwise one colour may seep into another. If a circle is broken, re-wax it.

Drip a few drops of wax over the fabric to make small white dots.

Paint inside the circles with a medium sized brush, using direct paint-on dyes. The colours can be used straight from the jar, or mixed, diluted or lightened by adding white to the basic colour.

When all the painted circles are dry, re-heat the wax and brush over each circle with wax. Wax further background areas to retain some of the pale pink colour from the first dye bath.

Remove from the frame and, when the wax has hardened, gently crumple the waxed areas in the hands to obtain the 'crackle' effect.

Make up the dark green dye bath.

Immerse the fabric in the dye bath for the amount of time specified in the manufacturer's instructions. Make sure this dye has penetrated the cracked lines in the wax before removing from the dye bath.

Dry off the fabric and remove the wax.

Steam, wash, rinse and then press with a hot iron while still slightly damp.

To complete

Mount the fabric on to the backing. Fold the surplus fabric over one of the side edges, then cut away any surplus fabric on the remaining three edges to fit the backing.

Cover the lampshade rings with tape.

Wrap the fabric and its backing round the top ring so that the top edge of the fabric is level with the ring. Hold in position with the clothes pegs. Repeat to fit the bottom ring in place so that it is level with the bottom edge of the fabric. While in position glue and press down the overlap so that it sticks to the underneath surface.

Remove the two rings and, using a clear adhesive, glue the outside edges of the taped rings and re-insert into position. Hold until glue dries.

Glue the braid round the top and bottom edges of the shade.

Right The poppy has been drawn straight on to the fabric with direct dyes. **Far right** The batik blind seen from outside.

each square = 1.25cm (½")

Fig. 5 Cushion design.

Cushion

This cushion has an attractive flower design combined with a controlled 'crackle'. The background is dyed in two colours whilst red and green dye paints are used for the poppies. The method can be adapted to fit a cushion of any size and the flower could be repeated on the back if desired.

You will need

● White silk, two pieces each 37 cm by 49 cm (15 in by 19 in) for front and back, four strips each 5 cm by 50 cm (2 in by 20 in) for the ruched edging
● down-proof cambric, two pieces each 37 cm by 49 cm (15 in by 19 in) together with feathers for filling *or*

Terylene fabric to the same measurements together with Terylene filling
● two cold water dyes in beige and brown
● two direct paint-on dyes in bright red and leaf green
● brushes, one fine and one about 2 cm (1 in) wide
● 1.5 m (1½ yd) piping cord
● batik equipment as given on page 99

Instructions

All the techniques required for this project are given on page 100.

Wash the fabric for the cushion and the ruched edging.

When dry, enlarge and transfer the floral design as shown in Fig. 5 on to one of the pieces of silk measuring 37 cm by 49 cm (15 in by 19 in).

Brush on the poppy design using red and green direct fabric dyes, as shown in the photograph, using a fine brush.

Leave to dry, then stretch this piece on to the frame.

It is important for the poppy design to remain free of 'crackle', so use beeswax over it on both back and front of the fabric.

When dry, remove the fabric from the frame.

Prepare the beige dye bath. It is best to use a wide shallow vessel so as not to disturb the waxing of the poppy.

Immerse the front and back pieces together with the edging strips.

When it is dry, re-stretch the front of the cushion on to the frame.

Using batik wax this time, and the wider brush, wax around the poppy to preserve some of the beige colour as shown in the photograph.

Repeat this waxing on the back half of the cushion.

When the wax has hardened, crumple to produce 'crackle', avoiding the poppy design.

Make up the brown dye bath.

Dye front, back and strips until the colour is of sufficient contrast to the first dye and the lines of 'crackle' clearly defined.

Remove the fabric from the dye bath, mop off and hang up to dry.

When dry, steam, rinse and iron while still slightly damp.

To complete

Join the strips of fabric together.

Cut the cord to fit all round the cushion, plus sufficient to allow for joining.

Fold the fabric strip in half lengthways and pin it over the piping cord, as shown in Fig. 6. Work a line of gathering stitches through both thicknesses along the strip, close to the cord. Then gather up the material evenly so that it fits the cord. Machine about 5 mm ($\frac{1}{4}$ in) from the cord. This makes the ruched edging.

Lay the ruched piping on the front of the cushion, all raw edges together and squaring off the corners neatly. To join the edging, fit one end inside the other, folding in the raw edges and slip-stitching together. Tack and machine into position between the first row of stitching and the cord.

Lay the back half of the cushion on top of the front half, right sides together. Tack all four layers of fabric together, leaving a large opening at one end.

Machine with a zipper foot as close to the cord as possible, still leaving the opening.

Turn the cushion cover to the right side through the opening.

Make up a cushion pad the same size as or slightly larger than the cover, using feathers and down-proof cambric or Terylene filling and Terylene fabric.

Insert the cushion pad into the cushion cover and hand stitch the opening with invisible stitches taken into the ruched piping cord.

Roller blind

A batik design on a roller blind is shown to best advantage when drawn across the window in daylight. It could, however, brighten up a dark area on a window or glass door or act as a room divider.

You will need
- A roller blind kit
- white firm cotton or linen to fit, allowing 4 cm ($1\frac{1}{2}$ in) for a hem at the bottom of the blind
- black fabric pen
- two cold water dyes in turquoise and dark blue
- three direct paint-on dyes in shades of grey, black and pale green
- batik equipment as given on page 99

Instructions
All the techniques required for this project are given on page 100.

Wash the fabric, dry and iron.

Cut the fabric for the blind on the straight of the grain, otherwise it will not hang correctly.

Make a hem at the bottom for the slat of wood to fit into.

Enlarge the stork and reeds design in Fig. 7 to fit.

Transfer it to the fabric using a fabric pen and varying the thickness of the lines as required. This outline will then show through the dyeing of the fabric.

Stretch the fabric on to the frame and paint the stork with direct dyes in shades of grey to black. Use a pale green behind the reeds as illustrated.

When dry, wax these areas with beeswax only, to avoid cracking.

Make up the turquoise dye bath and dye the fabric according to the manufacturer's instructions.

Remove from the dye and hang to dry.

When dried, re-stretch the fabric on to the frame.

Brush over areas of the background with batik wax, using a wide brush and making long strokes over the background, leaving the edges and the shadows free.

Gently crumple the waxed areas of the background to 'crackle', but avoid the stork and reeds.

Dye the fabric with the second colour, then iron out all the wax.

Do not steam the fabric, simply wash it in hot soapy water, then rinse well.

This will stiffen the blind slightly with the little wax left in.

To complete
Attach the top of the blind to the roller, with pin tacks or staples.

The ratchet on the roller blind must be mounted on the left for the material to fall from the front of the roller, or alternatively on the right, for the blind to hang from the back of the roller (Fig. 8).

Slip in the bottom slat and attach the pull cord.

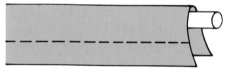
Fig. 6 Gathering fabric over cord.

Fig. 7 Roller blind design.

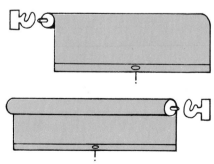
Fig. 8 Alternative mountings for ratchet.

Silk screen fabric printing

Silk screen printing on fabric has come a long way since the 18th century when Japanese stencil cutters first devised a way of cutting a solid ring from a stencil and preventing the middle from falling out by holding it to the main design with fine hairs. These fine hairs did not show on the pattern as the dye saturated the line left by the hair. Eventually an elaborate system of holding stencils to a grid of fine hairs led to a silk screen frame.

Nowadays, silk screen printing is highly mechanized. But with ingenuity and imagination, fabric printing at home, perhaps in the garage, can be achieved. Really, it is a craft which requires two people.

The appeal of the craft is that you can combine your own choice of fabric with your own designs in the colours of your choosing.

Materials and Equipment

The screen frame is usually made of either wood or metal. Wood should be well seasoned and resistant to warping and coniferous woods such as cedar are the best. Instructions for making a frame are given on page 106.

Strong wood glue and carpentry tools are needed to make the frame.

The mesh or screen gauze can be made from various fabrics such as cotton organdie, nylon silk or a Terylene polyester. It is important to use the correct mesh to suit the fabric being printed. Basically, for a fine, smooth fabric a high mesh number is used and the reverse for coarser fabrics. A fabric with a mesh count of 10 TT (number of holes per square centimetre) for polyester cotton, as used in the projects, is ideal.

The squeegee is the means by which the dye is screened on to the fabric. It consists of a wooden handle with a protruding rubber edge and should be approximately 4 cm ($1\frac{1}{2}$ in) shorter than the internal dimensions of the screen.

A spray gun is used for background and stencil dyeing.

Dyes and binders have about fourteen main groups, each with a specific print purpose. The pigment dyes used for the projects in this section are insoluble in water. A small quantity of dye is added to a binder which acts as an agent to fix the colour to the fabric when it is ironed after printing.

Waxed stencil paper is used for sprayed designs.

Stencil film (Stenplex) is a coated, translucent paper which has a removable backing sheet and which adheres to the mesh of the screen printing frame.

A staple gun (or drawing pins or tacks and a hammer) is used to attach the gauze to the frame and the padding to the printing surface.

Scouring powder is required to degrease the screen.

Sticky tape and brown gummed paper strip are used to mask the designs.

A stencil knife should be a fine, sharp bladed knife such as a scalpel.

Tissue paper and cardboard protect the screen and stencil when they are being ironed.

Methylated spirits removes the stencil.

The screen printing surface should be large and flat, ideally 3 m by 1.5 m (4 yd by $1\frac{3}{4}$ yd) although two of the projects could be printed on a smaller surface of about 1 m (1 yd) square. The surface is made up of a board with a soft covering of blanket and calico. Marine plywood is the best wood to use and should be a minimum of 12 mm ($\frac{1}{2}$ in) thick.

Clamps are needed to fix the printing surface to a trestle or table.

The work table or trestle used for cutting out and printing should be about 76 cm (30 in) from the ground.

The fabric used for all the projects is polyester cotton sheeting.

A large apron or overall should be worn to protect clothing.

Newspaper or polythene to protect floors and furniture.

General items can include tracing or drawing paper, pens, pencils, tape measure, ruler, a T square, needles, thread, sewing machine, dressmakers' pins and self adhesive labels.

Know how

Work area

It is not necessary for all the various stages to be carried out in the same area. Designing can be done anywhere but printing should take place in the garage or in any large space which is easily cleaned and near a water supply. Always wear overalls or a large apron and protect any furniture and the floor. Screens can be stored for further use either on shelves or by hanging on a wall.

The screen frame

The size of the screen is relative to the size of the design. Take the outside measurements of the design and add 15 cm (6 in) all round to find the outside measurements of the screen (Fig. 1).

To make a frame, mortise and tenon joint the four corners and glue with a strong wood glue (Fig. 2). Plane flat all sides and sandpaper all edges until they are smooth. The side pieces of the frame should be bevelled so that minimum contact is made with the table. A smooth surface prevents the gauze from snagging.

Stretching the mesh

The mesh can be stretched by hand over the frame but be very careful to keep the tension even. The warp and weft of the fabric (the vertical and horizontal threads) must be kept parallel to the sides of the screen. A loosely stretched, or even too tightly stretched, screen will give inaccurate printing.

Cut the mesh 3 cm (1¼ in) larger than the outside measurements of the screen and lay it on the screen. Fold the material over the edge of the frame at corner A (Fig. 3) and attach it to the frame using either staples or drawing pins positioned very close together. Next, pull the mesh over corner B, fold it over and secure. (This is when it really becomes necessary to have two people.)

Pull the material gently over corner D without stretching it in one particular direction and secure. Work the last corner in the same way. Finally, pin down the flaps at the four corners.

De-grease the screen with scouring powder to help the stencil to adhere. Rinse thoroughly and allow to dry.

Making the silk screen stencil

Draw out the design.

Place a film stencil such as Stenplex over the design, shiny side up. Cut out the necessary motifs, taking care not to cut through the backing sheet.

Prepare a pad of smooth cardboard slightly larger than the film. Place the film on it, cut side uppermost.

Lay the screen on top of the film, ensuring an equal border between the stencil and the screen edges. Place a sheet of tissue paper on the screen and, with an iron set at a temperature for silk, iron over the tissue paper. Always keep the iron moving. After a few minutes, and without excessive pressure, the design will be clearly visible through the screen. Continue until the entire film has been ironed and the design is completely visible.

Allow the stencil and screen to cool.

To remove the backing sheet, begin peeling it away at one corner. If the stencil has not stuck to the screen in any areas, replace the backing sheet and reheat the area.

Remove the tissue paper. Tape the border round the stencil on the top side of the frame and all the top surfaces of the frame with brown paper gummed strip (Fig. 4).

When this stencil is finished with it can be removed with methylated spirits.

To make the screen printing surface

Cover the piece of plywood with a blanket. Staple or pin it with nails or tacks to the underside of the board,

stretching it gently to prevent creasing.

Cut a piece of medium weight calico slightly larger than the board and secure it underneath the board too, as before.

Place the board horizontally on a large table or on bench trestles and clamp it in position. There should be no movement whatsoever.

Printing

Draw a straight pencil line on the calico about 15 cm (6 in) in from the long edges.

Lay the long edge of the fabric to be printed along this line and pin it with dressmakers' pins, stretching it slightly. Next pin the opposite edge, then the top edge and, finally, the bottom edge so that the fabric is stretched out under tension.

Registration

The next stage is to mark out the registration, that is, the lines at which the design is repeated.

Measure the design. The one used here is 50 cm by 65 cm (20 in by 26 in). The repeat will, therefore, be every 50 cm (20 in) and the width of the printed panel will be 65 cm (26 in).

Find the centre of the fabric along the short edge. Measure out 32.5 cm (13 in) on either side of the central point and make a faint mark. Do the

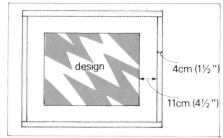

Fig. 1 Finding outside measurements of screen.

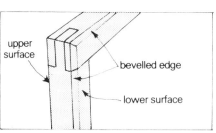

Fig. 2 Frame construction.

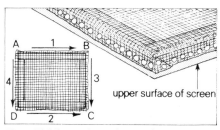

Fig. 3 Folding and securing mesh.

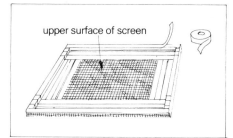

Fig. 4 Taping the screen and stencil border.

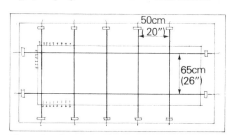

Fig. 5 Laying cotton for registration marks.

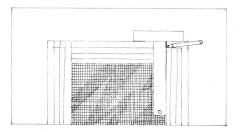

Fig. 6 Registration marks on screen.

same at the opposite end of the fabric.

Lay a line of cotton down either side of the fabric joining these marks as shown in Fig. 5. Secure the ends of the cotton with sticky tape.

Lay a length of cotton at right angles to these two long pieces of cotton, near the top short end of the fabric. Secure with tape. Measure down 50 cm (20 in) and lay another length of cotton.

Continue in this way until the length of the fabric has been divided up into pattern repeats (Fig. 5).

On the screen, using a T square, continue the lines of the edge of the design over the edge of the screen, being very careful to keep them straight. Mark these registration lines clearly in pen as shown in Fig. 6.

To ensure an accurate registration, always line up these marks on the screen over the cotton tapes (Fig. 7).

Printing

Mix the dyes. Use a half pint of binder with as many teaspoons of dye as necessary for the desired colour, trying one teaspoonful first. Stir until there is an even colour of paste. If the colour looks too weak, add a little more dye. Make up 0.25 litre (½ pint) of each dye and store in a glass container such as a marmalade jar. This quantity should be sufficient for all four projects. Made

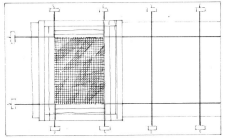
Fig. 7 Lining up screen and cotton tapes.

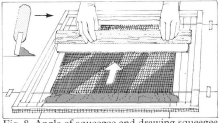
Fig. 8 Angle of squeegee and drawing squeegee across screen.

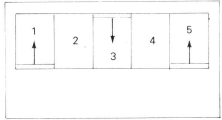
Fig. 9 Sequence of printing a length.

up dyes only keep for two days.

Test the dye first on a spare piece of fabric to find out how the dye and the fabric react. Put the spare piece under tension and place the screen over it, gauze side down.

Pour some paste at one end of the screen on top of the brown paper area, taking care that it does not spill on to the screen. One person should hold the screen while the other prints.

Place the squeegee, rubber side down, between the dye paste and the screen. The blade should be at a shallow angle (Fig. 8) with an even pressure on it. Draw the squeegee across the screen with a slow but smooth, flowing movement, pushing the dye in front so that it is transferred to the brown paper at the opposite end of the screen. Do not stop in mid screen as this will mark the fabric.

One pull across the screen should be sufficient for polyester cotton. If the printing is too faint, try again with two pulls. Too many pulls will cause an excess of dye on the fabric, blurring the crisp edges of the design. This is called 'bleeding'. Only this 'proofing' on spare fabric will determine how many pulls of the squeegee are needed.

To make the first print, with one person at each side of the screen, pick it up and lower it over the fabric. Do not rest it on the fabric until quite sure that the lines on the frame are in register with the cotton tapes. Place fingers between the frame and the fabric to keep the frame at the right height while it is being registered.

Lower the frame on to the fabric. One person should hold the screen firmly at the end furthest from the dye, the other should pull the squeegee across.

After printing, the person doing the printing should hinge the screen away from the table by lifting one side of the screen with the left hand while the other person holds down the opposite side with the right hand.

Lift the screen from the fabric and place it on newspaper. Then wash it thoroughly in cold water (see below).

Printing a continuous length

When the fabric is marked out, number each design repeat faintly in pencil (Fig. 9).

In the first sequence of printing, place the frame in panel 1 and draw the squeegee to the top edge of the fabric. Hinge off the frame and re-register it over panel 3. Draw the squeegee to the bottom of the fabric.

Remove the screen, re-register it over panel 5 and draw the squeegee to the top of the fabric. Continue in this way on all odd numbered repeats.

Before printing the even numbered panels, make sure that the fabric is completely dry. A panel printed adjacent to one that is still wet will bleed into the first panel and spoil the design. Do not touch the fabric as it dries or it will be marked. A stencilled fabric will take 10 to 15 minutes to dry if a fan heater is used.

When the printing is finished, leave the fabric to dry once more.

When completely dry, remove it from the printed surface and (according to the dye being used) iron with a medium hot iron on the right side to fix the dye.

Washing the screen

The screen should be thoroughly cleaned either at the end of the printing process or to change the dye colour. Wash it in a sink or bath large enough to take it.

Hose out the inside only with cold water and use a soft cloth to rinse off the dye, again, only on the inside. Continue hosing until all the dye has been washed out: then hose and gently wipe the other side.

Clean the squeegee in cold water. Replace the brown paper gummed strip if it has come away during the washing.

Dry the screen in front of a medium heat. If it gets too hot the tape will peel off and the screen will warp. Do not continue printing until the screen is completely dry.

Spray printing a background

Spray printing is done before stencil printing to give the fabric a varied background.

Make up the dye paste as before and store it in a glass container.

Take a small quantity of paste and add water to it so that it pours easily. It may be necessary to add more dye to strengthen the colour so that it still matches the paste. Fill a spray gun with the dye.

Pin the fabric to the print surface as before but do not lay the lengths of cotton.

Hold the spray gun about 30 cm (12 in) away from the fabric and spray across the fabric from left to right, then right to left and so on. If using a strong colour spray quickly; the movements can be slower for a paler dye.

The density of colour can be varied by making the to and fro movements

continued

close together or further apart. Also, different colours can be overlapped so that one merges into the other. To do this, fill the spray gun with the first colour and spray the top half of the fabric. Rinse out the spray gun and refill with the second colour. Spray the second half of the fabric but begin in the area of the first colour so that they overlap.

Spray printing a stencil

Cut out the design from a waxed paper stencil. Lay the stencil on the fabric, pinning if necessary.

Mask off a wide area around the stencil with sheets of paper to prevent the spray from dyeing unwanted parts.

Hold the spray gun close to the stencil and spray backwards and forwards as before. Again, experiment on scraps of fabric to get the dye consistency right.

Masking off

In this process an area of the fabric is masked off with a paper cutout or masking tape before it is sprayed or printed. This will result in a corresponding area of undyed fabric.

First work out the design on paper. Then cut out brown paper, masking tape or simply use sticky labels and position them in the design on the fabric.

Spray as before. Allow the fabric to dry, then remove the paper.

Printing two colours at once

Mix two dye pastes. Place them on the brown paper area of the screen, side by side, as shown in Fig. 10. As the squeegee is drawn across the colours will merge where they overlap.

Washing

If pigment dyes are used, all fabrics must be dry cleaned.

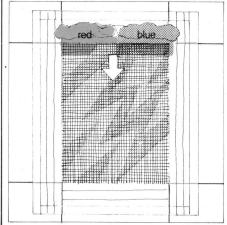

Fig. 10 Printing 2 colours on one stencil.

Coat hanger

Padded coat hangers are useful for keeping delicate clothes in good shape. The handle is covered with bias binding and the rest with fabric gathered round the padding. Both are spray painted with pink and blue to provide the basic background colour which is also used for the other projects.

You will need

- Pink and blue pigment dyes with binder
- 56 cm (22 in) white bias binding, 1 cm ($\frac{1}{2}$ in) wide
- two pieces white polyester cotton fabric each 10 cm by 70 cm (4 in by 28 in)
- wadding 18 cm by 43 cm (7 in by 17 in)
- wooden coat hanger
- silk screen printing equipment as given on page 105

Instructions

All the dyeing techniques required for this project are given on pages 106–8.

Pin the opened bias binding and the two pieces of white fabric on the print surface.

Make up both the pink and the blue dye and add enough water to make them runny.

Put the pink dye in the spray gun and spray all three pieces lightly all over.

Rinse out the gun thoroughly and refill with blue dye. Spray all three pieces lightly all over.

Allow the pieces to dry, using a fan heater if available. Iron with a medium hot iron on the right side to fix the dyes.

Cut off 10 cm (4 in) of the bias binding and set it on one side.

Wrap the remaining bias binding round the hook lengthways, with the folded edges on the inside of the curve. Oversew the edges together neatly, folding in the raw end at the top. Finish off firmly to prevent movement.

Fold the piece of wadding in half lengthways. Place it round the wooden part of the hanger with the cut edges uppermost. Oversew the edges together.

Pin the two pieces of fabric right sides together along two short edges and one long one. Tack 1 cm ($\frac{1}{2}$ in) from the edge, removing the pins.

Machine or hand stitch along the tacking line. Remove tackings and

Right The colours in the padded coat hanger and the caftan are repeated and developed in the matching pillowcases and duvet cover.

turn the fabric to the right side.

Turn in and press 1 cm (½ in) along the open edges. Find the centre and mark with pins.

Run a gathering thread along the long stitched edge through all thicknesses about 0.5 cm (¼ in) in from the edge. Place the coat hanger inside the covering and pull up the gathers to fit. Secure the thread and cut off the excess. Slip stitch the two open edges together making sure the hook is centred against the two marker pins.

Run a gathering thread through all thicknesses except the wadding about 0.5 cm (¼ in) down from the top edge. Draw up to fit, secure and trim the excess thread.

Fold the small piece of bias binding in half and oversew the edges together on all three sides. Turn the ends to the middle and attach to the coat hanger, directly below the hook, by oversewing the middle of the fold.

Caftan

The caftan makes an ideal subject for screen printing. The background has been masked and sprayed, then two different types of stencil applied and sprayed.

You will need
- 1 m (1 yd) white bias binding, 1 cm (½ in) wide
- 1.5 m (1¾ yd) of fine, white cord
- white polyester cotton 115 cm (45 in) wide. The length is twice the measurement from neck to hem plus 5 cm (2 in)
- dyes in pink, blue and sandy yellow
- silk screen printing equipment as given on page 105

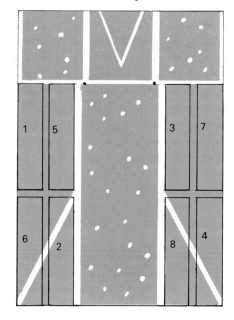

Fig. 11 Fabric division for caftan.

Measurements
To fit most sizes
length at centre back, 135 cm (54 in)

Instructions
All the dyeing and printing techniques required for this project are given on pages 106–8.

Cut the material to make two rectangles. Each rectangle is treated in the same way.

Pin out one of the rectangles on the print surface.

Divide the fabric into areas which will contain different designs, as shown in Fig. 11, as follows:

Mark off 35 cm (14 in) – a quarter of the length – down from the top at the side edges for sleeves. Lay a cotton thread across the width of the fabric.

The finished width of the caftan is 100 cm (40 in), the rest is taken up in seams. Divide this 100 cm (40 in) into three and mark with cotton thread from the top edge down to the horizontal thread.

Lay a piece of cotton down the length of the fabric to mark the centre. At the top, measure 10 cm (4 in) to either side of this line. Lay a piece of cotton at each of these marks and cross them on the centre line, 25 cm (10 in) down to form a V shape at the neck.

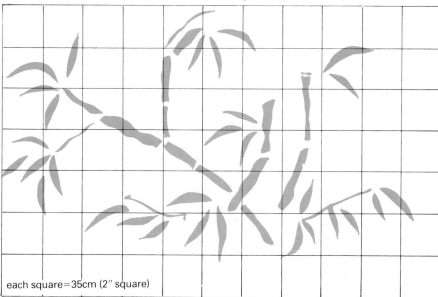

each square=35cm (2″ square)

Above Fig. 12 Design for sleeve and central panels.

Below Fig. 13 Design for side panels and pillowcase.

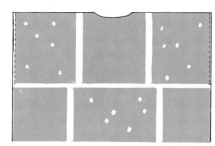

Above Fig. 14 Sequence of printing stencils.
Below Fig. 15 Neck shape.

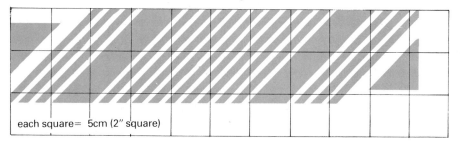

each square= 5cm (2″ square)

Measure out 20 cm (8 in) to either side of the central cotton and lay two vertical cottons from the sleeve division to the bottom edge. Measure up 50 cm (20 in) from the bottom of each of these cottons and lay two cottons diagonally from this point to the outside bottom corners.

Lay masking tape over all cottons except the central one, removing the cotton threads at the same time and making a double width of tape on the four vertical lines. Lay a single width of tape at the edge of the cloth on either side of the sleeve sections. Finally, stick self adhesive circles at random in the three areas indicated (Fig. 14).

Mix the blue and pink dyes and water them down. Spray lightly all over, first with pink and then with blue. Allow to dry.

When dry, peel off the tape and circles to reveal the white, undyed areas.

For the sleeve and central panels, enlarge Fig. 12 to 52 cm by 35 cm (21 in by 14 in). Transfer it to a paper stencil and cut out. The pattern of the stencil interlocks when laid the right way up on the left hand half of the fabric and upside down on the right hand half.

Lay it first on the left hand half of the sleeve panel, aligning the right hand of the stencil with the centre and taking in as much of the stencil as the width of the fabric allows.

Mix up the sandy yellow dye and water it down. Spray part of the shape with yellow and the rest with blue. Repeat on the lower half of the central panel, positioning the stencil vertically.

While these two areas are drying, cut a second stencil paper for the two side panels, enlarging Fig. 13 to 51 cm by 11 cm (20½ in by 4½ in).

When the fabric is dry, lay the new stencil and spray it with blue dye in the sequence shown in Fig. 14. Allow to dry.

Lay the bamboo stencil upside down on the right hand side of the sleeve panel and the top half of the central panel. Spray with sandy yellow and blue. Allow to dry.

Finally, to blend in the white stripes and circles, spray lightly all over with pink. Lay out the bias binding strip and the cord and spray pink. Allow to dry.

Press the fabric with a medium hot iron on the right side to fix the dyes.

Work the second rectangle in the same way.

Trim the edges of the front and back pieces to size, allowing 1.5 cm (¾ in) for turnings. Neaten the two sides of both pieces with either a narrow hem or a zigzag stitch and do the same with the shoulder seams.

With right sides together, pin and tack the sides seams from the bottom of the arm opening to the hem. Machine, remove tackings and press.

Make the shoulder seams in the same way, machining right across from one side to the other.

Make a narrow hem at the lower edge and press.

Fold in a narrow hem round the sleeve openings, machine and press.

Cut out the neck at front, following the V shape but leaving 0.5 cm (¼ in) for turnings.

Slightly hollow out the neck at the back as shown in Fig. 15.

Trim the neck edge with bias binding, mitreing it at the front.

On both back and front, make holes for the cord as indicated in Fig. 11. Buttonhole stitch round the holes, making them about 0.5 cm (¼ in) across. Thread cord through from the right side of the back through the holes to the front. Make a knot at each end of the cord and tie it in a bow at the front of the caftan.

Fig. 16 Pillowcase and duvet stencil design.

each square=5cm (2″ square)

Pillowcases

The pillowcases are designed to match the duvet cover in the next project. They are printed with a background of sprayed colour, a sprayed stencil and a silk screened picture in two colours. The backs are plain white.

You will need
● White polyester cotton 180 cm by 115 cm (72 in by 46 in)
● blue, pink and scarlet dyes
● silk screen printing equipment as given on page 105

Instructions
All the dyeing and printing techniques required for this project are given on pages 106–8.

Cut the white polyester cotton into four rectangles each measuring 57 cm by 90 cm (23 in by 36 in). Reserve two rectangles for the plain backs and pin the other two on the print surface.

Make up the blue, scarlet and pink dyes. Water a small quantity of the blue and fill the spray gun. Spray both rectangles lightly all over. Refill the spray gun with pink and give an even lighter spray of pink. Allow to dry.

Measure in 12.5 cm (5 in) from each short end and lay cotton threads to mark off the border areas.

Enlarge Fig. 13 to 51 cm by 11 cm (20½ in by 4½ in). Using stencil paper, cut out the design.

Lay the stencil centrally in each of the borders in turn and spray with pink dye. Allow to dry.

Enlarge Fig. 16 to 65 cm by 50 cm (26 in by 20 in). Using a film stencil, cut out the design. Fix the stencil to the frame.

Measure and mark each rectangle to centre the print (Fig. 17) and pro-

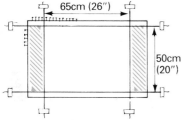

Fig. 17 Centring the print on the pillowcase.

vide registration lines. Mark corresponding lines on the frame.

Place two blocks of blue dye paste and two of scarlet alternately on the brown paper area at one end of the frame and make a test on spare fabric.

Print the design on each of the rectangles.

Allow to dry then iron to fix the dyes.

Machine a narrow hem along the left hand side of one dyed rectangle and the right hand side of the other.

On each of the two plain white rectangles fold in 1 cm (½ in) then 3.5 cm (1½ in). Pin and tack. Machine stitch 0.5 cm (¼ in) inside the folded edge. Remove tackings and press.

Place one white rectangle and one printed rectangle right sides and raw edges together with both hemmed edges at one end. Fold the printed border over the finished hem of the white rectangle. Pin and tack through all thicknesses, along the three remaining sides.

Machine a 1 cm (½ in) seam.

Neaten raw edges. Remove tacks, turn to right side and press.

Duvet cover

This has been made using three vertically printed panels, which are more manageable than a whole piece.

You will need
● 430 cm by 228 cm (172 in by 90 in) white polyester cotton
● blue, scarlet and pink dyes
● four press studs size 9
● silk screen printing equipment as given on page 105

Instructions
All the dyeing and printing techniques required for this project are given on pages 106–8.

Cut the fabric into two rectangles each measuring 215 cm by 228 cm (86 in by 90 in).

Cut one of them into three equal vertical panels each 76 cm (30 in) wide.

Lay one of the panels on the print surface and pin it under tension.

Mix the blue and pink dyes and water down a small quantity of each.

Spray the fabric pink to just over half way up then complete with blue, first overlapping the pink by several centimetres (inches). Allow to dry.

Make registration lines 65 cm (26 in) apart across the width of the fabric and repeating every 50 cm (20 in) up its length (four repeats). Number the panels.

Use the same film stencil as for the pillowcases (Fig. 16).

Mix the scarlet dye to a paste and place it at one end of the frame in the brown paper area. Add some blue paste next to it then some more scarlet and a little more blue. Make a sample proof.

Print the panel in the one, three, dry, two, four sequence. Allow to dry.

Enlarge Fig. 13 to 51 cm by 11 cm (20½ in by 4½ in). Using stencil paper, cut out the design. Lay it across the bottom of the design next to the last print. Spray pink and allow to dry.

Remove the fabric from the print surface. Wash the screen and the squeegee and do not use again until quite dry.

Lay out the second rectangle under tension. Spray the background as before and allow to dry.

Lay the stencil vertically against the left hand raw edge and spray pink. Repeat until the whole of the left hand side has a border of diagonal stripes. Allow to dry.

Make the registration lines on the second panel so that the print lies next to the printed border and has four repeats.

Print as before and allow to dry.

Finally, spray the paper stencil across the bottom of the panel, using pink dye.

When completely dry, remove the fabric.

Repeat the process with the third panel but print the diagonal border on the right hand edge.

Press the three panels with a medium hot iron to fix the dye.

To join the panels, fold in 1 cm (½ in) along the long printed (not border) edge of one of the side panels.

Carefully match up the design with the centre panel and pin. Slip tack the two edges right sides together and machine. Remove tacks, neaten seams and press.

Repeat with the other side panel, matching the outside edge of the printed panels (not the bordered side).

The fabric now measures approximately 215 cm (86 in) square. Cut the plain white rectangle to the same measurements. Turn over 0.5 cm (¼ in) along the right hand bordered edge of the printed fabric and one edge of the plain rectangle.

With right sides together, match, pin and tack the three raw edges. Machine 1 cm (½ in) from the edge. Remove tacks and neaten seams.

Mark the centre point of the open edges with pins. Divide the edges into four by marking the centre of each half with a pin. Pin and tack together the edges of the quarters. Machine 1 cm (½ in) in from the edge along both quarters, leaving the middle sections open. Fasten off and remove tackings.

Sew the four press studs at equal intervals to fasten the opening.

Beadwork

Beads are extremely versatile and come in many different shapes and sizes. They can be woven or threaded on wire, added as a decoration to other crafts or worked into a fringe. Bead fringes gained popularity in Victorian times when they were used on Tiffany lampshades and when jet beads gave a rich but subdued quality to black garments.

Making a bead fringe requires a lot of patience as the beads are small and the work progresses slowly. But once the simple techniques of this craft have been mastered, the end result is a glittering design, full of movement, which can decorate an article made specially or which can add a new dimension to something old.

Materials and Equipment

Beading needles are required to thread beads. These are long and fine and bend quite easily. They are available in various sizes from fairly thick, size 10, to extremely fine, size 13.

Polyester thread, strong and fine, is the most suitable. Colour will match either the beads or the fabric to which the beads are to be attached. When using transparent beads, the colour of the thread will show through so choose carefully.

The beads used must depend on the type of fabric with which they are being used – a larger bead for a heavy fabric, a smaller bead for a fine one. There is a wide variety of beads available, round, cut and bugle being the three most popular types. They are sold in many ways ranging from small packets, by the string or by weight. There is a wide range of colours and they can be transparent, opaque, pearl or matt. Work with beads all of the same size and if different types of bead are being used in the same project, make sure they are threaded in the same order or the pattern may be out of alignment and the fringe uneven.

Narrow cotton tape 0.5 cm ($\frac{1}{4}$ in) wide is used as a base for fringes destined for awkwardly-shaped articles.

An embroidery ring, in which a fabric remnant has been stretched, gives a stable background on which to work. The tape is tacked on to it.

Small containers (the ones the beads sometimes come in are ideal) are essential for keeping beads together while working with them.

Coloured pencils and squared paper are used for the designs.

Other items required can include scissors, tape measure, ruler, ordinary sewing needles and thread and glue.

Know how

Making designs

These can be worked out on squared paper, one square representing one bead and the colour of the bead indicated by using a coloured pencil. Start off with a simple design using one type of bead in different colours and gradually work up to more complex designs incorporating different kinds of beads.

When designing for small glass embroidery beads, bear in mind that these beads are broader than they are deep. Squared paper will not give an accurate representation of the final effect as the work will be shorter and more spread out than the squared paper shape.

Bugle beads are approximately twice as long as they are wide and so can be represented by being two squares long and one square wide on the graph paper.

To measure how many beads will be needed to fringe the edge of a specific article, lay the beads side by side, holes uppermost, to a length of 1 cm (1 in). Count the beads and multiply this number by however many centimetres (inches) the edge is to find how many rows of beads it will take to complete the edge. A design can be worked out accordingly.

If the design is geometric or symmetrical it is only necessary to work out half of the design on the graph paper as the second half will only be a repeat.

Preparation

There are two methods of working a fringe. It can be worked along a narrow cotton tape which is then attached to an object (for example, around the edge of a lampshade) or to an article which would be too awkward or too small to work on to directly.

Attach the tape to fabric stretched in an embroidery frame to give a stable background. Cut the tape a little longer than the projected fringe and tack it in position in the centre of the ring (Fig. 1). If the tape is too big for the ring, tack on the first section and when that has been worked, remove the tacking and place the next section of the tape on the fabric. Work along the entire length of the tape in this way (Fig. 2).

Alternatively, the beads could be worked directly on to the edge of an existing article when no preparation is necessary.

Working the beads

Work at a table covered with a cloth. The cloth will prevent the beads from moving around or rolling away, the table will support the work as it gains weight.

Separate the beads into their different colours and put each colour in a container.

Thread the needle with single thickness thread and secure with three or four small stitches on to the wrong side of the tape or edge.

Pick up the beads in the required sequence by pushing the needle into the hole of the bead while it is still in the container and pull it on to the thread. The ability to pick up several beads at the same time will soon come with practice (Fig. 3).

To secure a row of beads the thread has to be brought back to the edge. Insert the needle through the centre of the second to last bead to be threaded and return it back through all the beads to the beginning (Fig. 4). Work two or more small stitches into the fabric without pulling the thread so tight that the line of beads curves and hangs stiffly.

Take the thread through the hem to the starting point of the next row of beads, moving along the width of a bead. Bring the needle out, ready to work the next row in exactly the same way (Fig. 5).

Always make sure there is enough thread to work a complete row before starting the next one. If there is not, finish off securely at the end of the last row threaded and start a new thread at the top of the next row, one bead's width away from the last.

Place a ruler on the chart against the vertical line being worked to mark your place.

Finish the fringe by working a few small stitches at the end of the hem or tape and fasten off securely.

Loops

To make a loop at the end of a row, add four or more extra beads. Insert the needle back through the beads of the design, omitting the extra beads, which will form into a loop. Sequins can be added to loops. Place a sequin in the middle of the extra beads worked and proceed as above.

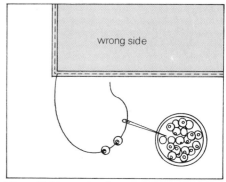

Fig. 3 Picking up beads on end of needle.

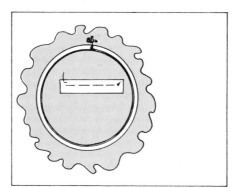

Fig. 1 Tacking tape to embroidery ring.

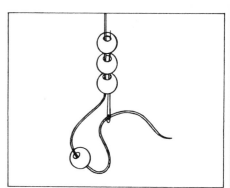

Fig. 4 Securing a row of beads.

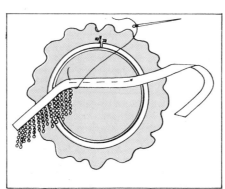

Fig. 2 Working a long tape in sections.

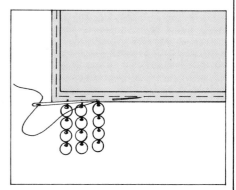

Fig. 5 Making a stitch through hem for new row.

Brooch

Two fringes, with reversed colour sequences, make up this unusual brooch. Only one type of bead is used but interest comes from the colours, the looped ends and the curved edge.

You will need

Small glass transparent embroidery beads:

- 15 g ($\frac{1}{2}$ oz) in colour A (blue)
- 15 g ($\frac{1}{2}$ oz) in B (mauve)
- 34 in C (red)
- 48 in D (green)
- two pieces of 0.5 cm ($\frac{1}{4}$ in) white cotton tape each 5 cm (2 in) long
- fabric 4 cm by 2 cm (2 in by 1 in) in A
- felt 3 cm by 1 cm ($1\frac{1}{4}$ in by $\frac{1}{2}$ in) in E (white)
- thick card 3 cm by 1 cm ($1\frac{1}{4}$ in by $\frac{1}{2}$ in)
- wadding 3 cm by 1 cm ($1\frac{1}{4}$ in by $\frac{1}{2}$ in)
- thin brooch mount about 2.5 cm (1 in) across
- needle size 13
- adhesive
- beading equipment as given on page 113

Measurements

Approximately 3 cm by 6 cm ($1\frac{1}{4}$ in by $2\frac{1}{2}$ in)

Instructions

The beading techniques required for this project are given on page 114.

Mount one length of the tape and bead, following Fig. 6. The six B beads at the end of each row form a loop (Fig. 7).

When complete, remove the tape and beads from the ring and repeat the instructions on the next piece of tape, using the second colour scheme.

Smear glue at either end of each tape near the beading. Allow it to dry and then cut off the excess tape (Fig. 8).

Glue the wadding to one side of the card and place this, wadding side down, on to the wrong side of the fabric. Bring the edges of the fabric over and glue to the back of the card. Allow to dry.

Glue the tapes on to the back of the card, allowing the A beads to fall from one edge and the B beads from the other (Fig. 9).

Cover the back with the pieces of white felt, sticking it securely.

Place the brooch mount in the centre of the back and stick it in place with a strong glue.

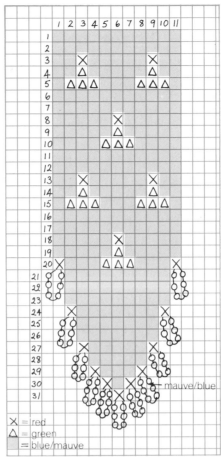

Fig. 6 Beading design for brooch.

X = red
△ = green
= blue/mauve

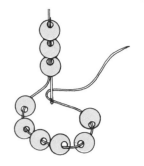

Fig. 7 Making loop.

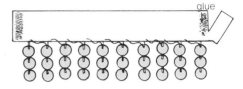

Fig. 8 Glueing and cutting tape.

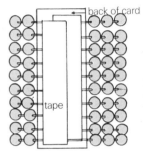

Fig. 9 Glueing 2 tapes to card.

This brooch is formed from two overlapping bead fringes.

Scarf

The fringe on either end of this richly decorated scarf is worked on the same principles as the previous project but is larger and more complex. The design uses mostly the same type of bead throughout with the exception of the beads in the end loops.

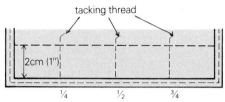

Fig. 10 Tacking lines on scarf end.

You will need
- Purchased scarf 140 cm by 31 cm (56 in by 12 in)
  small glass transparent embroidery beads:
- 390 g (13 oz) in colour A (gold)
- 90 g (3 oz) in B (red)
- 60 g (2 oz) in C (green)
  embroidery beads:
- 30 g (1 oz) in D (light green)
- 30 g (1 oz) in E (dark red)
- 15 g ($\frac{1}{2}$ oz) small bugle beads (brown)
- needle size 13
- beading equipment as given on page 113

Measurements
Depth of the fringe 12 cm ($4\frac{3}{4}$ in)

Instructions
The beading techniques required for this project are given on page 114.

Prepare the scarf by measuring 2.5 cm (1 in) in from the short ends and mark with a tacking line.

Fold the scarf in half lengthways to find the centre and mark this on the ends with a line of tacking going up to the 2 cm (1 in) line.

Fold the doubled scarf in half again to mark the quarter and three-quarters points with further lines of tacking (Fig. 10).

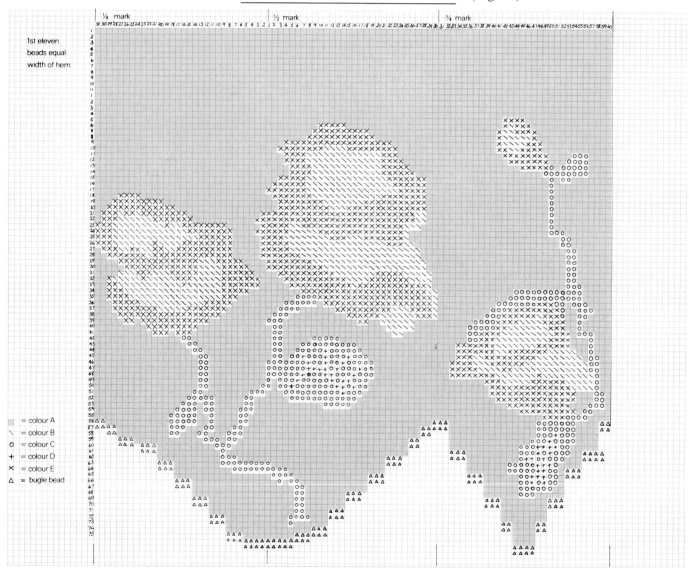

1st eleven beads equal width of hem

= colour A
\ = colour B
o = colour C
+ = colour D
× = colour E
△ = bugle bead

Fig. 11 Beading design for scarf.

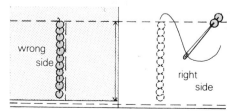

Fig. 12 Securing 1st 11 beads on wrong side.

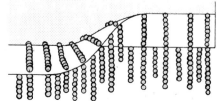

Fig. 13 Encasing alternate rows.

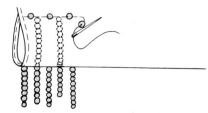

Fig. 14 Slip stitching hem with beads.

Enlarge the colour key pattern given in Fig. 11 (to count the squares more easily). Note that the left hand quarter is the same as the right hand quarter but in reverse.

Start the thread at the centre mark of the scarf end, on the wrong side.

First row. Start at row one in the middle of the chart.

Thread eleven A beads then insert the needle through the fabric on the 2 cm (1 in) tacking line directly above the starting point of the thread following the tacking line. Bring the needle through to the right side of the scarf before threading the remaining beads (Fig. 12).

At the end of the row thread three bugle beads to form a loop before returning the needle back through the row.

Second row. Thread all the beads without passing the needle through to the right side of the fabric and ending the row in a loop as before.

Work the beginning of the third row as the first row and the beginning of the fourth row as the second. Continue alternating in this way for the rest of the design. At the right hand edge of the scarf, secure the thread with a few small stitches and fasten off securely.

Return to the centre of the scarf and work the remaining half from right to left, alternating the beginning of the rows as before. Work from rows two to thirty-one on the left hand side of the design as shown in Fig. 11, then rows thirty-two to sixty reading the chart from left to right but working from right to left to reverse the design.

Work the other end of the scarf in the same way.

When the beading is complete, turn the scarf edge to the wrong side along the 2 cm (1 in) line, allowing the alternate rows of beads hanging from the edge to fall freely and encasing the first eleven beads of the other alternate rows (Fig. 13).

Slip stitch the hem in place. Each time the needle is brought through on to the right side of the scarf, thread on an A bead as shown in Fig. 14.

Work the other end to correspond.

The pattern of the fringe on each end of this scarf is asymmetrical. The two flowers in the middle are worked as a whole, whilst the design to the left is repeated in reverse on the right. Sparkling brown bugle beads are introduced in the loops at the end of the rows.

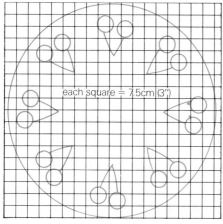

Fig. 15 Embroidery guidelines for cherries.

Fig. 16 Stitching shadow work on cherry.

each square = 7.5cm (3")

Cherry jam pot cover

This beaded food cover will bring a quaint, old fashioned air to the table. A cherry design has been worked into the bead fringe and is echoed in the shadow work on the organza. It can, of course, be adapted to any preserve or to make a cover for a milk jug or sugar bowl.

You will need
- A circle of white organza 13 cm (5½ in) in diameter
- a circle of white cotton lawn 13 cm (5½ in) in diameter
- bias strip of white cotton 50 cm by 1.5 cm wide (20 in by 1½ in)
- sewing thread in red, green and white
- beading needle size 13 transparent glass embroidery beads:
- 150 g (5 oz) clear beads
- 60 g (2 oz) red
- 60 g (2 oz) green
- 30 g (1 oz) dark red
- beading equipment as given on page 113

Measurements
Embroidered centre 12.5 cm (5 in) diameter
fringe 6 cm (2¼ in) deep

Instructions
The beading techniques required for this project are given on page 114.

Transfer the design for the cherries given in Fig. 15 on to the organza and

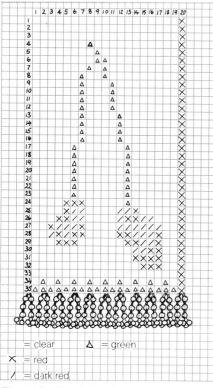

	1	2	3	4	5	6	7	8	9	10	11	12	13	14	15	16	17	18	19	20

= clear   Δ = green

✕ = red

∕ = dark red

Fig. 17 Beading design for jam pot cover.

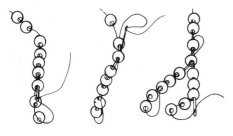

Fig. 18 3 stages of divided end to row.

stretch it in an embroidery ring.

Fill in the cherries with shadow work using red thread as follows:

Secure the thread on the wrong side with a few running stitches made on the outline of the shape and one back stitch. Make a back stitch along the line of the circle, close to and on the right of the running stitches. Work a similar back stitch on the left hand side of the running stitches. Continue in this way making back stitches on the right side of the fabric to form a close herring-bone on the wrong side (Fig. 16). Finish with a few back stitches in one place. Fasten off.

Turn the ring over and, using green thread, work the stems of the cherries in back stitch.

Tack the cotton lawn to the wrong side of the organza whilst it is still in the ring, sewing along the outer edge of the design.

Remove the fabric from the ring and trim the edge to 3 mm ($\frac{1}{8}$ in) from the tacking. Bind the edge of the cover with bias strip.

Divide the bias edge into eight equal parts, with a pair of embroidered cherries in each part, by folding the organza circle in half between the pairs of cherries and creasing gently between the fingers. Open and mark the crease with a small line of tacking stitches across the binding. Re-fold along the diameter at right angles to the last fold, crease and mark with tacking stitches in the same way. Repeat this process between the remaining four pairs of cherries.

*Start with the row of red beads at one of these marks and follow the graph pattern in Fig. 17, working from right to left. End each row of beads by threading three green beads and two transparent red beads, omitting the red beads return the needle back through the next five beads (Fig. 18a), pull the thread tight, miss one bead and then insert the needle and thread through the next bead (Fig. 18b). Thread three green beads and two red beads and return the needle back up through all the beads to the top, omitting the red beads (Fig. 18c).

Make sure that the working of each of the twenty rows of the design fills one eighth of the edge of the circle.

Repeat from * seven times more to encircle the cover.

Left Cherries are embroidered in the organza using shadow work and are beaded into the fringe of this jam pot cover. The use of opaque and clear red beads adds detail to the fruit.

Above A clever distribution of white, transparent and facetted crystal beads amongst the bugle beads adds detail to the fringes of this curtain.

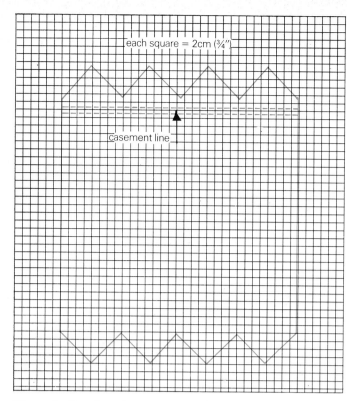

each square = 2cm (¾")

Casement line

Fig. 19 Outline of curtain.

Fig. 20 Beading design for half of diamond.

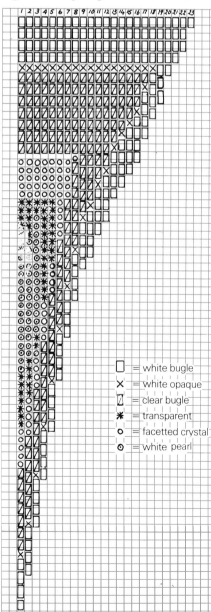

☐ = white bugle
✕ = white opaque
▨ = clear bugle
✳ = transparent
○ = facetted crystal
◉ = white pearl

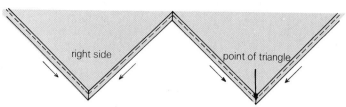

right side   point of triangle

Fig. 21 Direction of beading.

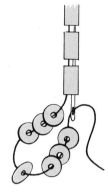

Fig. 22 Loop with sequin.

Curtain

The play of light on the transparent, white and pearly beads of this fringe elegantly outlines the geometric edging. Sequins have been threaded at the end of each row to add variety and interest. The design has been worked here on a small curtain but could be extended to any width.

Each diamond is worked in two symmetrical halves and an extra loop is added to each point.

Detail of curtain fringe.

You will need
- 1 m (1 yd) fine white fabric, 90 cm (36 in) wide
- 3.5 m (3½ yd) white bias binding
- 66 cm (26 in) white paris binding, 3 cm (1¼ in) wide
- white sewing thread
- 60 g (2 oz) each of white opaque bugle beads and crystal bugle beads
- 30 g (1 oz) each of small white pearl embroidery beads, small round transparent embroidery beads, small white opaque embroidery beads and faceted crystal embroidery beads
- one string of flat pearl sequins
- beading needle size 13
- beading equipment as given on page 113

Measurements
Depth of fringe 17.5 cm (7 in)

Instructions
The beading techniques required for this project are given on page 114.

Enlarge the outline of the curtain given in Fig. 19 to scale.

Trace the outline on to the fabric and cut it out.

Sew the paris binding along the wrong side of the fabric as indicated on the diagram.

Fold the bias binding in half to encase all round the curtain, folding the binding neatly at each point of the zig-zags. Machine stitch close to the edge of the binding.

Bead from the graph given in Fig. 20. Start at the highest part of the triangle and work towards the point as shown in Fig. 21, finishing one row's distance from the point. On the end of each row of beads and on each of the eight points of the curtain, thread three white opaque beads, one sequin, three white opaque beads, return the needle back up the row of beads omitting these six to form a loop (Fig. 22).

Leave a 0.5 cm (¼ in) space between each row of beads down the side of the triangle to allow the beads to hang correctly. This may be made easier if the fringe is worked with the end of the triangle mounted straight.

Quilting

Quilting is one of the oldest forms of embroidery. During the 13th, 14th and 15th centuries it was used both for the padding of knights' garments and for bedding. During the 16th and 17th centuries, silk and linen quilts were used by the wealthy in the great houses. Quilting at the end of the 16th and during the 17th and 18th centuries was used largely to enrich the clothing of men and women.

Towards the end of the 18th century, quilted clothing ceased to be fashionable and during the 19th century the bed quilt too gradually went out of use in many parts of Britain due, no doubt, to the introduction of factory machine-made bedcovers.

The quilting in this section is traditional to Britain and frequently referred to as 'English quilting'. This term is not strictly accurate as two of the main areas associated with the development and continuity of the craft are South Wales and Durham and Northumberland where the working of handmade quilts continued. Not the quilting for wealthy homes and wardrobes but the traditional utilitarian quilting for warmth and bedding in the farmhouses and cottages of the people. Each of these areas has developed its own distinctive designs although both use the same techniques.

Materials and Equipment

A frame is necessary for quilting. A traditional frame consists of two long rollers each with a strip of tape or webbing which form the top and bottom of the frame while two flat pieces with a series of holes for adjustment of size form the sides. Alternatively, make a rigid frame using four lengths of wood 2.5 cm by 2.5 cm (1 in by 1 in) in square section, joined to form a square.

Between needles are used for stitching, numbers 7, 8, 9 – the finer the fabric, the finer the needle. A heavier needle can be used to mark the design.

Thread was originally silk and strong cotton but today a good polyester sewing thread is suitable. To tack, use ordinary sewing thread.

Tailor's chalk can be an aid to marking the design.

Squared paper is used for designing.

Card is used for making templates.

Fabric should be plain and smooth, not shiny or very dull because the stitching design is the feature of this embroidery. It should show the light and shade of the quilted pattern and a dull satin, cotton or cotton polyester would be a good choice. A light colour often shows the quilting to greatest advantage. Traditionally the quilting should look the same on both sides with the same or contrasting material used as a backing. However, where the underside will not be seen, a cotton lawn can be used.

The padding originally used was carded sheep's wool or, for ordinary household quilts, an old blanket. Today wadding is readily available and Terylene can be bought in 45 cm (18 in) or 90 cm (36 in) widths. A single layer of wadding is usually adequate but a further layer can be used for a heavier effect. Household cotton wool is not recommended as a padding because it absorbs moisture.

General items can include scissors, tape measure, ruler, dressmakers' pins, drawing pins, glue and a sewing machine.

Know how

Designs

Designs are made up of main patterns and fillers. The fillers link the main patterns as well as giving them detail.

The main pattern is shown by a solid line. When making a template, trace the solid outlines and work the detail free hand.

Traditionally, quilters made use of everyday household items in their designs using the circles from cups, saucepans, plates and glasses to build simple units of the designs. One filler stitch of overlapping circles is actually known as the wine glass pattern (Fig. 1). Many of the traditional quilting patterns were given names by the old quilters and some of them are shown here. The scissors motif can either be used on its own (Fig. 2) or combined to make a circle. The Durham feather can be straight, curved or in a circle and worked to different lengths (Fig. 3). There are many variations on the circle as can be seen in the star, the rose, the whorl, the snail creep and the fan (Fig. 4).

Nowadays designs can still be built up from everyday objects, as shown in Fig. 5, where coins have been used to produce feathers of different sizes.

It is best to work out the whole design on squared paper first. It should fill the entire area using main pattern units and fillers. Unquilted spaces should be balanced and contrasted. As a guide for beginners, there should be no spaces wider than 5 cm (2 in) across as the prime purpose of the sewing is to hold the wadding in place. The main design patterns are often emphasized by using a smaller spaced simple filler. Try not to make all spaces the same size.

Making templates

Cut the design from the squared paper and glue it to cardboard. Cut round the outlines. If the design has a curved central line, such as in the freely worked Durham feather, it will help to trace it on to the template as well. Cut along this line to divide the template in two so that the curved line is marked on the fabric as a sewing guide.

A feature of traditional quilting is that a new design is planned for each piece of work. This is not a difficult task if motif templates are made from card and then their outlines drawn on the squared paper to make new combinations. When the design is completed, make templates of the main units.

Transferring the design

Accuracy is essential on a geometric or symmetrical design. A centre pattern must be exactly in the middle and borders should be kept the same width but at the same time there must be some freedom when filling in the units.

Needle marking makes the best line. If the material is suitable, once marked, the line will not disappear. When the fabric is on the frame, place the template on the right side of the top fabric and draw round with a sturdy needle.

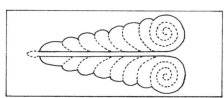

Fig. 1 Wine glass pattern.

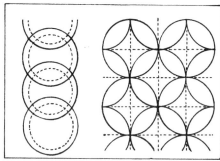

Fig. 2 Solo scissors pattern.

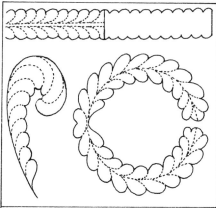

Fig. 3 Durham feather patterns.

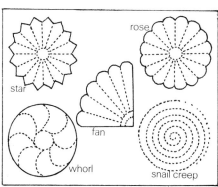

Fig. 4 Variations on a circle.

Alternatively, tailor's chalk can be used but it easily brushes off and the lines are thicker. The chalk is useful, however, for marking guidelines.

A further alternative is to pin the templates to the fabric before it goes on the frame and tack the outlines.

Setting up the frame

First iron the fabrics as any creases will spoil the design. The frame must be at least 4 cm (1½ in) bigger all round than the finished design and the fabric 4 cm (1½ in) bigger all round than the frame. The wadding can be smaller as it is tacked in position before mounting on the frame.

With the wadding in position between the top fabric and the backing, tack through all thicknesses (Fig. 6) in two central lines, one horizontal and

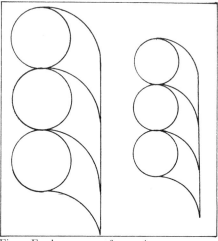

Fig. 5 Feather patterns from coins.

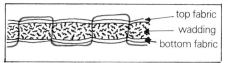

Fig. 6 Tacking stitches through all thicknesses.

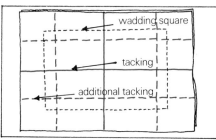

Fig. 7 Tacking lines.

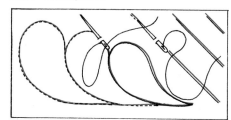

Fig. 8 Using two needles.

one vertical and then all round the edges (Fig. 7). Additional lines of tacking may be necessary on a larger piece.

The material should be mounted on the frame smoothly but not too tightly. For a rigid frame, place the tacked layers over it, the top fabric uppermost. Fold one edge over the top of the frame and secure with drawing pins. Fold over the bottom edge of the fabric and secure then fold over each of the side edges in turn and secure.

The stitching is worked with the right side of the top fabric facing and the frame is never turned.

Stitching

Begin all stitches with a small knot and finish with several small back stitches. On small pieces of quilting, work the main patterns first then the filler pattern. Start working either at the top or bottom of the quilting, but never turn the frame otherwise the work will 'cockle' (twist).

A running stitch is the main quilting stitch. Put one hand under the work to support it and guide the needle, keep the other hand above the frame. All the stitches must be the same length so that the spaces between the stitches are the same length as the stitches. This is more important than having very small stitches but do aim for the smallest stitch that the thickness of the padding will allow.

Ideally, pick up several stitches at once but they can be worked singly. To do this, put the needle through the material at right angles to the frame and pull it through to the back with the left hand. Without turning the frame, bring the needle through to the right side, again at right angles to it. It is important to develop rhythm and regularity so that the stitches are even.

Back stitch and chain stitch can also be used for quilting.

Working with two or more needles

To keep a large piece of quilting even, work on the design with two or more needles at once. Start the needles in the same area along the same level and gradually work up the design.

Begin with the main pattern and work some of the design then leave the needle in the fabric and begin filling in the pattern round this main design with the other needle(s). When the level of the first needle is reached, leave the other needle(s) in the fabric and continue with the first (Fig. 8).

Cleaning

Quilting should be dry cleaned.

Apron

The quilting for the apron is worked on seven separate squares which when completed are joined together and applied to the background material. This is a very suitable project for a beginner. The squares are worked with a number of motifs and fillers, including a traditional scissors design, a series of which often forms the centre design for a quilt.

These squares could be made up into many different projects.

You will need

115 cm (48 in) wide fabric in two contrasting colours:
- 1.5 m (1⅔ yd) in colour A (emerald)
- 0.75 m (¾ yd) in colour B (beige)
- 1 m (1 yd) cotton or cotton poly-ester lawn, 90 cm (36 in) wide
- 1.5 m (1⅔ yd) wadding, 45 cm (18 in) wide
- quilting materials as given on page 121

Instructions

All the quilting techniques required for this project are given on this and the facing page.

Enlarge the designs (Fig. 9) on to squared paper allowing a 0.5 cm (¼ in) border all round each square. Cut out

A patchwork of quilting for a party apron.

one of each motif and glue on to card.

Cut three squares in A, each 30 cm (12 in), five squares in B, each 30 cm (12 in), seven squares in lawn, each 30 cm (12 in) and seven squares of wadding, each 22.5 cm (9 in). Cut one of the B squares in half along the diagonal to make two equal triangles.

Transfer the designs to the right sides of the top fabric squares, making two of the first design and one of the fourth design on fabric A and two each of the second and third designs on fabric B. Alternatively, needle mark after mounting.

Fig. 9 Apron quilting designs.

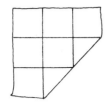

Fig. 10 Forming the skirt panel.

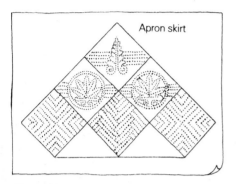

Fig. 11 Positioning the quilted panel.

Place wadding between one square of top fabric and one of lawn, tack and mount on the frame.

Work the design in running stitch. When all the stitching is completed, remove from the frame.

Repeat with the other six motifs.

To complete

From fabric A, cut a rectangle 97.5 cm by 70.5 cm (39 in by 27 in) and another piece 30 cm (12 in) square.

Using B, cut two 7.5 cm (3 in) strips each 122 cm (48 in) for the waistband and four 7.5 cm (3 in) strips each 60 cm (24 in) for the neckties.

Machine together six of the squares and the two triangles to form the apron skirt panel as shown in Fig. 10.

Trim the wadding and both layers of fabric on internal seams to 1 cm ($\frac{1}{2}$ in), tack them open and press lightly along the seam. On the outer edges trim the wadding and cotton lawn. Fold over the top fabric and tack.

Position the panel on the apron skirt and tack 0.5 cm ($\frac{1}{4}$ in) from the edge as shown in Fig. 11. Machine in place along two outer diagonal edges, between the squares and finally, along the bottom edge.

Tack and machine the remaining quilted square to the bib.

Turn a 1 cm ($\frac{1}{2}$ in) hem on all but the waistline edges of the apron and bib, tack and machine. Remove tacking.

Run a gathering thread along the top of the apron skirt and draw up to measure 42 cm ($16\frac{1}{2}$ in).

Place the two waistband strips right sides together, pin and tack. Find the centre and measure 21 cm ($8\frac{1}{4}$ in) to either side of it along the bottom edge of the strip and 14 cm ($5\frac{1}{2}$ in) along the top edge and mark with pins. Machine the two strips together all round except between the marker pins.

Remove tacking. Turn to the right side and press, with the seam allowance pressed under along the openings.

Insert the bib in the top opening, pin and tack. Insert the skirt in the bottom opening, pin and tack.

Top stitch the whole of the waistband, thus securing the bib and skirt.

Place two of the neckties right sides together. Pin, tack and machine, leaving one short end open. Turn to the right side and press, turning under the seam allowance on the open edges. Top stitch.

Make the second necktie in the same way.

Attach a tie at each end of the top edge of the bib and machine stitch them in place.

Remove all tackings.

Tote bag

The quilting on the bag uses the traditional Durham feather design but not in its traditional form. Durham feathers were originally used as part of regular patterns but in this design the feather shape has been adapted to a more free flowing design.

You will need

Cotton polyester medium weight fabric:
● two centre panels each 38 cm (15 in) square (A)
● three pieces each 42 cm by 46 cm (17 in by 19 in) (D)
● two 9 cm ($3\frac{1}{2}$ in) strips each 30 cm (12 in) long (B)
● two 6 cm ($2\frac{1}{2}$ in) strips each 46 cm (19 in) long (C)
● two 10 cm (4 in) strips each 44 cm (18 in) long (E)
● wadding 30 cm (12 in) square
● quilting equipment as given on page 121

Instructions

All the quilting techniques required for this project are given on pages 122 and 123.

Enlarge and draw the design (Fig. 12) on squared paper and make a tracing. Cut out the motifs and cut along the centre curved line.

Tack the outline of the motifs and the centre curved lines on the top fabric. Alternatively, needle mark after mounting.

Place the wadding between the two centre panel pieces, tack and mount on frame.

Cut a template 2 cm by 28 cm ($\frac{3}{4}$ in by 11 in). Place the template so that the top long edge joins two diagonally opposite corners of the square, passing through the central point. Mark a line on either side of the template in between the main patterns. Move the template down so that the top edge is on the second line marked and mark another diagonal. Continue in this way until the whole of the square is covered with diagonals in one direction.

Place the template to join the two opposite corners and repeat.

Work the design in running stitch. When the quilting is completed, remove the work from the frame and trim the panel to measure 30 cm (12 in).

To complete

Join a section B to both the top and the bottom of the quilted square with a 1 cm ($\frac{1}{2}$ in) seam allowance.

Join a section C to each side with the same seam allowance.

To scallop the top edge, place one of the D sections right sides together with the bag front. Stitch along the scalloped line at the top edge. Clip the curves, turn to the right side and press. Top stitch the scalloped edge.

Place the two remaining D sections right sides together and machine along the top edge. Turn to the right side and press.

Place the two sides of the bag right sides together and machine along the three sides of the bag. Trim and neaten the raw edges. Turn to the right side and press.

To make each of the handles, fold one of the remaining strips in half lengthways, right sides together. Stitch along the wrong edge, turn to the right side and press. Attach to the bag by sewing the bottom end of the handles to the lining on either side of the bag.

Cushion

On the cushion the motifs have been taken from a Welsh quilt design and linked together. The design incorporates the snail creep motif which is very popular on Welsh quilts.

Right A simple panel of Durham feathers features on the tote bag whilst the cushion has a more ambitious composite of motifs.
Far right The elegant jacket has a Durham feather border and beaded motifs.

each square = 1.5cm (⅝")

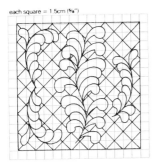

Fig. 12 Tote bag quilting design.

each square = 2.5cm (1")

Fig. 13 Cushion quilting design.

Fig. 14 Tacking lines for cushion front.

You will need

Dull satin finish furnishing fabric:
- one piece 60 cm (24 in) square
- one piece 45 cm (18 in) square
- 2 m (2¼ yd) crossway strip 4 cm (1½ in) wide for piping
- cotton lawn 60 cm (24 in)
- wadding 53 cm (21 in) square
- 2 m (2¼ yd) piping cord
- 30 cm (12 in) zip, optional
- cushion pad about 43 cm (17 in) square
- quilting equipment as given on page 121

Instructions

All the quilting techniques required for this project are given on pages 122 and 123.

Enlarge and draw the design (Fig. 13) on squared paper and make a tracing. Glue to card and cut out the major outlines marked with solid lines.

Place the wadding centrally between the larger squares of fabric and tack with horizontal, vertical and diagonal lines. Add an additional diagonal line 7.5 cm (3 in) away on either side of the top left to bottom right one and 6 cm (2½ in) away on either side of both the horizontal and vertical lines (Fig. 14).

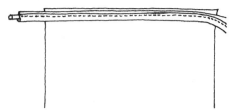

Fig. 15 Piping cord in casing attached to cushion.

Mount on to the frame and transfer the design to the fabric, using a straight template to mark the diagonal filler patterns as given in the tote bag instructions (see page 124).

Work the design in running stitch using more than one needle at the same time to keep the work even.

When the stitching is complete, take the fabric off the frame and trim to 45 cm (18 in) square.

To complete

Tack the piping cord into its bias casing. Tack it all round the quilting, with raw edges together, with the piping tacking on the 2.5 cm (1 in) seam (Fig. 15). Ease the piping at the corners.

Place the cushion back in position, tack and machine through all thicknesses, using a piping foot if available, and leaving an opening for a zip on one side. Remove tacking and turn to the right side.

Insert the zip or, if preferred, leave the seam open until the cushion pad has been inserted and then oversew.

Jacket

This design uses Durham feathers for a border pattern and has two beaded flower motifs on each front.

You will need

- 2 m (2 yd) dull satin, 115 cm (48 in) wide
- 2.75 m (3 yd) lining, 90 cm (36 in) wide
- 1 m (1 yd) wadding, 90 cm (36 in) wide
- packet of mixed gold and silver beads
- beading needle
- quilting equipment as given on page 121

Measurements

To fit bust 85 to 90 cm (34 to 36 in)

Instructions

All the quilting techniques required for this project are given on pages 122 and 123.

Cut all the pattern pieces except the fronts from the satin and lining (Fig. 16). Cut the two fronts as a 77.5 cm by 85 cm (31 in by 34 in) rectangle from the satin, wadding and lining.

Enlarge the design and make a tracing, including the outline of the jacket front (Fig. 17). Cut out round the main outlines and make further templates for the quilting patterns.

Tack the three layers of satin, wadding and lining together.

Allowing an extra 2.5 cm (1 in) on each side of the front for quilting shrinkage, tack the shape of the jacket front through all thicknesses. Reverse the pattern for the second side.

Place the work on a frame and transfer the design to the top fabric. For this size of project it is best to transfer the design in sections as work progresses, starting at the bottom of the frame and working to the top.

Work the design in running stitch. When the bottom half of the design has been quilted, move the work down the frame to work the remainder.

When all the stitching is completed, remove the quilting from the frame.

To complete

Trim round the quilted fronts leaving a 2 cm ($\frac{3}{4}$ in) seam allowance.

Tack the lining to the remaining jacket pieces along seam lines before making up.

Place one jacket front against the back, right sides together, and stitch the side seam and then the shoulder seam. Repeat with the second jacket front.

With each seam, trim the wadding and the satin to 0.5 cm ($\frac{1}{4}$ in). Turn in the raw edge of the lining and fold it over the wadding and the satin edges. Press, tack and machine to secure the flat fell seam (Fig. 18).

Sew the underarm seam in each of the sleeves and sleeve linings separately. Place the linings inside the sleeves, wrong sides together. With right sides together, set in the sleeves, trim the seams and neaten them with oversewing or zig-zag.

Cut 5 cm (2 in) wide strips on the cross for the binding. Join the strips, fold the binding in half lengthways and press. Place the raw edges of the binding so that they overlap the seam line of the jacket, with the folded edge on the opposite side of the seam line to the raw edge of the jacket (Fig. 19). Machine 2 cm ($\frac{3}{4}$ in) in from the edge. Trim the seam back to 0.5 cm ($\frac{1}{4}$ in), fold the doubled binding to the wrong side and slip stitch in position.

Turn a hem on the sleeves.

Bead the flower motif (see Fig. 20).

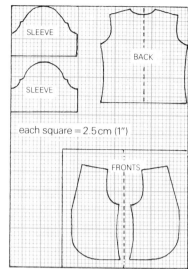

each square = 2.5 cm (1")

Fig. 16 Pattern piece cutting guide.

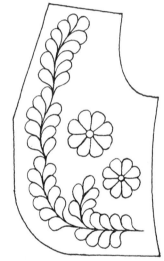

Fig. 17 Jacket quilting design.

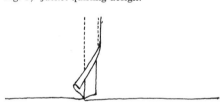

Fig. 18 Flat fell seam.

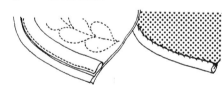

Fig. 19 Positioning doubled binding.

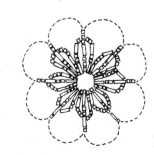

Fig. 20 Beading motif.

Smocking

The word 'smock' is derived from the Anglo-Saxon for a shift or shirt and the original smocks were overalls worn by agricultural and manual workers. They developed from being very basic garments to having intricate stitched decoration – smocking.

Smocking is a decorative method of controlling the fullness of fabrics in garments or other articles. The basic techniques are quite simple – evenly spaced gathers of cloth are drawn up by tacking and held in place by a variety of decorative stitches which have elasticity when completed.

In the 18th and 19th centuries the designs, which were passed from one generation to another, came to identify area and sometimes, occupation.

In the 20th century smocking has been particularly associated with children's dress because the elasticity provides room for growth. But there are many creative applications for the beginner or the experienced needlewoman.

Materials and Equipment

Fabric of most types (plain or patterned) can be smocked, so the choice will greatly depend on the article to be smocked. An ideal choice would have a repetitive design such as checks (e.g. gingham), spots or stripes as they provide a guide for drawing up the gathers and working the stitches. Fine fabrics such as voile, nylon, organza and lawn produce beautifully delicate results although heavier fabrics such as wool and velvet can also be used. Highly textured fabrics do not smock easily. However, never be afraid to experiment. Even fine leathers can be used, with practice, to stunning effect.

Threads for the smocking should match the weight and quality of the fabric. Stranded cotton is an old favourite as it can be split to a suitable thickness. It is, however, inclined to twist and there are numerous other embroidery cottons and fine crochet yarns which work very well.

Dotted transfers are ironed on to the wrong side of the fabric as a guide to making the gathers. There are various gauges, the most commonly used being 6 mm to 9 mm (approximately $\frac{1}{4}$ in to $\frac{3}{8}$ in) which are suitable for most fabrics. Choose a small gauge for fine fabrics, a larger one for heavier fabrics. Pencil, card and ruler can be used to make the dotted guidelines instead of a transfer.

Basic sewing equipment includes needles, thread, scissors, pins, tape measure and a sewing machine.

Know how

Estimating quantities

Generally the amount of fabric ought to be three times the width of the finished smocking, plus seam allowances. This rough guide depends on the weight of the fabric and the tension of the stitches used. Thicker fabrics will need slightly less and finer fabrics more. If the finished piece requires precise measurement it is wise to work a small sample first to ensure correct tension.

Marking the gathering lines

Carefully prepared fabric is essential to the success of smocking.

Transfers. Using a gauge suitable to the fabric, cut the transfer to the required width and depth before ironing on to the wrong side of the fabric.

Hand marking. Using a sharp pencil or fine brush and poster paint, make spots on the wrong side of the fabric. Measure these with a ruler or with a simple homemade template of a piece of card with regularly spaced holes punched throughout.

Counting threads. On even weave fabric threads can be counted. This is a traditional method which, although time-consuming, produces very even gathers on the straight grain of the fabric. Be very careful to place the rows directly under one another.

Fabric patterns. Spots, checks or stripes provide a good basis for smocking (Figs. 1 to 3). Attractive results are achieved by selecting to work on either a light or dark background and drawing up the relevant squares – picking up light squares will result in a dark background. On a striped fabric, guide dots will still be necessary to keep the horizontal lines straight.

Dotted papers. Tack the dotted paper through the dots to the wrong side of the fabric. Remove the paper before drawing up the threads.

Working the gathers

All smocking should be completed before the article is made up. Contrast gathering thread will be a helpful guide when smocking.

Starting with a secure knot at the top right-hand corner, work from right to left, picking up a small section of fabric at each dot. Work to the end of the row. Leave the thread hanging loose at the end of each row (Fig. 4). Repeat until all the rows have been completed.

Pull up the gathers to the required width and wind the threads in a figure of eight round the pin placed at the end of each row as shown in Fig. 5. Cut off excess threads.

Working the smocking

Smocking stitches are worked on the right side of the fabric across the gathers. The gathering threads can be used as a guide. The stitches should be selected not only for their decorative quality but for the degree of elasticity required.

Three stitch patterns form the basis of traditional smocking – rope stitch, basket or cable stitch and chevron – and these are all worked with the simple stem-stitch. Other stitches can include Vandyke, feather and herringbone, but combinations of the first three (some of which are given here) provide endless scope for experiment.

Stitches are usually worked from left to right, the threads secured on the back of the work and brought through to the left of the first fold.

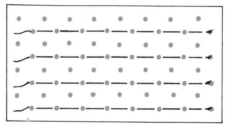
Fig. 1 Gathering lines on spotted fabric.

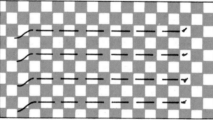
Fig. 2 Gathering lines on checked fabric.

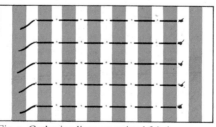
Fig. 3 Gathering lines on striped fabric.

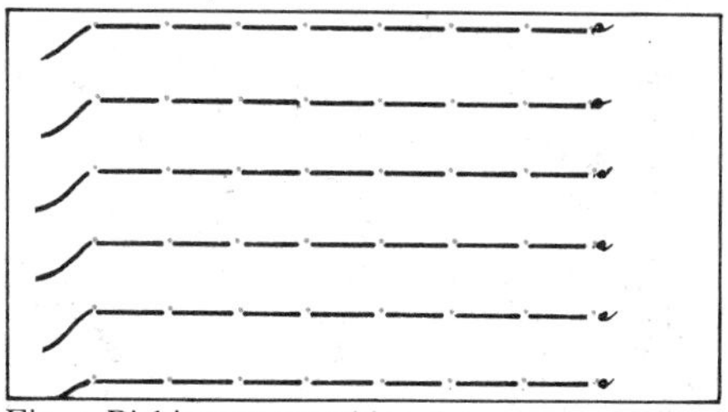

Fig. 4 Picking up smocking dots.

The stitches

Stem stitch (firm control). A useful stitch to establish a straight line at the top of a section and to keep the gathers firm. It is not suitable for a gentle flare such as on frills.

Keep the thread above the needle. Take the thread over two folds of fabric and insert the needle slanting downwards through the second fold (Fig. 6). Continue in this way always picking up one fold at a time. Although a simple stitch, it requires practice to keep an even tension and a straight line.

Cable or basket stitch (firm control). Working in stem stitch, take the thread over two folds of fabric and pick up one fold, inserting the needle diagonally. The stitches are worked alternately above and below one another (Fig. 7). To work the upper stitch keep the thread above the needle, below the needle for the lower stitch.

Several rows of this stitch can be

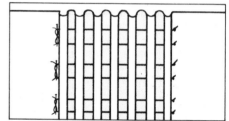
Fig. 5 Pulling up and securing gathered threads.

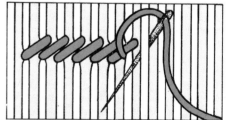
Fig. 6 Stem stitch.

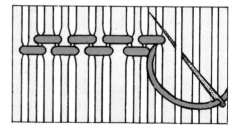
Fig. 7 Single row cable stitch.

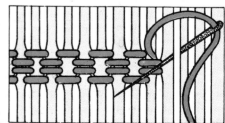
Fig. 8 Two rows cable stitch.

built up into various patterns, for example, cable stitch as in Fig. 8.

Chevron stitch (medium control). This consists of several stitches worked above one another and then below. Insert the needle diagonally. The thread is held below the needle when working upwards and above when working downwards (Fig. 9).

Once again this stitch makes interesting groups such as two-row chevron as shown in Fig. 10.

Wave stitch (light control). This is a further development of the up and down grouping of stem stitch. It is an ideal stitch for the release of gentle folds as in a pelmet or frill.

With the thread to the left of the first fold take it across the first and second folds and insert the needle slanting upwards as in Fig. 11. The thread is kept below the needle on the upward journey. On the sixth stitch, slant the needle downwards and keep the thread above the needle ready to work the downward journey.

Trellis stitch (light control). Alternate rows of wave stitch are worked first upwards and then downwards giving a diamond effect as in Fig. 12.

Honeycomb stitch (light control). Honeycombing is sometimes used incorrectly as an alternative word for smocking. It is another stitch which gives a cellular pattern and it is the play of light on the folds which creates the effect, rather than the stitch itself. It gives great elasticity.

This stitch is worked on two levels, using the gathering threads as a guide. Bring the needle up on the left side of the first fold. Take the thread over two folds and make a horizontal stitch, bringing the needle up just beneath the beginning of the first stitch. Take the thread over the folds again, but bring the needle out some distance below and to the left of the second fold with the thread above the needle (Fig. 13). Work two horizontal stitches over this fold and the next one, finally bringing the needle out above and to the left of the third fold and on a level with the first stitch, thread below the needle. Continue on two levels (Fig. 14).

Surface honeycomb stitch (light control). Begin on the lower level, work one horizontal stitch through the first two folds, keeping the thread below the needle. Insert the needle horizontally through the third fold on the higher level, thread above the needle, then through the fourth fold similarly as shown in Fig. 15. Work the fourth and fifth folds in the same way, thread below the needle, and so on to the end of the row.

Diamond stitch (loose control). This large stitch covers ground quickly and is therefore useful for large areas. It is worked in two stages, using the line of the gathering thread as a guide.

Bring the needle out to the left of the first fold and with the thread above the needle, take a back stitch through the second fold. Take the needle down to the second row and, thread below needle, back stitch through the third fold. Take the thread over two folds and make a back stitch through the fourth one. With the thread below the needle, work the next back stitch through fold five on the upper row. Continue to the end of the row.

The second stage is worked in the same way but beginning on its lower level at the third line of gathers. Alternate stitches meet the first row as shown in Fig. 16.

Using the stitches

Use stitches sparingly or the result will be cluttered and overworked. Remember also that the spaces are as much a feature of the design as the stitches.

Finishing off

Avoid pressing the smocking directly unless it is essential, in which case press before removing the gathering threads. Press the work face downward under a damp cloth and iron without pressing flat.

Remove the gathering threads, taking care not to damage the fabric. The smocking is now ready for making up. If the work is to be inserted into a yoke or band it may help to leave in the top row of gathers until the insertion is complete.

If the smocking is a frill (as in the valance project on pages 131 and 132) hem the top and bottom edges before gathering the folds of the fabric.

Fig. 9 Single row chevron stitch.

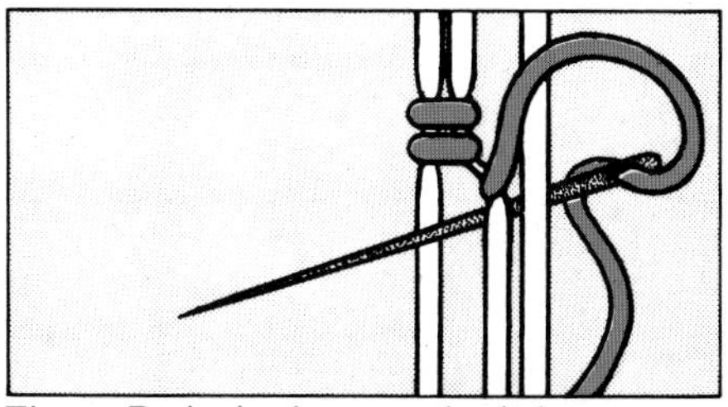

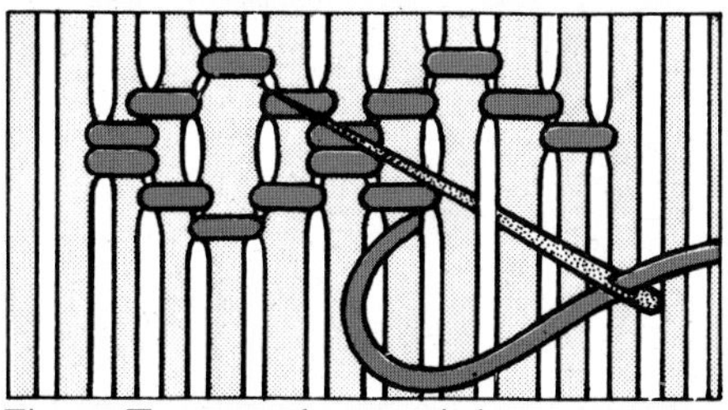

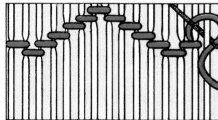
Fig. 10 Two rows chevron stitch.

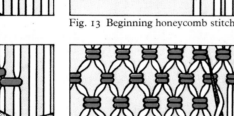
Fig. 11 Wave stitch.

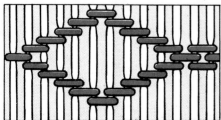
Fig. 12 Trellis stitch.

Fig. 13 Beginning honeycomb stitch.

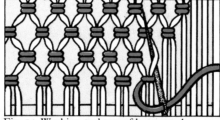
Fig. 14 Working 2nd row of honeycomb.

Fig. 15 Surface honeycomb stitch.

Fig. 16 2nd stage of diamond stitch.

Child's muff

The muff is worked in hidden honeycomb and will fit a child aged two to ten years. In appropriate fabric this would make an ideal bridesmaid's muff and could be adapted to an adult size by enlarging the dimensions, always a pretty idea for a winter wedding and one for which bridesmaids are usually grateful!

You will need

● 1.10 m (1¼ yd) light warm fabric (fine smooth wool or an equivalent synthetic fabric)
● 0.5 m (½ yd) warm soft lining fabric the same as outer fabric, brushed nylon, or equivalent (optional)
● Terylene wadding 20 cm by 40 cm (8 in by 16 in)
● thread for smocking
● smocking transfer with the dots approximately 13 mm (½ in) apart, if required. If this gauge is difficult to find, choose a smaller one and pick up alternate dots
● needle and thread
● 80 cm (32 in) of braid 2.5 cm (1 in) wide

Measurements

Width 21 cm (8¼ in), circumference 33 cm (13 in)

Instructions

All the smocking techniques required for this project are given on pages 128 and 129.

Cut the outer fabric to 23 cm by 101 cm (9½ in by 40¼ in).

If using a transfer, iron on the wrong side of the fabric, taking a long edge as top and leaving a 1.5 cm (⅝ in) seam allowance all round.

Make the gathers and draw up to 33 cm (13 in) – not including seam allowances – and secure.

Using the gathering threads as a guide, work honeycomb stitch all over except for the seam allowances. At the end of each row do not cut the remaining thread. When the smocking is complete, remove the gathers.

Place the two edges right sides together and hand stitch the 1.5 cm (⅝ in) seam between the gathers, using back stitch. Turn right side out.

To make the smocking continuous across the seam, pick up the loose smocking threads and take the stitches across the seam to join the first and last folds together, then fasten off.

Cut the lining to 23 cm by 45 cm (9½ in by 18 in).

Pin the wadding centrally to the lining and tack down the centre. Stitch the sides of the wadding to the lining. Stitch the 23 cm (9½ in) edges of the lining, right sides together, with a 1.5 cm (⅝ in) seam. Run a gathering thread around each end of the lining, place it inside the muff with the wadding next to the outer fabric and draw up the gathers to fit. Tack the edges together.

Cut two strips from the remaining fabric and join each into a circle to fit the end of the muff.

Place one circle round one end of the muff, right sides together. Space the folds evenly and stitch. Turn the binding to the inside, turn under a small hem and slip stitch in place.

Repeat for other end of muff.

The braid is attached so that the muff may be carried round the neck.

Fold the braid or ribbon in half lengthways and press. Pass one end through the muff and sew to the other end. This ring of braid can be secured inside the muff with a few stitches.

Child's dress

This is a highly adaptable design, which can be worn either as a sun dress or a pinafore dress. It could also be scaled up for an adult's evening dress or sun dress. The dress straps could be made in the same fabric as the garment with the ends attached to the inside and stitched in place below the top frill.

- Cotton or lightweight fabric, three times the chest measurement plus 1.5 cm ($\frac{5}{8}$ in) seam allowances
  Length depends on the height of the child. By leaving a generous hem allowance, this style will grow with the child
- smocking transfer in a medium gauge, if required
- thread for smocking in three colours
- 2 m ($2\frac{1}{4}$ yd) ribbon 5 m ($\frac{1}{4}$ in) wide
- needles and thread

Instructions

All the smocking techniques required for this project are given on pages 128 and 129.

Join the widths of fabric together. If using a transfer, cut it to a depth of about 6 cm ($2\frac{1}{4}$ in) and join strips to the necessary width.

Iron the smocking dots on the wrong side of the fabric approximately 3 cm ($1\frac{1}{4}$ in) from the top.

Turn a small hem at the top of the work. Make the gathers. Because of the width, more than one piece of thread will be needed for each row of gathers. Start the new thread at the same place in each row. Draw up and secure.

Begin at the top left hand corner of the gathering and leave a trailing thread at the end of each row.

Row 1. Stem stitch, colour A.
Row 2. Stem stitch, colour B.
Row 3. Stem stitch, colour A.
Row 4. Wave stitch with 5 steps up and down, worked in B.
Row 5. Wave stitch, in the same direction and with the same number of steps, in A.
Row 6. Wave stitch, in the opposite direction, but with the same number of steps, in A.
Row 7. Wave stitch, as given for Row 6, using colour B.

Rows 8 to 14. Repeat from the beginning. In the centre of each diamond, French knots highlight the design. Using colour C, bring the needle up in the middle of the diamond-shaped space, make a short stitch and bring the point of the needle out at the beginning of the stitch. Wind the thread round the needle 7 times. Holding the wound thread, draw the needle through and finish by inserting the needle through the fabric beside the knot. Repeat twice more to make a rosebud shape, then bring the needle up in the centre of the next diamond.

To complete

Join the side edges with a 1.5 cm ($\frac{5}{8}$ in) seam between the gathers.

Using the trailing thread at the end of each row, work some stitches over the seam to make the smocking continuous. Fasten off.

Cut the ribbon into four pieces, two long and two short, so that they will fit over the shoulder and hang free at back and front. Pin the ribbons in position and attach with back stitches over the first row of stem stitch.

Hem the dress to the required length.

Opposite page Two proud little girls, one keeping cosy, the other set for a party. **This page** A pretty dressing table and holdall.

Dressing table valance

This valance has been made for a rectangular dressing table, but it could be adapted to other shapes or a curtain pelmet. It is held in place on stretch wire slotted through a casing and the effect is completed with a plain curtain.

You will need
Lightweight cotton or synthetic fabric:
- **Valance.** Three times the measurement of the dressing table front and sides plus 1.5 cm ($\frac{5}{8}$ in) seam allowances. Depth, 25 cm (10 in)
- **Casing.** Strips of fabric to make the width of the finished valance (plus seam allowances) by 8 cm ($3\frac{1}{4}$ in) deep
- **Skirt.** Fabric same as for the valance by a depth of the dressing table to the floor, plus 10 cm (4 in) hem allowances
- thread for smocking in two colours
- two lengths plastic covered stretch wire and four hooks and rings
- needle and thread
- smocking transfer in a medium gauge, if required

Instructions
All the smocking techniques required for this project are given on pages 128 and 129.

Join together the valance pieces.

Turn a 1.5 cm ($\frac{1}{2}$ in) hem at the bottom of the fabric. Turn in the side edges and slip stitch in place.

If smocking transfers are being used, cut to a depth of 7.5 cm (3 in). Iron to the back of fabric. Smocking should begin 2 cm ($\frac{3}{4}$ in) from the top.

Run gathering threads across the width. Use more than one piece of thread for each row of gathers. Start the new thread at the same place in each row.

Draw up the gathers and secure.

Begin smocking at the top left hand edge.

Row 1. Stem stitch, with the thread above the needle, worked in colour A.

Row 2. Stem stitch with the thread below the needle, in colour B.

Row 3. Diamond stitch stage one, in B.

Row 4. Diamond stitch stage two, in A.

Row 5. Diamond stitch stage one, in A.

Row 6. Diamond stitch stage two, in B.

Rows 7 to 9. Three rows of extended wave stitch, using 13 steps up and down, the first two in B, the third in A.

To complete
Valance. Remove the tacking stitches.

Join the widths of the casing to the length of the finished valance plus 1.5 cm ($\frac{5}{8}$ in) turnings at either end. Turn in the ends and stitch.

Fold the casing in half lengthways, wrong sides together, and press.

Open out the casing. With right sides together, sew one edge to the valance 1.5 cm ($\frac{5}{8}$ in) from the raw edges. Turn to the inside along the crease. Turn in 1.5 cm ($\frac{5}{8}$ in) at the edge and stitch to the seam line.

Make a second row of stitching 1.5 cm ($\frac{5}{8}$ in) from the top.

Screw a hook into each end of the wire and insert the wire into the lower half of the casing. Extra hooks may be inserted at the corners and centre front of the dressing table to prevent the valance from sagging. Corresponding loops should be sewn on to the back of the casing.

Skirt. Join the pieces together to make the desired width in two sections.

Turn in and hem all side edges.

Turn over 5 mm ($\frac{1}{4}$ in) at the top edges, then make a 2 cm (1 in) hem leaving the ends open.

Turn up the lower hem to the required depth.

Screw a hook into each end of the wire and insert the wire into the casing. Fix it to the fittings on the dressing table. Extra hooks may be used around the dressing table to prevent sagging.

Jumbo Holdall

This multi-purpose bag could be made up for use on the beach or as a holdall for craft equipment. The shape of the handles illustrated reflects the shape of the bag but other designs are available and the dimensions depend on the handles chosen. The design is worked in a colour to match the fabric but a contrasting thread could be used.

You will need
- Two wooden handles
- heavy duty fabric (calico or twill) in two pieces each measuring 3 times the slit in the handles plus 3 cm ($1\frac{1}{2}$ in) turnings square plus enough fabric to make top casings (see INSTRUCTIONS)
- a piece of lining fabric (cotton or other lightweight fabric)
- thread for smocking
- smocking transfer, medium gauge, if required
- needle and thread

Instructions
All the smocking techniques required for this project are given on pages 128 and 129.

Round off the bottom of the squares by folding the fabric in half and cutting to shape.

If using a transfer, cut to about 8 cm (3 in) deep. Iron the transfers on the wrong side of the fabric, 2 cm (1 in) from the top.

Draw up the gathers and secure.

Beginning at the top left hand edge work as follows:

Row 1. Cable stitch.

Row 2. Cable stitch, worked in reverse of the previous row.

Row 3. Diamond stitch stage one.

Row 4. Diamond stitch stage two.

Row 5. Diamond stitch stage two.

Row 6. Wave stitch with five steps up and down.

Row 7. Wave stitch in same direction as previous row.

Row 8. Wave stitch in reverse to the previous two rows.

Row 9. Wave stitch in same direction as previous row.

Row 10. Wave stitch in same direction as previous row.

To complete
Remove the tacking stitches.

Match the two sections, right sides together. Stitch a 15 mm ($\frac{1}{4}$ in) seam round the lower edge to within 18 cm (7 in) of the top at both sides.

Fold over 15 mm ($\frac{1}{4}$ in) at each of the side openings and machine or back stitch round the edge of the opening to neaten and strengthen.

Cut two squares of lining slightly smaller than the original bag, rounding off the corners to correspond. Stitch together. Work gathering stitches along the top edges of the lining.

Place the lining inside the bag, wrong sides together, and draw up the gathers to fit.

Tack the raw edges together on both front and back.

Cut two strips of fabric each the width of the split in the wooden handle plus 3 cm ($1\frac{1}{4}$ in) for turnings, to a depth sufficient to cover all round the lower part of the handle plus 3 cm ($1\frac{1}{4}$ in).

Turn in the side edges and stitch in place.

Place one casing strip with right sides together against the top of the bag and stitch a 1.5 cm ($\frac{5}{8}$ in) seam.

Insert the casing through the slit in the handle, turn to the inside, fold in the raw edge and slip stitch to the lining.

Repeat for the other side of the bag.

Metal thread embroidery

Metal thread embroidery has been much used in Britain in the past for church and secular ceremonial dress and their accompanying furnishings. The Tudor and Elizabethan period portraits show lavish use of precious metals and pearls, a sumptuous richness in colour and texture. Evidence of the centuries of interest in metal thread in the Far East is often seen in Chinese restaurants.

Nowadays there are yarns available containing some precious metal but substitute yarns are often more easily available, often to no lesser effect. The main threads are laid on the surface of the work and stitched into place.

Materials and Equipment

A frame is essential to keep the work taut, ideally a slate frame or a stretcher as used by a painter or at least an old picture frame and drawing pins.

Crewel needles nos. 5 (for framing up), 8, 9 and 10 for general use and couching.

A ball of string for threading through calico and tightening it on the frame.

Felt is used for padding the embroidery.

A velvet board is made by sticking a piece of velvet of about 12 cm (5 in) square on to a piece of card to be used when cutting purls.

There are several types of metal threads. These include passing thread which is metal wrapped around a silk or similar yarn core; check, which is a similar thread crimped; twists which are two ply yarns; and T70 twists which are cabled yarns. Pearl purl is a coiled thread and has to be stretched slightly before use to allow the couching threads to fall between the coils. There are a number of purls which are coiled metal with no core and various surfaces. These are cut into lengths and used like beads. There are many cords and yarns intended for lampshade trimmings, knitting and crochet or even gift wrapping which can be used extremely effectively.

Silver threads come in the same range of qualities as gold.

Threads used for sewing down the metal yarns should preferably be silk, although synthetic and embroidery threads can be useful here too.

Background fabrics should be strong and smooth and in keeping with the richness of the yarns. Furnishing fabrics are often the most suitable.

General requirements should include an airtight box in which to keep the metal threads to prevent tarnishing; scissors, such as an old embroidery pair, able to withstand the blunting effect of cutting metal; also wax, tweezers, pencils, pins, tracing paper and tacking thread.

Know how

Preparation

Mounting up. Mount a backing fabric such as prewashed calico on to the frame using a no. 5 crewel needle as shown in Fig. 1.

Tack on the background fabric before tightening up the frame so that both fabrics will be stretched tight like a drum skin.

Mark the centre line in both directions with tacking thread.

Outlining the design. Draw or trace the design in hard pencil on to tracing paper.

Pin the paper in position on the background fabric. Tack the outlines of the design through the tracing paper, background and mounting fabrics making small stitches on the back and long stitches on the right side except on curves where all stitches should be short.

Prick the paper with the eye of a needle all the way round the design until the paper can easily be torn away leaving only the tacking stitches on the background fabric.

Couching

The metal threads are positioned on the fabric and held in place by means of couching stitches (see Fig. 2) which are worked over them with nos. 8, 9 or 10 crewel needles keeping the stitches close to the thread to hold it firmly in place.

Always draw the thread through beeswax three times to strengthen it against the friction of the metal and to stop it knotting up while the work is in progress.

Bring the thread through from the back of the work and make a small back stitch which will be covered by the couched thread once the work has been completed.

Always work two couching stitches close together at the beginning and end of a length of metal thread and leaving about 2.5 cm (1 in) spare at either end for finishing off once all the threads have been couched down.

End with a small back stitch in the background fabric before taking the thread to the back of the work.

Smooth threads. The couching stitches are worked at right angles to a smooth metal thread, usually over two threads at a time (Fig. 3). **Bricking** is when the stitches are alternated in position on consecutive rows to form a brick like effect (Fig. 4).

Pearl purl and twists. When using pearl purl or threads with a twist, the stitches are worked to match the angle of the twist so that they sink into it. Couch into every twist when using thick or medium weight threads, every other twist when using fine (Fig. 5). Once the work is complete the couching stitches will hardly be visible.

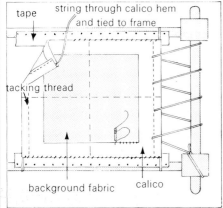

Fig. 1 Mounting up on frame.

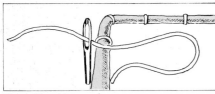

Fig. 2 Couching.

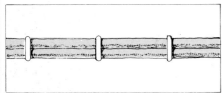

Fig. 3 Couching 2 threads at a time.

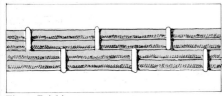

Fig. 4 Bricking.

Fig. 5 Couching pearl purl and twists.

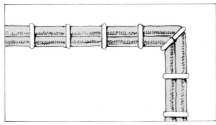

Fig. 6 Couching curves.

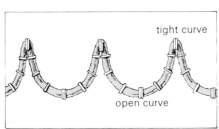

Fig. 7 Couching corners.

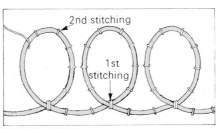

Fig. 8 Couching loops.

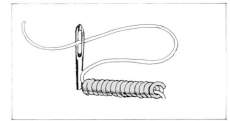

Fig. 9 Couching cut purl.

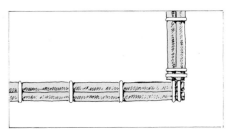

Fig. 10 Finishing off.

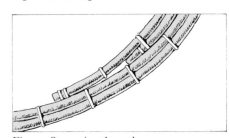

Fig. 11 Staggering the ends.

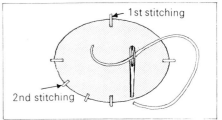

Fig. 12 Stitching felt padding.

It is usual to stretch a length of pearl purl before couching it down. Hold one end between the scissor blades and pull the other end with the other hand to open up the twists slightly.

Couching shapes. To couch a tight curve work two couching stitches very close at its turning point. A more open curve should have a double couching stitch positioned in the middle of the curve (Fig. 6).

To make a sharp angled corner, pinch the thread into shape with tweezers. If it is a double thread which is being couched take the outer one round first and couch it down before taking the second thread round and couching it down separately (Fig. 7).

To couch loops position the metal threads first with double couching stitches at the crossing points before couching round the rest of the loop to hold it in position in the usual way (Fig. 8).

Cut purl and beads. Cut purl just over the surface of the velvet board so that the pieces fall on its surface and do not roll away.

To couch, bring the thread through to the right side of the work, thread the needle through the length of the piece and take the needle back through the fabric the length of the piece away with the needle positioned at right angles to the fabric. Work beads in the same way (Fig. 9).

Finishing off
Leave all the metal thread ends on the right side of the work until it is completed.

After stitching closely to where the thread being couched ends, make two or three stitches. Then cut the end of the thread as near to these stitches as possible (Fig. 10).

To end on a curve such as on the picture frame (which is illustrated on page 137) stagger the ends of double threads, ending the inner one first as in Fig. 11.

Padding
Cut two or three layers of felt to the shape to be padded.

Trim each underneath layer slightly smaller than the previous one.

Stitch the smallest piece in place first using small stab stitches at right angles to the edge of the shape. Begin with four stitches, one at each of top, bottom, left and right, to ensure the shape is placed evenly, then fill in the other stitches (Fig. 12).

Stitch each layer in turn until the fully sized piece is in place, using rather more stitches for the final layer.

Clutch bag

This easily made clutch bag shows the initial of the bearer, illustrated here with an 'S'. However, the design could easily be adapted to any letter.

You will need
- Background fabric 51 cm by 31 cm (20 in by 12¼ in)
- lining fabric to the same measurements
- couching thread
- sewing thread to match bag
- selection of gold thread
- gold beads
- bronze beads
- small piece of felt
- interlining 48 cm by 28 cm (18¾ in by 11 in)
- stiff card 28 cm by 16 cm (11 in by 6¼ in)
- tacking thread

Measurements
28 cm by 16 cm (11 in by 6¼ in)
height of initial 11 cm (4¼ in)

Instructions
All the techniques required for this project are given on pages 134 and 135.

Frame up the background fabric.

Enlarge and draw out the initial (Fig. 13). Trace and tack it on to the background fabric (see Fig. 14).

Below An elegant evening bag.

Embroidery
Cut each of the first four threads the length of the circumference of the letter plus about 10 cm (4 in).

1st two threads. Leaving 5 cm (2 in) extra at the beginning, double and

Fig. 13 Layout of initials.

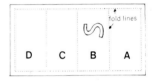

Fig. 14 Position of initial.

couch round the outline of the letter and outside the shaded area, then tie an overhand knot (Fig. 15) at each end. **2nd two threads.** Leave 5 cm (2 in) at the beginning as before, double and couch round the letter, bricking the couching stitches and taking it inside the shaded area (Fig. 15).

Continue to add doubled threads until the letter is filled but leaving a space for a single row of beads. Stitch on the beads.

Trim knotted ends to 2 cm ($\frac{3}{4}$ in).

Cut two pieces of felt to fit each shaded area and pad.

Stitch beads closely over both areas.

To complete
Remove work from the frame.

Turn under a narrow hem about 1.5 cm ($\frac{5}{8}$ in) on both sides and herringbone stitch.

Cut the interlining to size.

Turn the lining over the interlining. Place the lining and bag wrong sides together and slip stitch together.

Fold the quarter marked A over B to the centre of the fabric (see Fig. 16).

Herringbone stitch and insert card.

Herringbone a narrow hem at the other end (the 4th side).

Turn up section D to the centre. Oversew the two edges together.

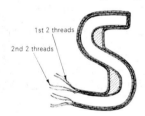

1st 2 threads
2nd 2 threads

Fig. 15 Positioning of 1st 4 threads.

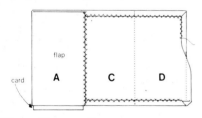

flap
card
A   C   D

Fig. 16 Make up of bag.

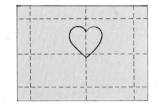

Fig. 17 Position of heart.

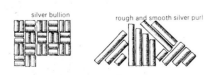

silver bullion   rough and smooth silver purl

Fig. 18 Arrangement of silver bullion and purl.

Pincushion

Silver threads, sequins and beads border the pincushion which contains a message spelled out in pins and would make a charming gift.

You will need
● Background fabric in two pieces, each about 28 cm by 17 cm (11 in by 6 in)
● inner cushion fabric in calico for holding sand, two pieces each about 22 cm by 14 cm (9 in by 5$\frac{1}{2}$ in)
● 3 small pieces of felt
● about 700 g (1$\frac{1}{2}$ lb) dry silver sand
● pins (lills) 14 mm ($\frac{1}{2}$ in) long
● 1 dram silver bullion
● 1 dram silver bright check no. 5
● 1 dram silver rough purl no. 8
● 1 dram silver smooth purl no. 8
● 1 m (1 yd) silver check 36 by 6
● 1 m (1 yd) T70 silver twists 2 by 2
● 14 5 mm ($\frac{1}{4}$ in) sequins
● 4 8 mm ($\frac{3}{8}$ in) sequins
● 50 seed pearl beads
● tacking thread
● sewing thread
● couching thread

Measurements
Design 18 cm by 11 cm (7 in by 4$\frac{1}{4}$ in)

pincushion about 24 cm by 17 cm (9$\frac{1}{2}$ in by 6$\frac{1}{2}$ in)

Instructions
All the techniques required for this project are given on pages 134 and 135.

Mount up background fabric.

Cut a heart-shaped template and draw on to tracing paper. Tack on to the background fabric, positioning as in Fig. 17.

Using the same template, cut three hearts in felt. Trim off about 3 mm ($\frac{1}{8}$ in) all round one and 6 mm ($\frac{1}{4}$ in) all round the other. Pad the heart shape and remove the tacking.

Embroidery
Cut silver bullion on a velvet board (see page 133) in 3 mm ($\frac{1}{8}$ in) lengths.

Stitch to the centre of the heart like a chequer board, surround this by a random row of bright check no. 5 in 4 mm ($\frac{1}{3}$ in) lengths then fill the remaining area with a mixture of silver rough and silver smooth purl no. 8 cut in lengths varying between 1 mm and 7 mm ($\frac{1}{16}$ in and $\frac{1}{3}$ in) as shown in Fig. 18.

Work the outer line of the border in silver check. Start at the bottom right hand corner and up the right hand side as this places the twist of the thread in

the correct direction for stitching. Couch.

Work the next row just inside the first using T70 silver twist. Couch and finish off ends.

Run a line of tacking thread 2 cm ($\frac{3}{4}$ in) up from the bottom line of the border.

Using silver check, make a circle of about 1 cm ($\frac{1}{2}$ in) across in the bottom right hand corner, then continue in serpentine curves between the row of silver twist and the tacking line, ending with another circle in the left hand corner.

Couch.

Complete the border in loops, small ones at either side, large ones on the top with a small one over the heart.

Finish off all ends.

To complete
Slacken frame.

Cut away the backing calico between couching and stitches holding top fabric to calico. Place a piece of fabric of finished size similar to top fabric, on the wrong side of the frame. Attach it on three sides between the two outer rows of the border, leaving the fourth end open.

Make up the calico bag to the measurements of the border. Fill with sand and close up. Place the bag in the cushion and close the open end.

Place a large sequin in each of the corner circles and secure by pushing a pin first into a bead and then through the sequin into the pincushion.

Place small sequins similarly in the loops on the lower border.

Pin a bead above each sequin on the lower border and in lines of five between the large loops and lines of three between the small loops as illustrated.

Complete the pincushion by spelling out a message in pins. Draw two parallel lines 1 cm ($\frac{1}{2}$ in) apart on tracing paper. Find the centre of the words by folding the paper in half, matching the first letter with the last and tracing the required letter between the drawn lines taking care to balance the spaces between letters.

Place in position on the cushion with several pins, then build up the letter by filling in the remaining pins, using seven to complete one vertical stroke. Tear away the tracing paper when the pinning is complete.

Fray out 1.5 cm ($\frac{1}{2}$ in) of fabric to end 1.5 cm ($\frac{1}{2}$ in) from the border.

Top right A pincushion with a special message makes a charming gift. **Bottom left** An unusual necklace. **Bottom right** Bands of gold make an unusual frame for that photo of someone special.

Necklace

This is made of different medallions suspended from a cord. They are worked with oddments of gold, silver and beads.

The background fabric is silk in a checked pattern and this was cut so that the colour change came exactly in the centre. The glass beads reflected the colour changes.

The medallions could be used as a bracelet or mounted individually on to a garment like buttons.

You will need
● 1 skein Anchor Stranded Cotton in each of two toning colours
● oddments of gold and silver thread and beads (see INSTRUCTIONS for details of the necklace illustrated here)
● stiff card
● felt
● 10p piece
● sewing thread
● tacking thread
● pencils

Measurements
Each medallion has diameter of a 10p piece

Instructions
All the techniques required for this project are given on pages 134 and 135.

Mount the background fabric on the frame.

Using a 10p piece, trace the circumference and tack five outlines on the background fabric.

Embroidery
Outer medallions. Using jap substitute and beginning from the outer edge, work six rounds of thread with bricked couching. Fasten off ends.

Fill the centre area with beads.

2nd and 4th medallions. Couch together one strand each of silver check and jap gold substitute 4K for one round. Do not fasten off ends. Sew one round of beads. Continue alternating a round of couching with a round of beads to the centre.

Fasten off ends.

Centre medallion. As for previous medallions but using doubled jap gold substitute 1K and gold metal beads.

Fig. 19 Making the cord.

To complete
Remove from frame.

Trim the background fabric to 6 mm ($\frac{1}{4}$ in) from the embroidery.

Run a gathering thread 3 mm ($\frac{1}{8}$ in) from the edge. Cut a piece of card to the size of a 10p piece and gather embroidery on to it. Fasten off.

Cut a piece of felt slightly smaller than a 10p piece and stitch in place on the back of the medallion.

Open out the two skeins of stranded cotton, cut through the loop at one end of each and knot the two skeins together. Put a pencil through the loops at either end and hold one steady while twisting the other (see Fig. 19). When tight fold the length in half and allow to twist up. Knot the ends together and trim off the loops.

Make a vertical buttonhole stitched loop near the edge at the back of each medallion and slot the cord through.

Alternatively, to make the medallions into a bracelet, place the loop centrally.

Photo frame

This design is illustrated in an oval frame but would easily adapt to a circular one. It is extremely simple to work with continuous rounds of thread couched to shape, with one wavy line and some beads for added interest.

You will need
● Picture frame, inside measurement 17 cm ($6\frac{1}{2}$ in) at widest point
● hardboard to fit frame
● brown paper to back frame
● background fabric to fit frame
● 2 m ($2\frac{1}{2}$ yd) gold passing thread 6S
● 1 reel gold substitute jap 1K
● 1 m (1 yd) gold T70 twist 2 by 2
● 1 m (1 yd) gold twist no. 2
● 1 m (1 yd) gold check 36 by 6
● 2 dram pearl purl no. 2 or 3
● 3 dozen small gold beads
● couching thread
● sewing thread
● tacking thread

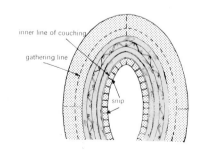

Fig. 20 Position of threads on background fabric.

Measurements
Width of embroidery 4 cm ($1\frac{1}{2}$ in)

Instructions
All the techniques required for this project are given on pages 134 and 135.

Mount up background fabric on frame.

Cut a hole in the hardboard 4 cm ($1\frac{1}{2}$ in) from where the frame inner edge will come.

Place the frame on tracing paper and mark the outline of the inner edge. Trace this on to the background fabric and tack. Repeat for the centre line taking it from the hardboard.

Embroidery
Measure out enough passing thread to go round the outer edge of the design 16 times plus about 2.5 cm (1 in).

Fold in half and position the thread just inside the outer line of tacking, beginning with the loop. Work the couching stitches 5 mm ($\frac{1}{4}$ in) apart.

Continue for eight rows in all, bricking the stitches.

Work one row of pearl purl.

Measure out substitute jap to go eight times round the inner edge of the design, remembering each row will take a little more than the previous one, plus about 2 cm (1 in).

Start with a loop as before and work from the centre out for four rows.

Next work one row of T70 twist, then five rows of gold twist no. 2, two rows of gold check and one row of pearl purl.

Using doubled jap substitute, work a wavy line between the two rows of pearl purl. Sew a bead inside each curve.

Finish off ends.

To complete
Remove the work from the frame.

Trim the background fabric to 4 cm ($1\frac{1}{2}$ in) from the outer tacking line.

Cut out the centre leaving a 1.5 cm ($\frac{1}{2}$ in) turning (see Fig. 20). Snip into this allowance to almost the first row of couching then fold to the back of the work.

Place a length of gold twist no. 2 round the edge and couch in place.

Run a line of gathering stitches 1.5 cm ($\frac{1}{2}$ in) from the outer row of couching (see Fig. 20).

Place the work over the hardboard and draw up the gathering thread to fit. Fasten off the stitches.

Place the embroidery in the frame.

Cut brown paper to fit the outer edge of the frame.

Stick photograph centrally on the paper and glue the brown paper to the back of the frame.

Needlepoint lace

Needlepoint lace is based on the humble button-hole stitch. It was the earliest form of lace and is still one of the most beautiful.

In its earliest form it was based on the drawn threads of a fabric and referred to as Greek lace or Cutwork. When threads are drawn from a fabric in two directions, the point where they cross becomes an open space and it is into this open space that the fillings are worked. As needle-work developed, the lace fillings became more important than the drawn threads and gave rise to Reticella lace.

In Venice, during the 15th century, the fabric part of the lace disappeared altogether and 'Punto in Aria' (stitches in the air) was created. The freedom from the basic warp and weft threads gave way to more flowing designs.

Reticella lace was brought from Venice to the Lake District. On his birthday of February 8, 1894, John Ruskin, the author, poet and artist, gave his name as a trademark to the craft so that it came to be known as The Ruskin Linen Work.

Both Punto in Aria and Ruskin Lace are covered in this section.

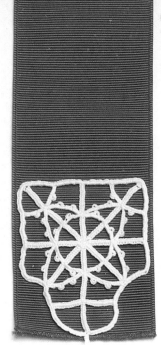
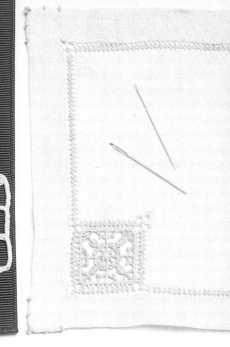

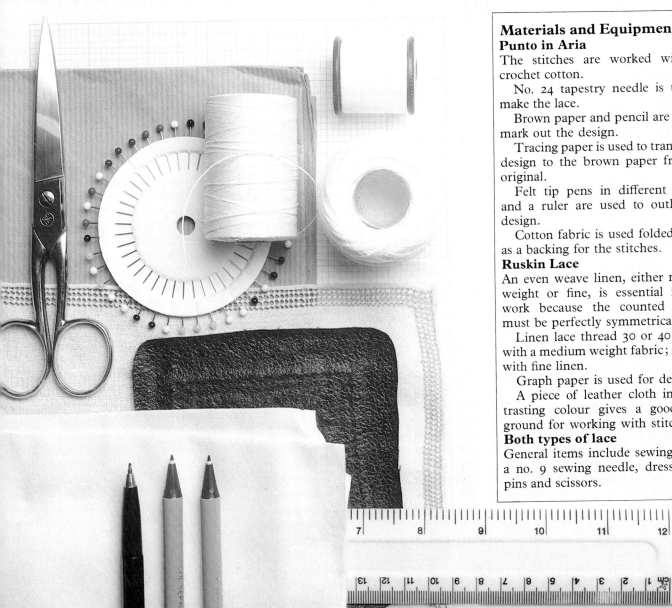

Materials and Equipment
Punto in Aria
The stitches are worked with 30s crochet cotton.

No. 24 tapestry needle is used to make the lace.

Brown paper and pencil are used to mark out the design.

Tracing paper is used to transfer the design to the brown paper from the original.

Felt tip pens in different colours and a ruler are used to outline the design.

Cotton fabric is used folded in half as a backing for the stitches.

Ruskin Lace
An even weave linen, either medium weight or fine, is essential for this work because the counted threads must be perfectly symmetrical.

Linen lace thread 30 or 40 is used with a medium weight fabric; 60 or 70 with fine linen.

Graph paper is used for designing.

A piece of leather cloth in a contrasting colour gives a good background for working with stitches.

Both types of lace
General items include sewing cotton, a no. 9 sewing needle, dressmakers' pins and scissors.

Know how

Punto in Aria
Designing and preparation
Work out a design on paper and transfer it, by tracing, to a piece of brown paper. Alternatively, work the design straight on to the brown paper. Draw over the pencil lines with a black felt tip pen and mark any picot points (see below) with a coloured pen. Trim the paper, leaving a 1 cm ($\frac{1}{2}$ in) margin all round the design.

Cut a piece of cotton fabric the same width as the brown paper and twice as long. Fold the fabric in half and place the paper on top. Using sewing cotton and a no. 9 needle, tack through all three layers round the edge of the paper, on all four sides.

Couching
Lay a length of 30s crochet cotton in a continuous line around the outline of the design.

To hold it in position by couching, thread a no. 9 needle with sewing cotton. Fasten the thread to the back of the fabric with a few small stitches and bring it straight up through the fabric and the paper on the line of the design. Pass the thread over the crochet cotton and take the needle back down through the same hole. Continue in this way along the crochet cotton, positioning the stitches 2 mm ($\frac{3}{16}$ in) apart and keeping the crochet cotton fairly tight for a smooth outline (Fig. 1a).

Whipping
Whipping is used when the couched thread needs doubling. Lay the crochet cotton back along itself and bring the needle to the top. *Pass the needle between the couched thread and the paper then over the new thread and the original couched thread. Repeat from * twice between each couched stitch (Fig. 1b).

Buttonhole stitch
This stitch is worked entirely over the couched thread without piercing the brown paper or fabric at all.

Using a no. 24 needle and crochet cotton, pass the needle under the crochet cotton from bottom to top, back over the crochet cotton and under the loose end as shown in Fig. 2a. Cover the loose end with the next few stitches.

Working from left to right, * make a loop round the left thumb, pass the needle over the crochet cotton, underneath it and up through the loop made by the thumb (Fig. 2b). Pull the

thread tight. Repeat from * to the end. Work in reverse for a right to left direction.

To finish off, push the needle through the back of two adjacent stitches and cut off the thread very close to the lace.

Where two couched threads cross or meet, make two buttonhole stitches round both threads to hold them together.

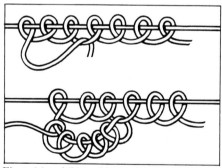
Fig. 1 (a) couching and (b) whipping.

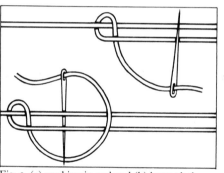
Fig. 2 (a) working in end and (b) buttonhole stitch.

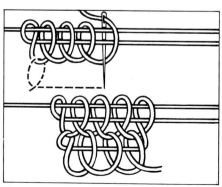
Fig. 3 (a) and (b) working a picot.

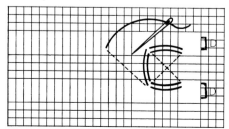
Fig. 4 (a) and (b) working cloth stitch.

Picot
A picot is a decorative loop. Work close buttonholing along the couched thread to the position of the picot. Pass the needle from front to back into the loop of the third stitch back, to form a small loop of single thread (Fig. 3a). Work five buttonhole stitches into the loop (Fig. 3b), then continue in buttonhole stitch over the couched thread. After working, form the picot by rubbing it

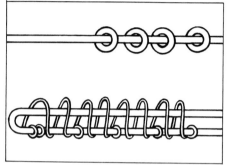
Fig. 5 Drawing single thread round square.

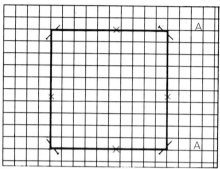
Fig. 6 Isolating 3 threads in either direction.

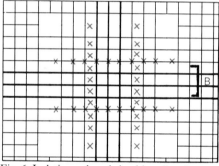
Fig. 7 Pattern of drawn threads.

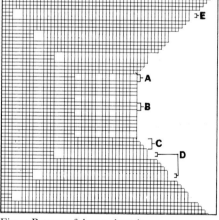
Fig. 8 Working single open hem.

flat with a fingernail.

Cloth stitch

When buttonhole stitch is worked over a laid thread into the previous row to build a solid area of stitches, it is called cloth stitch.

Begin by laying a crochet cotton thread from right to left across the area to be worked.

Take the needle over and under the couched thread and bring it up between the couched thread and the laid thread, to secure. Work buttonhole stitch from left to right over both the couched thread and the laid thread to the end of the row.

Take the thread back in a straight line and hook it into the loop of the first stitch as shown in Fig. 4a. On the next row work the buttonhole stitch into the loops of the first row and round the laid thread as shown in Fig. 4b.

Continue in this way for as many rows as are required.

Finishing off

Cut all tacking stitches by separating the two layers of cotton fabric and cutting between them. This prevents the lace being cut by mistake. Remove all loose pieces of cotton.

Discard the brown paper and the folded cotton fabric.

Ruskin lace
Designing

Ruskin work designs are created by cutting out squares and rectangles from the linen background and filling them with needlemade lace using geometric shapes. More advanced designs are made up from a combination of squares.

Whatever the shape of the cut-out area, it is always outlined by a padded roll to which the lace fillings are attached and this in turn is always framed by a single or double drawn thread hem.

Work out designs on squared paper the same size as the cut-out area of the finished work. Lace fillings need to be sufficiently concentrated not to give an empty appearance but they should not be overworked. It is also important that the eye is not drawn to any one particular unit but that the design is sufficiently balanced to be seen as a whole.

Drawing the threads

All round the four sides of the shape to be cut out, a single thread (A, Fig. 5) is drawn out as follows. Mark the threads with a pin at each corner, cut each thread at its centre, draw both ends back to the corners and cut them off where they meet.

Find the middle thread vertically and horizontally of the drawn thread square. Leave a thread on either side of these two central threads and draw the next one as before, so isolating three threads in either direction (B, Fig. 6) across the centre of the square. Leave the remaining threads between these central threads and the perimeter of the square.

Leave four threads outside square A undrawn (C, Fig. 7).

Draw the next two threads, leave four and draw another two all round the square (D, Fig. 7).

Leave the next four threads and draw the following two (E, Fig. 7).

Open hem

The open hem can be double or single. For a double open hem draw all the threads as given in Fig. 7 but for a single open hem, do not draw threads E. The hem is worked with a four sided stitch worked over four threads, as explained below. Use linen lace thread appropriate to the material being worked.

Single open hem. Bring the needle up in the top (outer) row of drawn threads D, between the fourth and fifth threads to the left of the top right hand corner. Leave a loose thread which can be sewn into the work once all the stitches are completed as shown in Fig. 8.

Work two straight stitches over the four threads to the right of the needle, take the needle down to the bottom row of drawn threads, bringing it out directly below the starting point. Work two straight stitches over the four threads to the right of the needle then take the needle back to the starting point. Work two straight stitches over the four threads below the needle then bring the needle up in the top row between the eighth and ninth threads to the left of the top right hand corner.

Double open hem. Bring the needle up in the top (outer) row of drawn threads (E), see Fig. 7, in between the fourth and fifth threads to the left of the top right hand corner.

Work two straight stitches over the four threads to the right of the needle, take the needle down to the next row of drawn threads, bringing it out directly below the starting point. Work one straight stitch over the four threads to the right of the needle then take the needle back to the starting point. Work two straight stitches over the four threads below the needle then bring the needle up in the top row between the eighth and ninth threads to the left of the top right hand corner.

For the second row of the hem, work a single straight stitch at the top of the four sided stitch to complete the stitch made in the first row.

At the corners of the open hem, work buttonhole stitch to secure the raw edges. At each side of the corner, work the first buttonhole stitch over two threads of the material, the next over three and the next over four, then decrease again to two threads. In the middle work over three, four and five threads, then graduate back to three threads.

Mounting

When the hem has been completed, tack a piece of leather cloth to the back of the square through the open hem. This firm but flexible backing remains in place while the lace filling is being worked.

Padded roll

It is most important to work the padded roll well because the lace is attached to the linen through it. It is worked over the four threads marked C in Fig. 7.

Cut three lengths of the working thread each a little longer than the perimeter of the square. Tie the three threads together and place these threads over the four threads of the linen. Secure with a stitch taken into each hole.

Work overcast stitches over both the material threads and the padding threads, taking the needle either into the fabric of the hem or the spaces. The stitches must be as close as possible so that there are no gaps between them.

Cut away the four small squares, one at a time.

The foundation structure

The three threads which cross the square horizontally and vertically (B, Fig. 7) form the foundation structure to the lace filling. They can be worked into either a woven bar or a whipped roll. Whichever is used, take care to keep the four smaller empty squares around the foundation structure equal in size and shape.

Woven bar

Add three more threads to the foundation structure in both directions, attaching the new threads through the padded roll.

Starting at the bottom, weave over

Needlepoint lace

three threads and under three from right to left, then over three and under three from left to right (Fig. 9). Keep the stitches as close as possible and make sure that the vertical and horizontal bars cross exactly at the centre.

Whipped roll
This is worked over four threads. Cut one of the original three threads and add two extra by attaching them

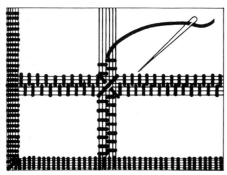
Fig. 9 Working woven bar.

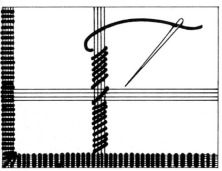
Fig. 10 Working whipped roll.

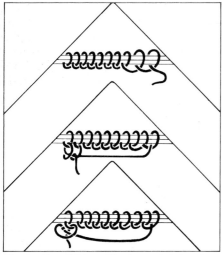
Fig. 11 (a) and (b) working buttonhole bar (c) increasing.

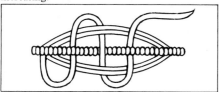
Fig. 12 Woven lozenge.

through the padded roll.

Whip over and over all four threads, keeping the stitches very close. Make sure that the horizontal and vertical bars cross exactly at the centre (Fig. 10).

Whipped rolls are also worked diagonally from corner to corner as part of the foundation structure. Attach three threads through the padded roll and carry them diagonally

Fig. 13 (a) and (b) beginning picot knot.

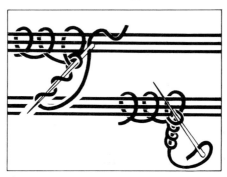
Fig. 13 (c) and (d) completing picot knot.

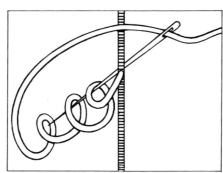
Fig. 14 Bullion knot.

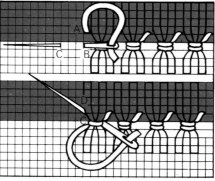
Fig. 15 Starting and Fig. 16 finishing pin stitch.

from corner to corner of the large square and whip over them. At the centre cross over the vertical and horizontal rolls with one stitch either way, or go under the woven bars likewise.

Buttonhole bars
Attach three foundation threads in the required position on the foundation structure. Work buttonhole stitch over the three threads (Fig. 11a).

This can be extended to form solid shapes such as points and petals by decreasing or increasing the number of stitches at the beginning and end of each row (Fig. 11b and Fig. 11c), working as for cloth stitch in Punto in Aria.

Woven lozenges
These are worked over whipped rolls. Add three foundation threads to the whipped roll in the shape of a lozenge and then weave the thread over and under the foundation threads and the whipped roll as shown in Fig. 12.

Finally, work buttonhole stitch round the edges of the lozenge.

Picot knot
A picot knot is made during a row of buttonhole stitches.

Work buttonhole stitch to the desired position, pass the needle through the bottom of the stitch to make a loop (Fig. 13a). Push the needle through this loop as shown in Fig. 13b. Wind the thread round the end of the needle three or four times (Fig. 13c) and finally pass the needle through the original loop made at the bottom of the buttonhole stitch (Fig. 13d).

Bullion knot
The bullion knot can be worked at the very centre of the pattern or at any point on a roll or bar.

Bring the needle up and make a tiny stitch on the roll or bar, leaving the needle in. Twist three or four loops on to the end of the needle (Fig. 14), then pull the needle through the loops, drawing the thread up tight. Fasten the thread with a knot at the back of the roll and cut the thread.

Pin stitch
Fold over a hem and tack.

Bring the needle up through the hem at A (Fig. 15), close to the edge. *Take the needle over one horizontal thread and insert it below the hem, directly below A at B. Take the needle under four vertical threads and bring it up at C. Work two backstitches between C and B, pulling tight. After the second stitch bring the needle out directly above C at D (Fig. 16) and repeat from *.

Book mark

The dark blue of the book mark makes an ideal background for this Punto in Aria motif which is worked first and then attached to the fabric. The motif could be used as an edging on a guest towel as the work is strong and can easily be washed.

You will need
● White crochet cotton
● cotton fabric 20 cm by 10 cm (8 in by 4 in)
● 30 cm (12 in) of Petersham or ribbon, 5 cm (2 in) wide
● Punto in Aria equipment as given on page 139

Measurements
Motif 6 cm by 7 cm ($2\frac{1}{4}$ in by $2\frac{3}{4}$ in), excluding tassel

Instructions
All the Punto in Aria techniques required for this project are given on pages 140 and 141.

Enlarge the design given in Fig. 17 on to brown paper. Cut out the brown paper, place it on the doubled cotton fabric and tack.

Lay the crochet cotton in a continuous line in the sequence given in Fig. 18, starting at A and ending at Z, couching single threads and whipping double threads, and leaving a 7.5 cm (3 in) tail at A.

Couch thread down round the petals and then round the inner circle, whipping over petal and circle where the couching threads meet.

Join in thread 7.5 cm (3 in) above A. Work buttonhole stitch along the line to B, wrap the thread once round the end and return along the other side of the bar, placing one buttonhole stitch between each stitch made before.

Work TR/S, MK/L, UI/JH and PN/CO in the same way.

Work the two small curves E/DF and W/VX in close buttonhole stitch, making picots at the marks shown in Fig. 17.

Work the petals and circle in buttonhole stitch with picots as marked.

Take three 30 cm (12 in) lengths of crochet cotton. Leaving a 7.5 cm (3 in) tail at A, lay them round the outside of the motif, buttonholing over them at the same time. Leave another tail

of the same length at the end on returning to A. Tie one of these ends round the other six to secure the tassel. Trim the tassel.

Remove the lace from the backing.

Trim both ends of the Petersham either by satin stitch on a sewing machine or blanket stitch by hand.

Place the lace motif in position at one end of the Petersham. Attach it with a few small stitches at the four corners and at the tassel point, working from the back of the Petersham and catching the back only of the stitched bar.

Finish off all ends.

Paperweight

This Punto in Aria motif incorporates cloth stitch to give a more solidly worked appearance. It has been displayed under a glass paperweight and is held in place with red felt to show it to its best advantage.

You will need
● White 30s crochet cotton
● cotton fabric 20 cm by 10 cm (8 in by 4 in)
● glass paperweight
● red felt to fit the base of the weight
● clear-drying glue
● Punto in Aria equipment as given on page 139

Measurements
Lace 6 cm ($2\frac{3}{8}$ in) diameter

Instructions
All the Punto in Aria techniques required for this project are given on pages 140 and 141.

Enlarge the design given in Fig. 19 on to brown paper and cut out. Tack to the doubled cotton fabric.

Fold 2 m (2 yd) of crochet cotton in half. Catch the folded loop down at A and couch the double thread in the sequence given in Fig. 20.

On reaching C, take one of the two threads and couch it down to I then whip back along itself to C. Continue with both threads to D then take a single thread to B and whip back as before. Continue in this way for each dotted line so that when complete there is a double thread all round.

Work buttonhole stitch along A/B. On reaching B, wrap the thread once round the end and return along the other side of the bar, placing one buttonhole stitch between each stitch made before.

Work H/E in the same way.

Buttonhole stitch the semicircle K/L, making picots as marked in Fig. 19. Work the triangle between L and M in cloth stitch, starting with 17 buttonhole stitches along the couched thread then lay the thread back along the row and hook into the last but one stitch. Work the second row to the second last stitch. Continue in this way decreasing two stitches on each row to reach a point at the outer of the two inner circles. Catch the last stitch to this circle. Bring the needle and thread up the edge of the triangle to work the semicircle M/N.

Continue working motif triangles and semicircles all round.

Work the two inner circles so that the cording of the buttonhole stitch is on the inside of the curve.

Pad the outside circle with three extra lengths of crochet cotton and work buttonhole stitch all the way round.

Remove the lace from the backing.

Mount the motif on the circle of felt and glue it to the base of the paperweight.

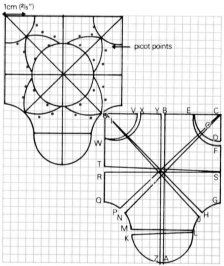

Fig. 17 Design and Fig. 18 laying crochet cotton.

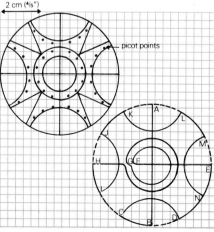

Fig. 19 Design and Fig. 20 laying thread.

Needlecase

The lace filling for this Ruskin lace square is made up of four repeats surrounded by a single open hem.

You will need
- Two pieces of medium weave linen each 12 cm ($4\frac{3}{4}$ in) square
- two pieces of coloured silk for lining each 12 cm ($4\frac{3}{4}$ in) square and one piece 6.5 cm ($2\frac{1}{2}$ in) square as backing to lace
- two pieces of card each 12 cm ($4\frac{3}{4}$ in) square
- two pieces of white felt each 7 cm by 8 cm (3 in by $3\frac{1}{2}$ in)
- small button
- linen lace thread no. 30 to match linen
- pinking shears (optional)
- Ruskin Lace equipment as given on page 139

Measurements
Needlecase 11 cm ($4\frac{1}{4}$ in) square lace inset 5 cm (2 in) square, excluding open hem

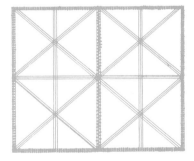

Fig. 21 Division of original square.

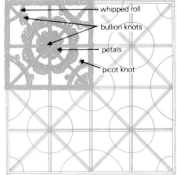

Fig. 22 Ruskin lace for needlecase.

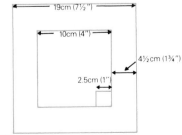

Fig. 23 Position of glass mat square.

Instructions
All the Ruskin Lace techniques required for this project are given on pages 141 and 142.

Fold 0.5 cm ($\frac{1}{4}$ in) and pin stitch all round one of the squares of even weave linen.

Pink round both felt pieces.

Fold 0.5 cm ($\frac{1}{4}$ in) all round each of the 12 cm ($4\frac{3}{4}$ in) squares of silk lining and press.

On one of the squares of medium weave linen, mark off the central 5 cm (2 in) square with pins at each corner, counting the threads along each side to ensure there are an equal number. Cut and draw threads as given in Fig. 7 in the Know How, omitting E.

Using linen lace thread, work a single open hem outside the 5 cm (2 in) square over the D threads.

Attach a piece of leather cloth to the back of the square.

Work a padded roll on the C threads.

To work the lace foundation structure, make a vertical and horizontal woven bar over the 6 central threads. Cut out the small squares.

Add three threads to make a diagonal from one corner of the padded roll to the other. Repeat in the opposite direction. Work a whipped roll over each of these diagonals.

Make four short diagonals across the small squares and work as whipped rolls.

Make and work four more whipped rolls as vertical and horizontal divisions to each of the four small squares (Fig. 21).

Make and work a whipped roll in the outside corner of each small square (Fig. 22).

Attach three foundation threads in a semicircle and in the centre of each side of the padded roll. Work these in buttonhole stitch with picot knots in each space between threads as shown in Fig. 22.

Attach three threads to make a circle at the centre of the design. Work in buttonhole stitch with picot knots as before.

Attach three threads to make a circle at the centre of each small square. Work a petal in each space between threads by working seven buttonhole stitches in the first row, decreasing to six in the second row and five in the third.

Make a circle of 8 bullion knots at the centre point of each small square and again at the centre of the large square one knot between each roll.

Work two bullion knots on the rolls in the space between the petal and the

whipped roll at each corner.

Remove the lace from the backing and attach coloured silk behind.

To complete
Take the plain square, turn under a 0.5 cm ($\frac{1}{4}$ in) hem all round and tack in place. Secure the hem with pin stitch.

Place silk lining and lace square wrong sides together and tack. Secure along three sides, leaving the left hand side free. Insert the card. Repeat with silk lining and plain linen square, leaving right hand side free. Make bullion knots at 1 cm ($\frac{1}{2}$ in) intervals round the outer edges, working two together at each corner.

Attach the two halves with two bullion knots together at 1.5 cm ($\frac{5}{8}$ in) intervals along the free edges.

Attach a small button at the centre of the right hand side of the lace square.

Work a corresponding loop of three threads to fit over the two edges and round the button to the left hand side of the plain square. Work the loop with buttonhole stitch and picot knots.

Table linen

This table linen develops the art of Ruskin Lace with rather more complicated designs worked on finer linen. The designs could be repeated on other pieces of table linen such as place mats or a tablecloth.

You will need
Fine even weave linen:
- **glass mat** 19 cm ($7\frac{1}{2}$ in) square
- **napkin** 41.5 cm ($16\frac{1}{2}$ in) square
- linen lace thread no. 60 to match the linen
- Ruskin Lace equipment as given on page 139

Measurements
Glass mat 14 cm ($5\frac{1}{2}$ in) square
napkin 41 cm (16 in) square

Instructions
All the Ruskin Lace techniques required for this project are given on pages 141 and 142.

Glass mat
Measure out, and mark out the corners with pins, a 2.5 cm (1 in) square in the bottom right hand corner of the linen, leaving a 4.5 cm ($1\frac{3}{4}$ in) border between the square and the edge (Fig. 23). Draw a single thread round the perimeter of the square.

Cut and draw threads as given in Fig. 7 in the Know How omitting E.

Mark out a larger square measuring 10 cm (4 in), starting at the bottom right hand corner of the small square (Fig. 23). Draw two sets of two threads for a single open hem, continuing the single open hem of a small square on two edges.

Work the open hem round the larger square and the two remaining sides of the smaller square, working buttonhole stitch at the corners.

Attach a piece of leather cloth to cover the back of the small square.

Work a padded roll round the small square. Cut out the four sections after isolating the central threads each way.

Make a whipped roll over the foundation structure.

Add four threads to make a diagonal from one corner of the padded roll to the other. Repeat in the opposite direction. Work whipped rolls over each of these diagonals.

Attach three threads to the padded roll to make an arc across each end of the diagonal whipped rolls. Work each arc in buttonhole stitch (Fig. 24).

Make a semicircle with three threads at the end of each of the remaining whipped rolls. Work each in buttonhole stitch with two picot knots (Fig. 24).

Make a circle of two threads in the middle of the square and work a petal in each of the eight spaces between the whipped rolls.

Work a woven lozenge on each diagonal whipped roll.

Work a bullion knot in each corner between the arc and the padded roll.

Work a circle of eight bullion knots at the centre of the square.

To complete

Remove the lace from the backing.

Turn the hem to the back of the work to the edge of the open hem. Slip stitch neatly in place and secure the overlap at the corners with slip stitch.

Decorate each hem corner with two bullion knots at the point and two others each at 0.5 cm (¼ in) intervals on either side.

Napkin

Measure out, and mark the corners with pins, a 5 cm (2 in) square in the bottom right hand corner of the linen, leaving a 3.5 cm (1½ in) border between the square and the edge.

Draw a single thread round the perimeter of the square. Leave four threads for the padded roll.

Measure 2.5 cm (1 in) to the left of the bottom edge of the large square. Mark with a pin and draw the cut thread to this point and cut. Extend the top right hand corner of the square

in the same way. This marks two sides of each small square. Draw a single thread along each of the other two sides to complete.

On the three outer sides of the two small squares count in four threads from the single drawn thread and pull one thread for the continued padded roll. This gives the shape outlined in colour in Fig. 25.

Leave four threads all round then draw two more.

Work a single open hem, with buttonhole stitch at each outward pointing corner.

Attach a piece of leather cloth to the back of the work.

Work a padded roll round the outside of the shape, inside the open hem.

On the original 5 cm (2 in) square, isolate the centre three horizontal and vertical threads of the foundation structure and work them as a woven bar.

Add two threads to the four threads between the large square and the small square and work this as a woven bar. Repeat with the other small square.

Cut out the six small squares divided by these woven bars.

Work three diagonals as whipped rolls in one direction and, at right angles to these, a further five diagonals (Fig. 26).

Work three vertical whipped rolls across the centres of the squares and across these at right angles with the further three whipped rolls as indicated in Fig. 26.

In the two outside squares, work a central ring over three foundation

threads with buttonhole stitch petals, four woven lozenges on the diagonals, two bullion knots on the remaining four whipped rolls, two buttonhole stitch arches with two picot knots in the corners and eight bullion knots at the centre, one between each roll.

In the centre of the 5 cm (2 in) square work a ring of buttonhole stitches over three threads to make a circle. On this, in each of the four spaces between the woven bars, work a triangle of cloth stitch: work three rows with the same number of stitches, ending with a picot knot at the end of the third row, decrease the next row by one stitch at each end and end with a picot knot. Continue decreasing in this way, making a picot knot at the end of the seventh and eighth rows. Continue the end of the triangle to work a circle at the centre of the four smaller squares.

Work a petal in each of the remaining spaces between diagonals in each of the four smaller squares and fill in the remaining spaces with arcs, semicircles and bullion knots.

To complete

Remove the lace from the backing.

Measure in 0.5 cm (¼ in) from each edge of the linen. ★ Working inwards, draw two threads all round the square of linen, leave four threads. Repeat from ★ until four pairs of threads have been drawn in all. Work three rows of open hem stitch.

Roll the 0.5 cm (¼ in) hem to the wrong side of the work to meet the first row of open hem. Slip stitch in place.

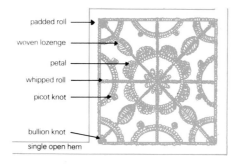

padded roll
woven lozenge
petal
whipped roll
picot knot
bullion knot
single open hem

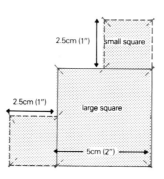

2.5cm (1″) Small square
2.5cm (1″) large square
5cm (2″)

Fig. 25 Dimensions of napkin squares.

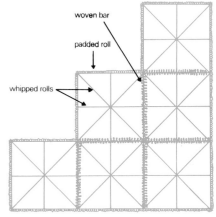

woven bar
padded roll
whipped rolls

Fig. 26 Ruskin lace for napkin.

Australian cross stitch

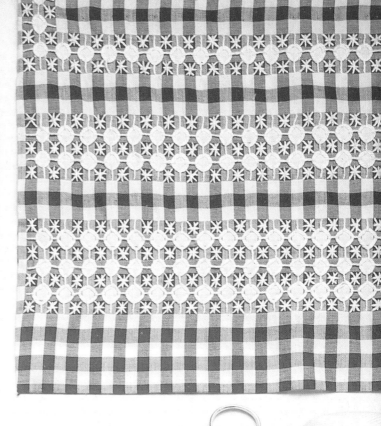

Australian cross stitch is a form of gingham embroidery, the history of which is virtually unknown. As a technique, it goes back only to the late 19th century and is related to the then popular counted thread peasant embroidery.

Peasant work was almost always made to fulfil a well recognized purpose in the social and domestic economy of the household. The best illustrations of this were the dowry articles made and embroidered by young girls for themselves, personal objects and those needed in the home. In those days, home-spun linen was worked in cross stitch, displaying an extraordinary wealth of brilliant colour on the white fabric.

In this particular form of gingham embroidery, white threads are worked on the gingham squares in the shape of roses, daisies, butterflies and snowflakes. The patterns combine and transform the gingham squares into a distinctive design.

Materials and Equipment

Fabric for Australian cross stitch is always polyester cotton gingham with 6 mm (¼ in) squares. Pure cotton fabric should not be used as it is likely to shrink when washed thereby ruining the embroidery.

Twilley's Lyscordet crochet cotton in white is used for the embroidery.

Sewing cotton to match the coloured squares is used for making up the articles.

Needles required include a no. 4 crewel needle which has an eye large enough to take the embroidery thread and smaller needles for use with the sewing cotton.

General items can include scissors, thimble, dressmakers' pins and tape measure.

Know how

Preparation

Cut sufficient fabric to enable the back of the stitches to be covered by hems.

Use no more than an arm's length of embroidery thread, approximately 90 cm (1 yd) at any one time. Tie a knot at the end of each new thread and use the squares on the gingham as the stitching line. All stitches on the back of the work should be straight.

Fastening off

To fasten off, make a loop and pull the thread through to form a loose knot (Fig. 1). Slide the knot down on to the fabric with the thumb on top of the work and index finger underneath. Cut off the excess thread.

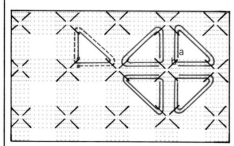

Fig. 1 Fastening off.

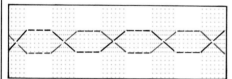

Fig. 2 1st stage of broken cross stitch.

Fig. 3 2nd stage of broken cross stitch.

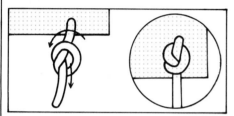

Fig. 4 Beginning 2nd row.

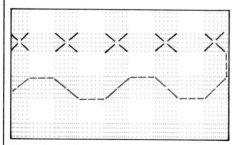

Fig. 5 Rose design.

Broken cross stitch

Three rows of broken cross stitch form the foundation of the rose, daisy and butterfly designs. Each broken cross is worked on coloured squares.

The rows of stitches are worked in two stages. Make a knot at the end of 90 cm (1 yd) of the crochet cotton.

First stage. ★ Bring the needle out at the upper right hand corner of a dark coloured square at the right hand end of the row to be worked. Take a small diagonal stitch in the centre of the square, then insert the needle into the lower left hand corner of the square. Bring it up at the lower right hand corner of the next coloured square. Take a small diagonal stitch in the centre of this square, then insert the

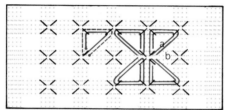

Fig. 6 Butterfly design.

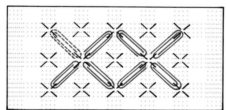

Fig. 7 Plain daisy design.

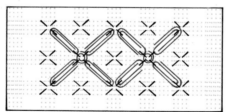

Fig. 8 Daisy with small centre.

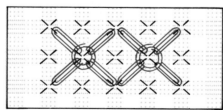

Fig. 9 Daisy with large centre.

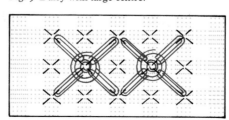

Fig. 10 Daisy with double centre.

needle into the upper left corner. Repeat from ★ to the end of the row ending at the lower left hand corner of a square. Always work an odd number of squares (Fig. 2). Dotted lines represent the thread at the back of the work.

Second stage. Continue by taking the thread up to the upper left hand corner of the same square and work from left to right across the stitches of the first stage as before but reading left for right and right for left (Fig. 3).

To begin the second row, take the thread straight down behind the light coloured square and bring it out at the upper right hand corner of the next dark coloured square (Fig. 4).

Work three rows of stitches in all. Fasten off.

Rose design

Work three rows of broken cross stitch.

The pattern is formed around the centre cross of nine, working from right to left across the row.

Bring the needle up in the middle row, just to the left of the upper right hand spoke of the second cross (point A, Fig. 5). Pass the eye of the needle through the lower right hand spoke of the second cross in the first row, then the upper left spoke in the first cross in the second row and back through the upper right spoke of the first cross.

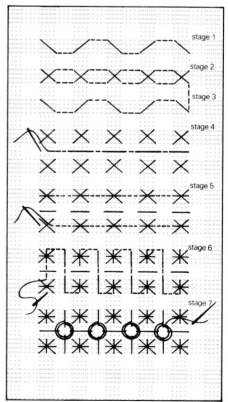

Fig. 11 7 stages of snowflake design.

Take the thread through these spokes again then insert the needle close to the right hand side of the upper right spoke of the first cross (point B, Fig. 5). This completes one petal.

Work three more petals around this first cross so that it forms the centre of a block of nine crosses as shown in Fig. 5. Work each petal and the sequence of the petals in a clockwise direction. The spokes of the centre cross should be visible after the rose is completed, therefore the thread should not be worked over them.

Start the next rose in the next unthreaded cross in the middle row, using this cross as the centre one of nine as before.

Butterfly design

Work three rows of broken cross stitch.

The pattern is formed around the centre cross of nine, working from right to left across the row.

Bring the needle up in the middle row, close to the left of the upper right hand spoke of the second cross (point A, Fig. 6). Pass the eye of the needle through the lower right hand spoke of the second cross in the top row, then the lower left spoke of the first cross in the top row and back to the centre cross.

Take the thread through these spokes again then insert the needle close to the right of the upper right spoke of the centre cross (point B, Fig. 6). This completes one wing.

Work three more wings around this first cross so that it forms the centre of a block of nine crosses as shown in Fig. 6. Work each wing and the sequence of the wings in a clockwise direction.

Start the next butterfly in the second unthreaded cross in the middle row, using this cross as the centre one of nine as before.

Plain daisy design

Work three rows of broken cross stitch.

The pattern is formed around the centre cross of nine, working from right to left across the row.

Bring the needle up in the middle row, close to the left of the upper right hand spoke of the second cross. Pass the eye of the needle through the lower left hand spoke of the first cross in the first row, then back through the upper right spoke of the centre cross.

Take the thread through these spokes again then insert the needle close to the upper right spoke of the centre cross. This completes one petal.

Work three more petals around this first cross so that it forms the centre of a block of nine crosses as shown in Fig. 7. Work each petal and the sequence of the petals in a clockwise direction.

Start the next daisy in the second unthreaded cross in the middle row, using this cross as the centre one of nine as before.

Daisy with small centre

Work the plain daisy design.

Bring the needle up just to the right of the upper left spoke of the centre cross and pass the eye of the needle clockwise under the spokes of the centre cross twice before taking the thread to the back of the work (Fig. 8).

Daisy with large centre

Work the plain daisy design.

Bring the needle up close to the left of the first petal worked. Pass the eye of the needle clockwise under the petals of the daisy twice before taking the thread to the back of the work (Fig. 9).

Daisy with double centre

Work the plain daisy design with both small and large centres (Fig. 10).

Snowflake design

This pattern differs from the other patterns in that the foundation consists of only two rows of cross stitch. This is worked in the same way as broken cross stitch but without the tiny stitch in the centre of the squares.

The pattern is worked in stages as shown in Fig. 11.

Stages one to three. Make two rows of plain cross stitch.

Stage four. Make a row of straight stitches between the two rows of cross stitch, taking the thread over the coloured squares and fractionally over the edges of the white squares.

Stage five. Make a horizontal straight stitch across the centre of each cross.

Stage six. Make a vertical straight stitch across the centre of each cross and across the coloured squares between the cross stitch, taking a longer stitch into the white squares.

Stage seven. Using the eye of the needle, pass the thread clockwise under the four straight stitches twice, beginning and ending on either side of the top straight stitch.

The thread can be wound round three times for a larger ring.

Washing

Hand wash the embroidered gingham and allow to drip dry. It can be pressed very lightly on the wrong side.

Tablecloth and napkin

The rose design forms a border round the tablecloth and the toning napkins. A cluster of rose motifs could also be worked in the centre of the tablecloth. The design could be adapted to make kitchen curtains; a nice touch if the table linen is used in the kitchen.

Close up of the rose design.

You will need
- 1.5 m (1¾ yd) polyester cotton gingham, 115 cm (45 in) wide
- one ball Twilley's Lyscordet
- Australian cross stitch equipment as given on page 147

Measurements
Table cloth 102 cm by 86 cm (40 in by 34 in)

napkins 32 cm by 29 cm (12½ in by 11½ in)

Instructions
All the Australian cross stitch techniques required for this project are given on this and the facing page.

Tablecloth
Cut a piece of gingham 106 cm by 115 cm (41 in by 45 in).

Count out a centrally positioned rectangle of 69 by 51 coloured squares and mark with a pin at each corner.

Work broken cross stitch on the three rows of coloured squares immediately outside this rectangle, thus giving an odd number of crosses on each side.

Work a row of the rose design all round, taking the thread round three times for each petal.

Napkins

Cut two pieces of gingham each 46 cm (18 in) square.

Count out a centrally positioned rectangle of 15 by 17 coloured squares and mark with a pin at each corner.

Work the embroidery as given for the table cloth but taking the thread round twice for each petal.

Work another napkin to match.

To complete

Press fabric lightly on wrong side.

Turn in each edge of the tablecloth so that three rows of white squares and two rows of coloured squares are left between the embroidery and the edge of the cloth and so that the back of the embroidery is covered. Slip stitch in place.

On the napkins, turn in each edge so that two rows of white squares and one row of coloured squares are left at the border.

Slip stitch in place.

Aromatic cushion

This cushion has the butterfly design worked on it and is filled with aromatic dried herbs and soft wadding. It will both decorate and perfume any room in the house but is specially pleasant if left on a pillow during the day.

You will need

● 0.5 m ($\frac{3}{8}$ yd) polyester cotton gingham, 115 cm (45 in) wide
● one ball Twilley's Lyscordet
● 1 m (1 yd) bleached cotton wadding, 90 cm (36 in) wide
● dried herbs such as sage, bay leaves, lavender or any other sweet smelling dried flowers
● Australian cross stitch equipment as given on page 147

Measurements

32 cm by 25 cm (12$\frac{1}{2}$ in by 10 in)

Instructions

All the Australian cross stitch techniques required for this project are given on pages 148 and 149.

Cut two pieces of fabric each 29 cm by 37 cm (11$\frac{1}{2}$ in by 14$\frac{1}{2}$ in).

Count out a centrally positioned rectangle of 15 by 11 coloured squares on one piece of fabric and mark with a pin at each corner.

Work broken cross stitch on the three rows of coloured squares immediately outside this rectangle.

Work a row of butterfly design on each of the long borders of cross stitch, taking the thread round twice for each wing.

Leave one row of white squares free at each corner before working the butterfly design on each of the short borders.

To complete

Place the two pieces of fabric right sides together, matching squares and

Above An apron worked in the snowflake design and a work bag which features the daisy design in its various forms. **Right** The butterfly design brings a distinctive touch to an aromatic cushion.

leaving two rows of white squares and two rows of coloured squares all round between the embroidery and the seam. Stitch round three sides, leaving a short edge open.

Cut 15 cm (6 in) off the width of the wadding and fold the remaining material in half then half again, width ways. Stab stitch round three sides through the four thicknesses of wadding, leaving a short edge open.

Stuff the dried herbs and flowers between the layers of wadding.

Place the wadding in the cushion cover and stab stitch the wadding to close its open edge.

Slip stitch the remaining seam of the cushion cover.

Summer bag

This bright summer bag incorporates all the different permutations of the daisy design. It can be adapted to any size of handle.

You will need
● 0.5 m ($\frac{3}{8}$ yd) polyester cotton gingham, 90 cm (36 in) wide
● one ball Twilley's Lyscordet
● one pair 31 cm ($12\frac{1}{4}$ in) wooden bag handles
● 0.5 m ($\frac{3}{8}$ yd) white fabric, 90 cm (36 in) wide, for lining
● Australian cross stitch equipment as given on page 147

Measurements
Depth, 33.5 cm ($13\frac{1}{4}$ in) excluding handles
width, 41 cm (16 in)

Instructions
All the Australian cross stitch techniques required for this project are given on pages 148 and 149.

Cut a piece of fabric 81 cm by 46 cm (32 in by 18 in).

Fold the fabric in half width ways and mark the centre row of white squares on the fold line with a coloured thread.

Miss one row of coloured squares from the centre row and start the embroidery on the next row of coloured squares. Work in broken cross stitch for seven rows each with twenty-five crosses, positioned centrally on the width of the bag.

Starting at the centre cross of nine at the right hand side of the work, and taking the thread around twice for each petal, work daisy pattern as follows:

First row. Daisy with large centre.
Second row. Daisy with double centre.
Third row. Daisy with large centre.
Miss one row of coloured squares and work three more rows of broken cross stitch.

Work a row of daisies with small centres through these crosses.

In the opposite direction from the centre marked row, work the other side of the bag to correspond.

To complete
Press the work lightly on the wrong side.

From the lining fabric cut a piece 81 cm by 46 cm (32 in by 18 in).

Place it right sides together with the gingham and tack. Stitch together round three sides. Turn out to the right side and slip stitch the fourth side

to close. Press the seams.

Make a line of running stitches 1 cm ($\frac{1}{2}$ in) from each top edge. Gather in to fit the handle slots. Insert the fabric through the slots. Making sure that the coloured thread marking the lower edge of the bag is on the fold line when the two handles are placed together, stab stitch through the four thicknesses of material to hold the handles in place.

Remove the coloured thread.

Turn the bag wrong side out and slip stitch the side seams, leaving 18 cm (7 in) open at the top of each side to allow for easy opening.

Turn right side out.

Apron

This unique snowflake pattern skilfully accentuates the white squares of the gingham design to produce wide bands of embroidery which appear more like insets than part of the rest of the fabric. The idea would make a charming border on a summer skirt, a child's dress, straight cuffs or short sleeves.

You will need
● 90 cm (1 yd) polyester cotton gingham, 115 cm (45 in) wide
● one ball Twilley's Lyscordet
● Australian cross stitch equipment as given on page 147

Measurements
Depth 66 cm (26 in) including waistband
width of waistband 53 cm (21 in) excluding ties

Instructions
All the Australian cross stitch techniques required for this project are given on pages 148 and 149.

Cut the apron pieces as shown in Fig. 12.

On the apron skirt the embroidery begins on the eighteenth row of

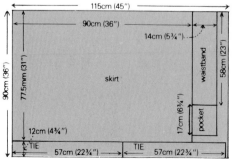

Fig. 12 Apron pattern pieces.

coloured squares up from the bottom and begins and ends on the third coloured square in from each of the side edges.

Taking the thread round twice, work the snowflake design to include the next four rows of coloured squares, miss one row of coloured squares, work the design to include the next three rows of coloured squares, miss one row of coloured squares, then work one row of the design.

Starting immediately above this last row of embroidery, work the snowflake design up the sides of the apron skirt.

Fold the waistband in half lengthways immediately above a row of white squares. Work the snowflake design over the next four rows of coloured squares so that the row of white squares is at the top of the right side of the waistband. Do not catch in the back half.

Embroider snowflakes around three sides of the pocket, leaving two squares, one as a border, the other to turn under.

To complete
Press the work very lightly on the wrong side.

Turn in the sides of the apron to cover the embroidery and slip stitch in place.

Turn the hem to leave a border of three white squares and three coloured squares free of embroidery on the right side and slip stitch in place.

Turn under one square along the top edge of the pocket and slip stitch. Turn under one square along each of the three sides of the pocket and slip stitch in place on the apron about 13 cm (5 in) away from the right hand side and 3 cm ($1\frac{1}{4}$ in) above the single line of snowflakes.

Gather the top of the apron about 12 mm ($\frac{1}{2}$ in) away from the edge and draw up to 53 cm (21 in). With the right side of the waistband to the right side of the apron, machine stitch the waistband to the apron along the line of the gathers. Fold the waistband in half, turn under 12 mm ($\frac{1}{2}$ in) along the edge and slip stitch in place along the line of machine stitching.

Turn 12 mm ($\frac{1}{2}$ in) to the wrong side along the two long edges and one of the short edges of the ties. Fold raw sides together and top stitch close to the edge.

Turn in 12 mm ($\frac{1}{2}$ in) at both ends of the waistband. Place the raw edges of the ties into the ends of the waistband and slip stitch in place.

Press all seams.

Weaving

Weaving is a method of making fabric by interlacing horizontal and vertical strands of yarn. It has probably been in existence since primitive man first experimented with trailing vines.

Simple loom weaving was certainly in existence at the time of the ancient Egyptians as we can tell from the cloth used to enshroud the mummies. The Greeks and Romans produced fine damasks and tapestries and there were beautiful muslins from India.

Until about 1850, almost all weaving was done by hand loom. The first power loom, invented in 1784, eventually contributed to the industrial revolution and spinning and weaving gave birth to the huge mills of the Victorian north.

Today the interest in crafts such as spinning and weaving by hand has been revived. Despite the wide range of manufactured goods available there is enormous satisfaction in creating a fabric to one's own exact specifications.

Materials and Equipment

Threads used for the warp (see Know How) of a tapestry should be strong, smooth and even such as cotton, wool or linen. Ordinary knitting wool is not suitable. A good type of weft (see Know How) thread is rug yarn which is available as a continuous thread or as 'thrums'. Thrums are remnant lengths, varying from short thrums of about 10 cm to 50 cm (4 in to 20 in) to lengths of several metres (yards). The great advantage of thrums is the wide variety of colour available in small quantities for little expense.

Simple frame looms are suitable for small to medium-sized tapestries and have the advantage of being inexpensive, portable, easily stored and not requiring additional equipment. An ideal, ready-prepared frame can be made with painters' canvas stretchers. These have the advantage of being made with smooth wood and have mitred corner joints, enabling them to be assembled and dismantled using various lengths of side for different pieces of work. A useful size for the beginner is 60 cm by 75 cm (24 in by 30 in) and is the size used for all the projects described in this section.

A tape measure is needed to place the warp threads accurately.

A ruler checks the accuracy of the warp.

A clamp fixes the frame to the table edge whilst winding the warp.

General items include pen or pencil, adhesive tape, darning needle and scissors.

Know how

Weaving is a method of producing cloth by interlacing two sets of threads at right angles to each other. One set is called the warp and these travel along the length of the cloth. The warp threads on each edge are called the selvedges (self-edges). The threads which travel across the width of the cloth (from selvedge to selvedge) are called weft.

The sett
The number of warp or weft threads used per centimetre or per inch is called the sett.

To calculate the warp sett, wind one warp and two weft threads around a ruler side by side without any empty space between them. Continue winding until two or three centimetres (one or two inches) have been covered (Fig. 1). For very thick yarns, wind more to fill four or five divisions of the ruler. Count the number of warp threads and divide by the number of centimetres (inches) covered to find the average. This is the ideal number of warp threads for the project.

Preparing the frame
Assemble the frame, making sure the corners are square.

Use a metric tape measure and fix it along one of the 60 cm sides with a piece of adhesive tape at each end. (For imperial measurements use an inch tape stuck along the 24 in side.)

Using a pen or pencil, mark off 1 cm (1 in) units across the width of the frame, starting 8 cm (3 in) from one end and finishing the same distance short of the other.

Do the same along the opposite end of the frame as shown in Fig. 2. The outer marks on these two sides represent the widest possible weaving width of the loom.

Making the warp
Warping a frame loom is easier if the frame is secured with a clamp on its unmarked edge to the edge of a table (Fig. 2). If the entire width available for weaving is not to be used, plan to place the warps centrally on the frame, marking the width of the project with a coloured thread (Fig. 2).

Tie the warp thread to one end of the frame, using the mark which represents the selvedge which will be directly opposite one of the coloured threads (Fig. 2).

Wind the warp around the frame in a continuous figure of eight movement, placing the threads parallel with each other and spaced according to the sett (Fig. 3).

Because the warp is wound in a figure of eight, every second thread passes over the front of the frame and the alternate threads return from the back of the frame so that only half of the threads will show on the face of the loom. Remember, therefore, to space the threads around the ends of the loom at half the sett. For example, a warp sett of two threads per centimetre would be wound around the frame placing one thread on each centimetre mark on the edge of the frame.

It is important to wind the warp with as even a tension as possible. It should be reasonably tight so the threads 'twang' if plucked but not too tight for comfortable weaving. The spacing can be adjusted when the warp is completed but only before it is fixed to the frame. Experiment with various tensions on different warps to find the most comfortable.

When the correct number of warp threads have been wound, tie the last thread to the same end of the frame as the starting thread. This will be the bottom edge of the loom when weaving. Check the spacing of the warp threads on both the upper and lower sides of the frame and push any badly spaced threads into the correct position.

When satisfied with the spacing, fix the threads on the edges of the loom by placing strips of adhesive tape across each side of the loom over the threads, making sure that the tape is well stuck down. Unclamp the frame.

Heading cords
These give a firm base to the weaving and prevent the weft from sliding to the bottom of the loom.

Tie the first cord to one of the unmarked sides of the frame, about 10 cm to 15 cm (4 in to 6 in) above the bottom edge of the loom.

Pass the first heading cord through the space between the upper and lower warp threads (Fig. 4) which is called the 'shed'. Pull the cord as tight as possible and tie it to the other side of the frame directly opposite the starting point. Tie a second heading cord just above the first. Counting from the side to which the thread is tied, pick up the first four back warp threads in the left hand and slide the fingers down towards the first heading cord, so raising the back threads above the front set. Pass the second heading

cord underneath the raised threads, called the 'counter shed' (Fig. 5), with the right hand. Continue across the width of the warp to the other edge. Pull this second cord tight and tie it to the frame.

Place a ruler into the open shed to check the spacing of the warp at the heading cords, which will probably be uneven. Re-arrange as required. Use the ruler to pull the second heading cord close to the first, making a straight edge against which to weave (Fig. 6).

Weft finger skeins
To make a neat manageable bundle of weft thread, cut a length of about 2 m (2 yd). Leave a 15 cm to 20 cm (6 in to 8 in) length of yarn across the palm of the left hand and wind the rest in a figure of eight round the thumb and forefinger which are held about 5 cm (2 in) apart. Leave another 15 cm to 20 cm (6 in to 8 in) piece free at the end.

Carefully remove the figure of eight from the fingers. Making sure the starting end is hanging free, firmly wrap the last end around the middle of the skein, making a half-hitch with the end.

Lengths of 3 m to 4 m (3 yd to 4 yd) can be wound into a skein but lengths of less than 50 cm (20 in) are not worth winding and can be used loose.

Weaving
Insert the fingers of the left hand into the open shed near the top of the loom and pick up four threads. As before, slide the fingers down the warp, this time to within about 15 cm (6 in) of the weaving. Separate the fingers to make the shed large enough to pass the weft thread skein through with the right hand. Hold the skein between the tips of the middle and ring fingers of the right hand. Pass the skein into the shed from the right and pick up from the left with the thumb and forefinger of the right hand.

As each section of weft is inserted, beat it into position with the fingertips of the left hand.

To pick up the counter shed, the warp threads which lie in the upper half of the open shed have to be depressed one at a time while the alternate lower threads are picked up with the fingers of the left hand. Pick up about four at a time and separate the fingers to deepen the shed as before.

It is extremely important that the weft is allowed to bend over and under the alternate warp threads in each row. If it is pulled too tight and not allowed to bend, the fabric will narrow, which is called waisting.

When weaving the alternate rows from left to right, the movements of the right hand are reversed.

Weft splices

Break, rather than cut, the ends of the weft so that the tapering ends can be lapped over each other in the weaving to produce a neat, invisible and strong join (Fig. 7a). If the yarn will not break easily, cut both the old end and the new end and unravel the threads of each a little. Splice (overlap) the ends of the old thread with those of the new across 2 cm to 3 cm (1 in) of the warp, as shown in Fig. 7b. When the weaving is completed, trim off the ends flush to the fabric.

Weaving in ends

There are two ways of fixing the starting and finishing ends of each colour into the fabric. Firstly, the ends can be darned in with a needle after the weaving is completed. If a colour area is very narrow, darn the thread along a warp thread so that the colour does not show through. The ends have to be darned in this way in a colour area of less than six warp threads wide.

Alternatively, the starting ends of a new colour can be tapered (or thick threads spliced) into the second row of the colour area for 2 cm to 3 cm (1 in) as shown in Fig. 8. The finishing end should be tapered or woven back into the last row of weaving. In order to return into the same row without undoing the weaving of that row, the weft has to travel around two warp threads before starting the weaving sequence (Fig. 9).

Cutting and knotting. A simple method of finishing off is to cut and tie the thread, leaving a loose fringe at the end of the work.

Cut one or two warp loops at a time close to the outside edge of the frame. Tie either two or four threads together with an overhand knot, close to the edge of the weaving, making sure the knots are firm. Trim the fringe to the length required.

Woven border. This gives a firm neat edge to the fabric. Turn the frame over to work from the back of the weaving, using the warp as the weft.

Start at what is now the left selvedge. Cut the first loop of warp where it travels around the frame to release the two warp threads forming that loop. Take the edge thread and, using it as

a weft, weave it to and fro as shown in Fig. 10, to build up the triangle for the corner.

Weave the second thread once down the diagonal formed by the first thread. Leave the ends hanging where the border joins the edge of the weaving.

Continue across the width of the warp, cutting one loop (two warps) at a time and weaving them in sequence. The last nine warps (four loops and end thread) will have less and less to weave through. These nine threads are left hanging from the right hand selvedge of the border. When all the warp has been cut from the loom, knot the very last thread around the other eight threads to hold them together, as shown in Fig. 11. Divide the nine threads into three groups of three and plait for several centimetres (inches). Fasten at the end with an overhand knot and stitch the pigtail to the back of the work unless otherwise stated.

Trim all the other ends close to the point where border meets weaving.

Abbreviations

To simplify the instructions abbreviations are used to indicate the number of warp threads to be woven and the direction of the weave.

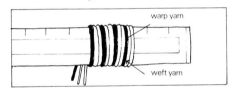

Fig. 1 Calculating the warp sett.

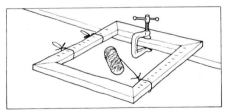

Fig. 2 Marking the frame.

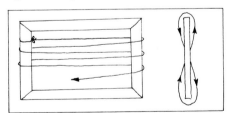

Fig. 3 Figure-of-eight warping of frame.

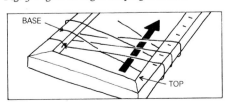

Fig. 4 1st heading cord through shed.

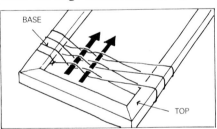

Fig. 5 2nd heading cord through countershed.

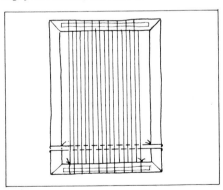

Fig. 6 Heading cords in place.

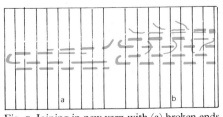

Fig. 7 Joining in new yarn with (a) broken ends and (b) spliced ends.

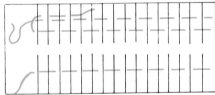

Fig. 8 Tapering ends into 2nd row of new colour.

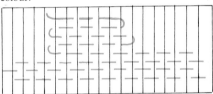

Fig. 9 Weaving tapered end back into last row.

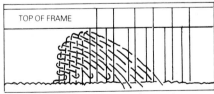

Fig. 10 Woven border – weaving 1st 6 warp threads.

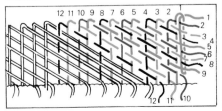

Fig. 11 Woven border – weaving last 12 threads.

continued

lr means weave a row from left to right; rl means weave a row from right to left. The figure following this will indicate the total number of warp threads in the row. Because the sheds are formed by lifting alternate warp threads, the weft will pass under half (and over the remainder) of this total number.

As this will not always be an even number, the shed may be divided into odd and even groups of threads. For example, in Fig. 12 the first row – lr 9 – travels under five warp threads and over four. The second row – rl 8 – travels under four and over four. The third row – lr 5 – only travels over and under a total of four threads. The fifth thread is not actually included in the third row, but the weft must go round it to begin the fourth row, so it is added into the third and fourth rows.

The starting place of a shape will be given by the number of the warp threads, counting from the left edge, unless otherwise stated. However, when working at the right of the fabric only, it makes more sense to count the threads from the right hand edge. Instructions will always state when the warp thread has been numbered from the right.

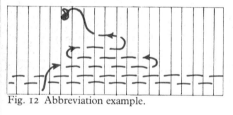
Fig. 12 Abbreviation example.

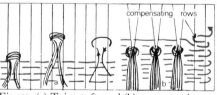
Fig. 13 (a) Tying tufts and (b) compensating rows.

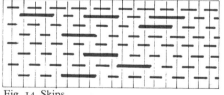
Fig. 14 Skips.

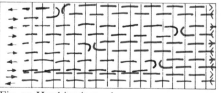
Fig. 15 Hatching in 2 colours.

Tufting

Cut a number of lengths 20 cm to 23 cm (4 in to 5 in) for the tufts. The effect will be more natural if the lengths are not exactly the same.

To tie the tuft, select two adjacent warp threads and pass the left end of the tuft over and under the left warp thread and the right end over and under the right warp thread (Fig. 13a).

Tufts can be worked across the whole warp or in any part of it but if only part of the warp is used, the weft will be uneven and compensating rows must be woven. To the left of the tuft, weave two rows over the empty warps. Weave the next row across the whole width. To the right of the tuft, push this row down over the empty warps to the previous level of weaving and compensate by weaving two short rows across the empty warps to the right of the tuft (Fig. 13b).

Skips

To produce a skip, weave the main weft over three warps instead of the usual over-under-over sequence (Fig. 14). Skips should not be made too often or too close to one another or the weaving will be very loose.

Fleece weft

Pieces of fleece can be woven in with the main weft. Pull a small quantity of dry, lightly washed fleece to form a bulky strand, thickest at the centre and tapering off at each end. Use this as weft across part of the warp. It will be easier to insert the strand into an open shed. The placing and arrangement can be more easily adjusted. The main weft is also woven into the same shed with the fleece but across the full width of the warp. The next main weft row is then woven and is pushed down firmly over the fleece to keep it in place.

The addition of fleece rows means the weft will not be level, therefore occasional compensating rows will be required at the edges. Stagger the positions of fleece so that compensating rows are not required in the centre.

Hatching

The basis for the hatching effect is the 'meet-and-part' rule. In any one shed, or counter shed, two adjacent wefts weave either towards or away from each other as shown in Fig. 15. Because two colours meet in the first row of hatching and part in the second, they can meet at a different point in the third row, part in the fourth and meet at a new point in the fifth, etc. In this way the two colours will be interlinked.

Shoulder bag

The bag is woven in two panels which are stitched together. The first panel consists of stripes in two colours. Some stripes are plain and other wider stripes show some of the basic patterns achieved by using two colours. The second panel uses plain stripes, some with various diagonals to produce a zig-zag.

You will need
Warp:
- 100 g (3½ oz) high twist rug yarn
weft:
- 75 g (2⅔ oz) brown single 'Berber' wool, A
- 75 g (2⅔ oz) beige 'Berber' wool, B
- 75 g (2⅔ oz) orange rug yarn
- weaving equipment as given on page 153

Measurements
31 cm by 35.5 cm (12¼ in by 14 in), excluding fringe

Instructions
All the weaving techniques required for this project are given on pages 154–156.

First side
1st band. Using high twist rug yarn, wind the warp 30 cm (12 in) wide, to a sett of two threads per centimetre (5 threads per inch).

Insert the heading cords about 10 cm (4 in) from the bottom edge of the frame.

Using A and starting at the left selvedge, weave 2.5 cm (1 in), approximately 18 rows. Leave a tail of about 2.5 cm (1 in) hanging from the selvedge on the first row to weave in when the second row is complete.

2nd band. Starting B from the right selvedge, work two rows and weave in the loose end as before. Do not break the thread at the end of the two rows.

Weave two rows A and catch in B with the edge warp thread by turning the working weft around the non-weaving weft (Fig. 16).

Continue the horizontal stripes in this way, weaving two rows B, two rows A for 4.5 cm (2 in), ending with two rows B. Do not break the thread.

3rd band. Weave another 2.5 cm (1 in) stripe of A only, carrying B up with the thread on the right selvedge.

4th band. Work one row of each

colour alternately to produce a thin vertical stripe equal in width to the sett of the fabric. Interlock the rows of the weft on the selvedges as shown in Fig. 17. Continue for 4.5 cm (2 in), ending with an A row.

5th band. Weave a 2.5 cm (1 in) stripe in B, carrying A up the selvedge as before.

6th band. Weave two rows A, one row B for 4.5 cm (2 in) to produce a pattern of staggered dots of beige on a brown background.

7th band. As 5th.

8th band. This band combines all three previous patterns. It is divided into three sections, the first and the third having the same sequence of weft colours and the middle one having the same sequence but with the colours reversed.

For the first section work, 2 rows A, 1 row B, 1 A, 1 B, 2 A, 1 B, 1 A, 1 B, 1 A, 1 B, 2 A, 1 B, 1 A, 1 B, 2 A.

For the second section, work 2 B, 1 A, 1 B, 1 A, 2 B, 1 A, 1 B, 1 A, 1 B, 1 A, 2 B, 1 A, 1 B, 1 A, 2 B.

Repeat the first section beginning with 2 rows A.

To complete the first side of the bag, weave a 2.5 cm (1 in) stripe of A, 5 rows of B and then, using A, weave until the fabric measures 38 cm (15 in) from the beginning.

Work a woven border to finish off.

Cut the warp from the lower edge of the frame and tie the ends in pairs using a reef knot. Make the knots firm and close to the edge of the fabric.

Second side
Make the warp as for the first side.

1st band. Weave 18 rows in A, starting and finishing at the left edge and remembering to weave in the starting ends.

2nd band. Weave 18 rows in B, carrying the dark weft up the edge.

To weave the triangle in the centre, work lr 46, rl 31, lr 28, rl 25, lr 23, rl 20, lr 17, rl 14, lr 12, rl 9, lr 6, rl 3.

Break off the weft and darn in the end.

3rd band. To fill in to the left of the triangle, using A work lr 15, rl 15, lr 18, rl 18, lr 21, rl 21, lr 24, rl 24, lr 27, rl 27, lr 30, rl 30. Leave the weft thread.

With a new A thread start at the right selvedge and weave to fill to the right of the triangle for twelve rows. Weave a 13th row to the centre, break the thread and weave the end into the 12th row of the left hand side.

The weaving should now be level across the width of the fabric and about 5 cm (2 in) deep.

Work another triangle, using A in the same sequence as for the first one.

4th band. Using orange rug yarn double, fill in on either side of the triangle to bring the weft back to the horizontal, making the fabric about 7.5 cm (3 in) deep.

Weave another triangle in the doubled orange weft, using the same base of 31 warps but reducing the number of warps by two and one alternately on the left side and by two each time on the right side.

5th band. Build up each side with separate A threads as before until these are level with the orange apex.

Weave a triangle with A on the same base of 31 warps. Reduce the number of warps by one each time on the left side and in a repeating sequence of 2, 1, 1, on the right hand side.

6th band. Using B, fill in each side as before.

The triangle is worked on the same base of 31 warps. To make the steeper sides work as shown in Fig. 18 – two turns (4 rows) and then one turn (2 rows) alternately on the left slope, with a step reduction of one warp at a time and two turns (4 rows) with a step of one warp on the right slope. The apex of this triangle is two warps wide and should be about 23 cm (9 in) from the lower edge of the fabric.

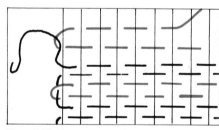

Fig. 16 Taking non-weaving colour up side of work.

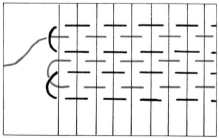

Fig. 17 Interlocking weft on selvedge.

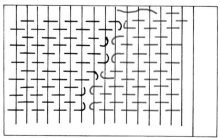

Fig. 18 Triangle sides with fill-in weaving.

7th band. The fill-in sequence again uses separate wefts of A for each edge but the horizontal areas are only 21 rows deep (Fig. 18).

Continue to fill in with A following the steps of the triangle and forming parallel outside edges (instead of returning to the selvedge) by weaving over only eight warps (Fig. 19).

When both A threads reach the apex of the triangle, break the right weft and weave it in.

Continue with the left weft and complete the triangle, ending with an apex three warps wide, about 27 cm (10½ in) from the beginning.

8th to 11th bands. Fill in with orange on each side for 14 rows then change to B (carrying the orange up the side) for ten rows, then work in orange (carrying B up the sides) for 14 rows. Complete with B on both sides and weave a further ten rows the full width of the fabric once the apex has been reached.

Complete the fabric with 12 rows A, 10 rows orange, 12 rows B and continue with A until the work measures 38 cm (15 in).

Finish off as given for the first side.

To complete

Using a steam iron, press both pieces lightly on the wrong side.

Place the pieces wrong sides together so that the warp pigtails are at opposite corners. Stitch side and bottom edges together using the same yarn as the warp. For added strength to the bottom of the bag, tie the warp threads (two from the fringe of each panel) in overhand knots.

To make the shoulder strap, cut 24 lengths of orange rug wool each 3 m (3 yd). Place the threads to form a 24 strand bundle, tie them together about 10 cm (4 in) in from one end of the lengths with an overhand knot. Divide the strand into three groups of eight threads each and make a plait ending in another overhand knot about 10 cm (4 in) from the other end.

Place one of the knots just below a bottom corner of the bag and stitch the plait up the side seam to the top edge. Repeat for the other side, adjusting the length if required by tying an overhand knot in the correct position and unravelling the unwanted plaiting. To make the strap more secure at the top corners, take the warp fringe plaits around the shoulder strap plait at each corner and stitch these to the strap and back down inside the bag.

Trim the tassels of the shoulder strap and the warp fringe to an equal length.

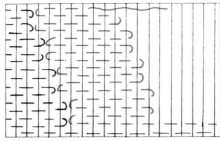

Fig. 19 Forming parallel outside edge.

Wall hanging

In this wall hanging the warp shows where the fleece weft is inserted so choose a warp colour to blend in with the general colour scheme.

You will need
- 100 g (3½ oz) 2 ply rug yarn (ordinary twist) for warp and main weft
- 75 g (2⅔ oz) mixed thrums (ordinary and high twist rug yarn) for tufting
- small quantity of fleece, about 10 g (⅓ oz). This can be gathered from hedgerows, washed gently in warm soapy water, rinsed thoroughly but gently and allowed to dry naturally
- 5 mm (¼ in) dowelling, 45 cm (18 in) long
- weaving equipment as given on page 153

Measurements
About 56 cm by 36 cm (22 in by 14 in)

Instructions
All the weaving techniques required for this project are given on pages 154–156.

Warp the frame to a sett of two threads per centimetre (5 threads per inch).

Insert the heading cords about 10 cm (4 in) above the bottom edge of the frame.

Weave the first 16 rows – about 3 cm (1½ in) deep – starting from the left edge. Beat gently to allow the warp to show between weft rows to make a softer, more pliable fabric.

Cut a number of lengths of yarn each 25 cm (10 in) for the tufts. Using three strands of weft for each tuft, tie a row of tufts on every pair of warp threads. The colours illustrated have been blended at random but the first and last few knots of every row have the same colour in order to outline the shape.

Weave eight rows across the full width of the warp and taking the weft up the selvedge past the row of knots.

Tie a row of tufts as before.

Weave eight rows; make another row of tufts but with 20 cm (8 in) strands; weave eight rows. The fabric will now be about 10 cm (4 in) deep.

Using 20 cm (8 in) strands, tie a row of tufts on all but the first and last pair of warp threads. To compensate on the left edge, weave two rows using the first two warp threads only, weave a row across the full width then weave two rows on the last two warps at the right hand edge.

Weave a further seven rows across the full width to make a total of eight rows above the knotted area, ending at the left again.

Tie the next row of tufts using 15 cm (6 in) strands and leaving four empty warps at each end of the row. Weave the compensating rows at each end and eight full rows as before.

Tie a row of tufts using 15 cm (6 in) strands, leaving eight untufted warps at each edge. Compensate and weave six rows for the full width.

Leave 14 empty warps each side and tuft with 12 cm (5 in) strands on the remaining warps. Compensate and weave four rows for the full width.

Leave 22 empty warps each side and tuft the remainder with 12 cm (5 in) strands. Compensate and weave four rows.

Leave 32 empty warps each side and tuft the central 14 warps. Compensate and weave six rows to complete the tufted area.

In the next 12 rows of weft, produce skips at random at both sides of the fabric. Make only one or two skips at each side in the first and last couple of rows, more in the in-between rows without them being too frequent or too close to one another. Weave some rows without skips to prevent the fabric becoming loose.

Weave two rows without skips to complete this area.

With the main weft at the left, place a small quantity of fleece into the open shed and secure it with the next two rows.

Weave four rows, then weave in more fleece, this time using two slightly shorter strands placed towards either end of the first one.

Weave another six rows.

Continue in this way until, over 12 cm (5 in) of weaving, there are about eight rows of fleece in all, placed at random and in varying lengths. Separate the fleece rows by four or six rows of plain weft and leave about four warps between lengths in any one row. Weave compensating rows where necessary.

After the last fleece row, level the cloth with compensating rows then continue with the main weft until the work measures 40 cm (16 in) deep.

Finish off by cutting four warps at a time and tying an overhand knot close to the edge of the cloth, first at the top of the frame, then at the bottom.

When the work is off the loom, make three more rows of overhand knots, using two threads from each of the previous knots to alternate them and form a latticed fringe. Trim the fringe level.

Trim the lower edge fringe to match the tufted pile.

Thread the dowel rod through the latticed fringe. Use a length of warp yarn as a hanging cord.

Place mat

The hatching, or shading, which characterizes the design of this place mat is a very versatile technique. Two versions are used, straight hatching for the purple and blue wefts and curved for the green shapes.

You will need
- 50 g (1¾ oz) 3/3/9s warp cotton dishcloth cotton:
- 50 g (1¾ oz) blue, A
- 90 g (3¼ oz) purple, B
- 25 g (1 oz) green, C
- weaving equipment as given on page 153

Measurements
28 cm by 38 cm (11 in by 15 in)

Abbreviations
Because this weave always uses two rows of a colour which starts from and returns to a selvedge, two rows are shown as lr/rl (or rl/lr depending on the starting and finishing point).

Instructions
All the weaving techniques required for this project are given on pages 154–156.

Warp the frame to a sett of two threads per centimetre (five threads per inch).

Using two strands of B together as one, work 16 rows, starting and ending at the left edge.

Straight hatching. B lr/rl 43, A rl/lr 17, rl/lr 12, B lr/rl 48, lr/rl 30, A rl/lr 30, rl/lr 15, B lr/rl 45, lr/rl 52, A rl/lr 8, rl/lr 45, B lr/rl 15.

Repeat the sequence once more.

Turn the frame over and work a third and fourth repeat of the pattern but in the reverse colour proportions, reading B for A and vice versa.

When all four repeats are complete, the work should measure about 8.5 cm (3½ in).

Turn the frame over again so that B is to the left and A to the right.

Weave the next 11.5 cm (4½ in) using the same technique but to a random pattern, using more of B than A, as illustrated.

When half the mat has been worked, a third colour is introduced together with the curved hatching. The A and B weft continue to hatch in straight weft towards the left hand edge.

Curved hatching. B lr/rl 20, lr/rl 16, lr/rl 13, lr/rl 11, lr/rl 9, lr/rl 8, lr/rl 7, lr/rl 6, lr/rl 5, A rl/lr 8.

Work B lr 52, weaving down the slope and across to meet A, creating a curved edge. Because the weaving concept is new, the actual warp thread number is given in brackets after each step of the sequence.

With a finger skein of C, starting at the sixth warp from the left, weave lr 18 (23rd), rl 8 (16th), lr 5 (20th), rl 8 (13th), lr 5 (17th), rl 7 (11th), lr 4 (14th), rl 6 (9th) as shown in Fig. 20.

B rl 38 (15th), lr 18 (32nd), rl 15 (18th), lr 12 (29th), rl 9 (21st) then lr to hatch with A in a free continuation of the previous area, keeping it clear of C.

C lr 22 (30th), rl 5 (26th), lr 3 (28th), rl 5 (24th), lr 3 (26th), rl 5 (22nd), lr 3 (24th), rl 5 (20th), lr 3 (22nd), rl 10 (13th).

B rl to 23rd warp, lr to hatch with A, rl to 26th, lr to A.

C lr 25 (37th), rl 30 (8th), lr 27 (34th), rl 8 (27th).

B rl to 30th, lr to A, rl to 33rd, lr to A, rl to 36th, lr to A, rl to 39th, lr to A, rl to 42nd, lr to A.

C lr 16 (42nd), rl 8 (35th), lr 4 (38th), rl 6 (33rd), lr 8 (40th), rl 6 (35th), lr 4 (38th), rl 14 (25th).

Continue to hatch B with A and weave until the B is level with the highest point of C (Fig. 21). This completes the first half of the C shape.

To weave the remainder of it, bring B to the 27th warp, then lr to A, rl to 31st, lr to A, rl to 34th, lr to A, rl to 38th, lr to A.

C lr 9 (33rd), rl 6 (28th), lr 9 (36th), rl 20 (17th).

B rl to 19th, lr 13 (30th), rl 10 (21st), lr 7 (27th), rl 5 (23rd), lr to A.

C lr 11 (27th), rl 13 (15th), lr 15 (29th), rl 23 (7th).

B to 12th, lr to A, rl to 15th, lr 11 (25th), rl 4 (22nd), lr to A.

C lr 15 (21st), rl 13 (9th), lr 10 (18th), rl 13 (16th), splice starting ends back into this row to finish C.

Weave B across to the left selvedge and then fill in until the edge of the weaving is reasonably level.

The remainder of the mat is woven in a similar way, making variations on the first C shape with the curved weft technique or reverting to the straight weft hatching.

Complete all hatching by the time the work measures 38 cm (15 in) so that it can be levelled off before 40 cm (16 in).

Weave 2 cm (1 in) in B only.

To finish off, cut one loop at a time and tie an overhand knot close to the edge with each pair of warps at both ends and then trim the fringes to 2 cm to 3 cm.

Trim off all spliced weft joins.

The mat is reversible, the curved shapes taking on a different significance depending on which way up they are.

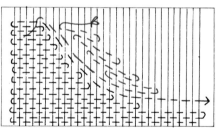
Fig. 20 Curved hatching.

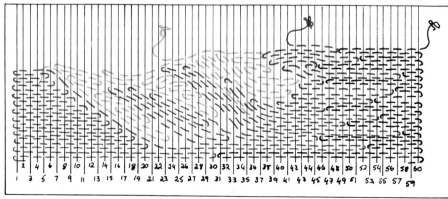
Fig. 21 1st half of curved hatching motif.

BLK

Crochet

Crochet has been with us since ancient Egyptian times. It spread through Renaissance Europe to the west, particularly Ireland where a distinctive form of crochet developed which was really a form of lace. Victorian England felt crochet was a fitting occupation for any gentlewoman and crochet trimmings and accessories abounded.

Today the craft encompasses all aspects from delicate lacy openwork to firm close fabrics, using anything from fine silky threads to chunky rug wool. Items range from fashion garments to household goods and sometimes it is used as an art form to create pictures and even 'sculptures'.

It is easy to learn as, in fact, there is really only one stitch, made with yarn and a hook.

Materials and Equipment

Yarns suitable for crochet include knitting wools and cottons and, for fine work, mercerized crochet cotton. Interesting effects can also be achieved by experimenting with other materials such as garden twine or ribbon.

Crochet hooks come in a number of thicknesses but are generally all the same length. They are made of aluminium or plastic in the middle to large sizes, the very fine ones are made of steel. Generally speaking, the correct size of hook relates to the thickness of the yarn. Nowadays, the range of sizes is numbered metrically to an international standard although some hooks will still show the old English sizing as well.

General items include a blunt-ended needle, scissors, tape measure, dressmakers' pins, pressing cloth and iron.

Know how

Holding the work

All crochet stitches are based on the principle of drawing one loop through another. The hook is held in the right hand. Left-handed people may find they can still learn to crochet using the right hand. Those who prefer to hold the hook in the left hand will have to reverse the directions, reading left for right and right for left, and place the diagrams in front of a mirror and work from the reflection.

Begin by making a slip loop at the end of the yarn (Fig. 1).

Hold the hook in the right hand like a pencil (Fig. 2), put the hook through the loop and pull the yarn tight with the left hand and turn the palm of the right hand towards you.

Wind the yarn round the little finger of the left hand, across the palm and behind the forefinger (Fig. 3). Hold the loop at its base close to the hook between thumb and forefinger.

The stitches

Chain. Take the hook under the yarn so that there is a loop of yarn over the hook (Fig. 4). This is described as 'yarn round hook'.

Draw the hook through the slip loop taking the yarn caught in its curve with it and passing the slip loop over the end of the hook (Fig. 5). This makes one chain.

To make another chain, take the yarn round the hook and draw the yarn through the loop on the hook, so passing the loop off the hook.

Continue in this way, always moving the left thumb and forefinger up the work to hold the most recently made stitch close to the hook.

Foundation chain. Crochet usually begins with a length of chain into which the first row of stitches is worked and this is called a foundation chain. The hook is inserted into the centre of the chain as shown in Fig. 6 so that there are two threads on top of the hook and one below.

Turning chain. Because crochet stitches are worked from the top down, chain are used to take the yarn up to the top level of the work at the beginning of each row. These are called turning chain. The number of chain used depends on the depth of the stitch to follow (Fig. 7). The turning chain count as the first stitch of the row and it is important to remember to work into the top turning chain at the end of the next row otherwise a stitch is lost.

Slip stitch. This stitch has almost no depth and is, therefore, used to move invisibly from one position in the work to another or for joining stitches together. It requires no turning chain.

Make four chain. Insert the hook into the next chain from the hook from front to back, yarn round hook (Fig. 8) and draw the yarn through both the chain and the loop on the hook (Fig. 9).

Double crochet. Make 12 chain. Insert the hook in the third chain from the hook, yarn round hook (Fig. 10), draw the yarn through so that there are two loops on the hook, yarn round hook again (Fig. 11) and draw it through both loops, slipping them off the hook (Fig. 12). This makes one double crochet. Work nine more to complete the row.

Double crochet requires two turning chain.

Half treble. Make 12 chain. Yarn round hook (Fig. 13), insert the hook in the third chain from the hook, yarn round hook and draw yarn through (three loops on hook) yarn round hook (Fig. 14) and draw yarn through all the loops on the hook. This makes one half treble (Fig. 15).

Half treble requires two turning chain.

Treble. Make 12 chain. Yarn round hook, insert hook in the fourth chain

Fig. 9 The finished slip stitch.

Fig. 1 Making a slip loop.

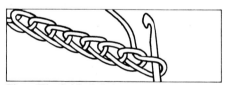
Fig. 5 The finished chain.

Fig. 10 Yarn round hook ready to make 4th double crochet.

Fig. 2 Holding hook like a pencil.

Fig. 6 Beginning the 1st row of stitches.

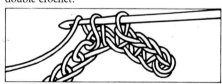
Fig. 11 2 loops on hook and yarn round hook.

Fig. 3 Winding yarn round left hand.

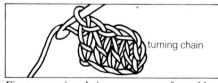
Fig. 7 3 turning chain are necessary for trebles.

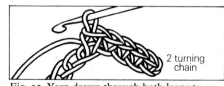
Fig. 12 Yarn drawn through both loops to complete.

Fig. 4 Winding yarn round hook.

Fig. 8 Yarn round hook ready for a slip stitch.

Fig. 13 Yarn round hook ready to start 4th half treble.

a

from the hook, yarn round hook and draw yarn through (three loops on hook), yarn round hook (Fig. 16) and draw through the first two loops (two loops on hook), yarn round hook (Fig. 17) and draw yarn through both loops (Fig. 18). This makes one treble.

Treble requires three turning chain.

Working into previous stitches

Viewed from above, the stitches have a chain formation along the top and in subsequent rows the hook is inserted under both threads of this chain as shown in Fig. 19.

Sometimes, however, the pattern requires a stitch to be worked either *between* stitches or into a space which is usually formed by chain and this would mean working *round* the chain (Fig. 20).

Sometimes, too, stitches are worked into either the back loop only (Fig. 21) or the front loop only (Fig. 22).

Working in the round

Sometimes crochet is worked in rounds instead of rows and the end result will generally be either circular or square.

To begin, make a length of chain and join to the first chain with a slip

stitch to make a circle (Fig. 23). Stitches are then usually worked into the centre of the circle rather than each individual chain.

Tension

There is much more variation between different people's tension in crochet than there is in knitting and it is therefore much more likely that the size of hook will have to be adjusted. The important thing is to get the correct number of stitches and rows to a given measurement so that the article works out to the required size.

Work a sample square to a minimum of 10 cm (4 in) square with the recommended hook size. If there are too many stitches try a larger hook, if too few, try a smaller hook.

Changing colour

To give a clear colour change, use the new colour for the last 'yarn round hook' of the last stitch in the old colour.

Crochet seams

To join two sections together by crocheting rather than sewing them, place the pieces right sides together. Pass the hook through both stitches of the edges, yarn round hook and draw through then draw the short end through this loop to secure.

Insert the hook through both these stitches again and draw the yarn through, insert the hook in the next two stitches, yarn round hook and draw through both the stitches and

the loop on the hook. Continue working in this way to the end (Fig. 24).

Filet crochet

This form of crochet works in rows of blocks and spaces which build up into geometric patterns. The stitches used are the same as in ordinary crochet but the instructions are given in chart form.

It begins as usual with a foundation chain. A block consists of three treble and a space is made with two chain separated from the next block or space by one treble. Once the first few rows are established with instructions written out in full it is very easy to follow the pattern through from a chart – easier, in fact, than wordy instructions.

Extra stitches are added by making a length of chain at the beginning of the row – three chain to stand for the new edge treble and one chain for each of the other extra stitches (Fig. 25).

To decrease, slip stitch across at the beginning of the row to the required place and begin with three chain to stand for the first treble (Fig. 26.)

Finishing off

After the last stitch, break off the yarn about 10 cm (4 in) from the hook and draw the end through the loop on the hook, pulling tight to secure.

Using a blunt-ended needle, darn the end along the back of the work for about 5 cm (2 in), working a back stitch at some point along the darn. Cut off the excess yarn.

Fig. 14 3 loops on hook and yarn round hook.

Fig. 15 Yarn drawn through 3 loops to complete.

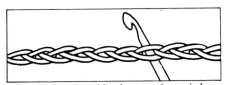
Fig. 19 Normal working into previous stitches.

Fig. 23 Joining to 1st chain with slip stitch.

Fig. 16 3 loops on hook and yarn round hook.

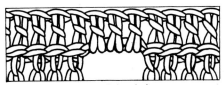
Fig. 20 Working round the chain.

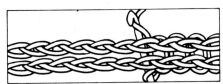
Fig. 24 Working a crochet seam.

Fig. 17 Yarn drawn through 2 loops and yarn round hook.

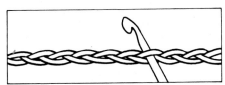
Fig. 21 Working into back loop only.

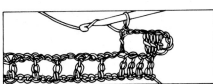
Fig. 25 Increasing at beginning of a row.

Fig. 18 Yarn drawn through next 2 loops to complete.

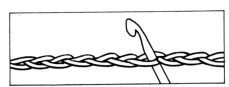
Fig. 22 Working into front loop only.

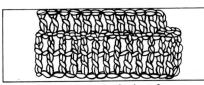
Fig. 26 Decreasing at beginning of a row.

Both the spectacle case and the slippersocks are worked in the round for minimum making up.

Abbreviations

Abbreviations will always be given at the beginning of a purchased pattern but these are some of the most commonly used:

beg – beginning
ch – chain
dc – double crochet
patt – pattern
rep – repeat
RS – right side
ss – slip stitch
sp – space
st(s) – stitch(es)
tr – treble
WS – wrong side
yrh – yarn round hook

Spectacle case

The simple cylinder shape of this spectacle case has many adaptations, some of which are suggested here. Worked in double crochet throughout, it is the ideal project for a beginner.

You will need
● Scraps of 4 ply wool in five toning shades, weighing 13 g ($\frac{1}{3}$ oz) altogether
● no. 3.00 crochet hook

Measurements
9 cm by 15 cm ($3\frac{1}{2}$ in by 6 in)
Tension
5 dc and $5\frac{1}{2}$ rows to 2.5 cm (1 in)

Instructions
All the techniques required for the crochet stitches in this project are given on pages 162 and 163.

Make 32 ch, join into a ring with a ss.

1st round 1 ch, 1 dc in each ch, ss to top of first ch. (32 sts.)

2nd round 1 ch, 1 dc in each st, ss to top of first ch.

Rep the second round working 5 rounds in each colour then another 5 rounds in the first colour.

To complete
Placing the seam line at one side, press the work under a damp cloth, using a warm iron.

Using the colour of the first and last stripes, work in dc through both thicknesses down the seam, across the bottom and up the other side on the fold, making 3 dc in the same st at each corner. Do not break off yarn.

Make ch for 55 cm (22 in), join with ss to first dc over seam.

Fasten off.

Adaptations
The basic pattern could be adapted for other items. A stronger, firmer fabric would be achieved by laying an extra thread across the top of the previous row from right to left and working over it. This would be advisable for the items suggested below and could be incorporated in the spectacle case, too, if desired.

Purse. This would measure 9 cm by 7.5 cm ($3\frac{1}{2}$ in by 3 in) and take 20 g ($\frac{2}{3}$ oz) of wool.

On 32 sts work 3 rounds in each of 5 colours then in the first colour work across 16 sts, turn, then 15 sts, turn and so on to make a flap, decreasing until 8 sts remain. Work round the purse and the flap in dc, making a small chain loop in the centre of the flap to go round a button, then make the cord.

Shoulder bag. This would measure 20 cm by 23 cm (8 in by 9 in) and take 100 g ($3\frac{1}{3}$ oz) of wool.

On 80 sts work 8 rounds in each of 5 colours and another 8 in the first colour. Work round the bag in dc as for the purse. Make a cord handle by using the yarn double to make 5 ch, join with a ss to make a circle, work 1 dc in each ch then 1 dc in the back loop only of each dc in a continuous spiral for the length required. Stitch the ends securely to the sides of the bag, trimming each one with a tassel.

Baby's slippersocks

These little socks have a suede sole which makes them ideal for the tot whose feet need protection but manages to shake off one shoe even before the second one is put on! They are mostly worked in double crochet with a star pattern square featured on the uppers.

You will need
● Suede leather 11 cm ($4\frac{1}{4}$ in) square
● leather punch
● scraps of 4 ply wool in four toning colours, weighing about 28 g (1 oz) in all
● no. 3.00 crochet hook

Measurements
Size 2
Tension
5 dc to 2.5 cm (1 in)

Instructions
All the techniques required for the crochet stitches in this project are given on pages 162 and 163. When

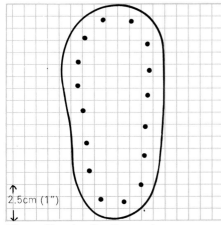

Fig. 27 Template for slippersock.

2.5cm (1")

changing colour, the ss at the end of the round is worked in the new colour for a tidy join.

Upper
Using colour A, make 3 ch, join into a ring with a ss.

1st round 3 ch, 2 tr into the centre of the ring, 1 ch, *3 tr into the ring, 1 ch, rep from * twice more, ss into third of 3 ch.

2nd round Ss across first 2 tr of previous round then, using colour B, ss into 1 ch sp, 2 ch, (1 htr, 1 ch, 2 htr) in 1 ch sp, (1 htr between tr) twice, *(2 htr, 1 ch, 2 htr) in 1 ch sp, (1 htr between tr) twice, rep from * twice more, join with ss to second of 2 ch.

3rd round Ss across next st then, using colour C, ss into 1 ch sp, 2 ch, (1 htr, 1 ch, 2 htr) in 1 ch sp, (1 htr between htr) 5 times, *(2 htr, 1 ch, 2 htr) in 1 ch sp, (1 htr between htr) 5 times, rep from * twice more, join with ss to second of 2 ch.
Fasten off.

Inner sole
Using D, make 16 ch.

1st round 1 dc into third ch from hook, 1 dc in each of next 12 ch, 5 dc in last ch, 13 dc down other side of ch, ss to top of turning ch.

2nd round 2 ch, working into the back loop only of the previous row throughout 1 dc in each of next 14 dc, 2 dc in each of next 4 dc, 1 dc in each of next 13 dc, 2 dc in next st, join with ss to top of 2 ch.

3rd round 2 ch, 1 dc in each of next 15 dc, (2 dc in next st, 1 dc in next st) 4 times, 1 dc in each of next 13 sts, 2 dc in next st, 1 dc in next st, join with ss to 2 ch.

4th round 2 ch, 1 dc in each of next 16 sts, (2 dc in next st, 1 dc in each of next 2 dc) 4 times, 1 dc in each of next 13 sts, 2 dc in next st, 1 dc in each of next 2 sts, join with ss to top of 2 ch.
This should make a sole to fit the template but if for reasons of tension it

does not fit, add or subtract a row.
Sock
Cut a cardboard template of the sole from Fig. 27.

Cut two soles, drawing round the template on the suede with ball-point pen.

Mark 16 holes spaced evenly round each sole and punch with the leather punch.

Using D, make 3 dc into each hole, starting at the centre back, join with a ss. Use a larger hook if necessary to keep the sole flat. Fasten off.

Place the woollen inner sole against the WS of the leather sole.

1st round Using B, draw the wool through the centre back stitch, 1 ch, crochet the soles together with dc going into the back loop only of each dc on the leather sole. (48 sts).

2nd and 3rd rounds 1 ch, 1 dc in each dc, ss to 1 ch.

4th round Using D, 1 ch, 1 dc in each of next 8 dc, then join in the upper by crocheting three sides of it together with the next 30 sts, 9 dc, ss to 1 ch.

5th round 1 ch, 8 dc, 10 dc across the instep (fourth side of square), 9 dc, ss to 1 ch.

6th to 22nd rounds Continue in rounds of 28 sts, working 5 rows B, 3 rows C, 3 rows B, 5 rows C and 6 rows B.

23rd round Continue in B to work 1 ch, miss 1 dc, *5 tr in next dc, miss 2 dc, 1 dc in next dc, miss 2 dc, rep from * 3 times more, 5 tr in next dc, miss 1 dc, ss to 1 ch.
Fasten off.

Bedspread

The closely worked crochet of this bedspread makes it extremely warm and weighty. As it is made up of squares to which a border is added it would easily adapt to any size of bed or cot.

***

You will need
Good quality dishcloth cotton:
- **Single bed.** 29 100 g hanks
- **Double bed.** 37 100 g hanks
- **Queen size bed.** 45 100 g hanks
- **King size bed.** 54 100 g hanks
- no. 4.00 crochet hook

***

Measurements
Single bed. Approx. 200 cm by 250 cm (6 ft by 8 ft)
Double bed. Approx. 250 cm (8 ft) square

Queen size bed. Approx. 250 cm by 300 cm (8 ft by 10 ft)
King size bed. Approx. 300 cm (10 ft) square
Note: in-between sizes can be achieved by using a larger or smaller hook or by adding or subtracting rounds. For example, to make 25 cm (10 in) squares for a cot, work only rounds 1 to 13
Tension
7 tr to 5 cm (2 in)

Instructions
All the techniques required for the crochet stitches in this project are given on pages 162 and 163.
Squares
Work into the back loop only throughout.

Make 6 ch, join into a ring with a ss.

1st round 3 ch, 15 tr into the centre of the ring, ss to top of 3 ch.

2nd round *3 ch, miss one st, 1 dc in each of next 3 sts, rep from * 3 times more.

3rd round *3 ch, miss one st, 2 tr in next st, 1 tr in each of next 3 sts, 2 tr in next st, rep from * 3 times more.

4th round *3 ch, miss one st, 1 dc in each of the next 9 sts, rep from * 3 times more.

5th round *3 ch, miss one st, 2 tr in next st, 1 tr in each of next 9 sts, 2 tr in next st, rep from * 3 times more.

6th round *3 ch, miss one st, 1 dc in each of next 15 sts, rep from * 3 times more.

7th round *3 ch, miss one st, 2 tr in next st, 1 tr in each of next 15 sts, 2 tr in next st, rep from * 3 times more.

8th round *3 ch, miss one st, 1 dc in each of next 2 sts, 3 ch, (yrh, insert hook in next st, yrh and draw through, yrh and draw through two loops on hook) twice, yrh and draw through two loops, yrh, insert hook in same st, yrh and draw through, (yrh and draw through two loops) 3 times – 1 bobble made – **1 dc in each of next 3 dc, 1 bobble in next st, rep from ** 3 times more, 1 dc in each of next 2 dc, rep from * 3 times more.

9th round *3 ch, miss one st, 2 tr in next st, 1 tr in each of next 21 sts, 2 tr in next st, rep from * 3 times more.

10th round *3 ch, miss one st, 1 dc in each of next 27 sts, rep from * 3 times more.

11th round *3 ch, miss one st, 2 tr in next st, 1 tr in each of next 27 sts, 2 tr in next st, rep from * 3 times more.

12th round *3 ch, miss one st, 1 dc in each of next 33 sts, rep from * 3 times more.

13th round *3 ch, miss one st, (1

The curtains echo the pattern of the squares in
the bedspread and the two are linked by an
identical border.

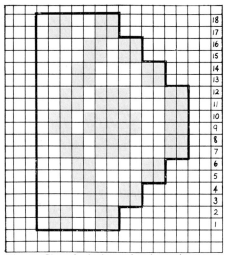

Fig. 28 Chart for bedspread and curtain border.

tr, 1 ch, 1 tr) all in next st, (1 ch, miss one st, 1 tr in next st) 16 times, 1 ch, miss one st, (1 tr, 1 ch, 1 tr) all in next st, rep from * 3 times more.

14th round *3 ch, miss one st, 1 dc in each of next 41 sts, rep from * 3 times more.

15th round *3 ch, miss one st, 2 tr in next st, 1 tr in each of next 41 sts, 2 tr in next st, rep from * 3 times more.

16th round *3 ch, miss one st, 1 dc in each of next 47 sts, rep from * 3 times more.

17th round *3 ch, miss one st, 2 tr in next st, 1 tr in each of next 47 sts, 2 tr in next st, rep from * 3 times more.

18th round *3 ch, miss one st, 1 dc in each of next 2 sts, 1 bobble in next st, (1 dc in each of next 3 sts, 1 bobble in next st) 12 times, 1 dc in each of next 2 sts, rep from * 3 times more.

19th round *3 ch, miss one st, 2 tr in next st, 1 tr in each of next 53 sts, 2 tr in next st, rep from * 3 times more.

20th round *3 ch, miss one st, 1 dc in each of next 59 sts, rep from * 3 times more.

21st round *3 ch, miss one st, 2 tr in next st, 1 tr in each of next 59 sts, 2 tr in next st, rep from * 3 times more, 2 ch, ss to top of first tr.

22nd round 4 ch, 1 tr in same st, 1 ch, 1 tr in next st, (1 ch, miss one st, 1 tr in next st) 30 times, 1 ch, miss one st, (1 tr, 1 ch, 1 tr) all in next st, *3 ch, miss one st, (1 tr, 1 ch, 1 tr) all in next st, (1 ch, miss one st, 1 tr in next st) 31 times, 1 ch, miss one st, (1 tr, 1 ch, 1 tr) in next st, rep from * twice more, 3 ch, ss to third of 4 ch.

Border

Make 23 ch. Work in both loops of each st in the usual way throughout.

1st row 1 tr in 4th ch from hook, 1 tr in each of next 4 ch, 2 ch, miss 2 ch, 1 tr in next ch, 2 ch, miss 2 ch, 1 tr in

each of next 7 ch, 2 ch, miss 2 ch, 1 tr in next ch, turn.

2nd row 5 ch, 1 tr in each of next 7 tr, 2 ch, 1 tr in next tr, 2 ch, 1 tr in each of next 5 tr, 1 tr in top of 3 ch.

Continue working from chart (Fig. 28), starting at row 1 again but thereafter only repeating rows 1 to 18.

Single bed. Work two lengths of 6 patt repeats each and two lengths of 8 patts repeats each.

Double bed. Work 4 lengths of 8 patt repeats each.

Queen size bed. Work 2 lengths of 8 patt repeats each and 2 lengths of 10 patt repeats each.

King size bed. Work 4 lengths of 10 patt repeats each.

All sizes. Always work the first 2 rows of the pattern repeat twice at the beginning only of each length of border.

To complete

Single bed. Make 12 squares and join into 4 rows of 3 squares each.

Double bed. Make 16 squares and join into 4 rows of 4 squares each.

Queen size bed. Make 20 squares and join into 5 rows of 4 squares each.

King size bed. Make 25 squares and join into 5 rows of 5 squares each.

All sizes. Either sew or crochet the squares together, right sides facing. Add the borders in the same way, ending the ends of each border piece level with the outer edge of the squares.

Curtains

The pattern of these curtains echoes that in the bedspread so that they would look well together.

You will need
- Good quality dishcloth cotton: one 100 g hank per 90 cm (36 in) of each patt repeat
- no. 4.00 crochet hook
- curtain tape to the curtain width

Measurements

Each patt is 50 cm (20 in) wide.

The curtains are very heavy and will drop for at least three days after hanging, getting narrower in the process.

For example, the curtains illustrated have 3 patt repeats across each. They were 150 cm (60 in) wide and 170 cm (68 in) long before hanging. After three days they measured 100 cm (40 in) by 185 cm (74 in).

To calculate the number of patterns to repeat, add half the required finished width. For example, for a curtain 90

cm (36 in) wide, crochet one 135 cm (54 in) wide. Deduct about 15 cm (6 in) from the required length.

Border. 20 cm (8 in) deep.

Tension

8 tr to 5 cm (2 in)

Instructions

All the techniques required for the crochet stitches in this project are given on pages 162 and 163.

Main section

For the first patt make 75 ch and add 68 ch for each additional patt repeat.

1st row 1 tr in the seventh ch from hook, *1 tr in each of next 12 ch, 2 ch, miss 2 ch, 1 tr in each of next 36 ch, 2 ch, miss 2 ch, 1 tr in each of next 13 ch, 2 ch, miss 2 ch, 1 tr in next ch, rep from * to end, turn.

2nd row Work into the back loop only throughout the row. 4 ch to count as first dc and 2 ch sp, *1 dc in each of next 6 tr, 3 ch, (yrh, insert hook in next tr, yrh and draw through, yrh and draw through 2 loops on hook) twice, yrh and draw through 2 loops, yrh, insert hook in same st, yrh and draw through, (yrh and draw through 2 loops) 3 times – called 1 bobble – 1 dc in each of next 6 tr, 2 ch, miss 2 ch, 1 dc in each of next 6 tr, 1 bobble in next tr, 1 dc in each of next 22 tr, 1 bobble in next tr, 1 dc in each of next 6 tr, 2 ch, miss 2 ch, 1 dc in each of next 6 tr, 1 bobble in next tr, 1 dc in each of next 6 tr, rep from * ending last (or only) repeat 2 ch, miss 2 ch, 1 dc in third of 5 ch.

3rd row Work into the front loop only of each st throughout the row. 5 ch, *1 tr in each of next 13 sts, 2 ch, miss 2 ch, 1 tr in each of next 36 sts, 2 ch, miss 2 ch, 1 tr in each of next 13 sts, 2 ch, miss 2 ch, rep from * ending last repeat 1 tr in second of 4 ch.

Rep the second and third rows for the length required.

Border

Work as given for Bedspread (see left).

Heading

Join in yarn to the foundation chain of the Main Section and work in alternate rows of dc and tr to the depth of the curtain tape.

To complete

Machine the tape to the heading, tape uppermost and using the largest stitch.

Press the edges under a damp cloth using a warm iron.

Hang up the curtain for three days. After it has dropped, measure the length and add on the depth of the border, then either undo or add a few rows, as required.

Sew on the border.

Knitting

Knitting is one of the oldest crafts with known examples dating from ancient Egyptian times. It was spread throughout Europe by the Crusaders and sailors, with the result that fishing villages particularly have had a long tradition of knitting. In 16th century France, professional knitters served a three-year apprenticeship although this should not put off the would-be learner of today. The early Victorians were actually legally obliged to teach their children, boys and girls, to knit.

In its simplest form, knitting is an easy craft to learn which can provide relaxation as well as an economic and creative source of clothes and household items. It can, however, be developed into an art form with endless creative satisfaction.

Both aspects of the craft are covered here, giving a beginner the basic necessary grounding and, hopefully, inspiring the more experienced to expand the scope of their ideas.

Materials and Equipment

Knitting needles come in a variety of shapes: thin, thick, double-ended and circular, mostly in pairs. However, only a few, usually just one pair, are needed for any one project although a collection can be built up over a long period as the requirements of different projects vary. The choice of needle depends on the yarn being used.

Knitting yarn is available in assorted balls and cones of different thicknesses and textures. It can be of natural fibres or man-made. Often the thickness is described as 'ply' with a number, the lower the number the finer the yarn. A 2-ply yarn consists of two threads twisted together as one, a 3-ply has three strands and so on. Four-ply is the thickest, next comes double-knitting, triple-knitting, double-double-knitting and thicker-knit although nowadays many yarns have a non-generic trade name.

A stitch-holder is like a very large safety pin and is used to hold stitches which are not required until later. Sometimes a spare needle will suffice although there is always the risk of stitches falling off but this can be avoided by winding a rubber band on to the end of the needle.

General items can include a large wool sewing needle, tape measure, scissors, ruler, dressmakers' pins, needle gauge, row counter, paper, pencils, pens and graph paper.

Know how

This basic knowledge of knitting is all that is required to produce the most beautiful and complex patterns. However, it takes experience to achieve an even tension so practise making small sample squares first or simple articles such as the liquorice all-sorts before going on to anything more ambitious.

Casting on

To practise, the learner should choose thick wool and use large needles about 7 mm (no. 2).

Make a slip loop near the end of the yarn (Fig. 1) and pull it up firmly round the end of one needle, held in the left hand.

Hold the long end of the wool with the right hand and wind it round the fingers as shown in Fig. 2. With practice this will come automatically and will ensure an even tension.

Keep the yarn to the back of the right hand needle and with the right hand, insert the right hand needle into the slip loop below the left hand needle. Wind the wool under and over the right hand needle (Fig. 3). Pull the new loop through the first loop (Fig. 4) and place it on to the left hand needle (Fig. 5), pulling it close round the needle to match the first loop.

Insert the needle between the two stitches (Fig. 6), then wind the wool over and under again to make the third loop in the same way.

Continue in this way until the required number of stitches has been cast on.

The knit stitch

Knitting is worked from right to left. Hold the needle with the stitches in the left hand and place the point of the right hand needle from front to back through the first stitch, holding the yarn and the needle with the right hand as before. Wind the wool under and over as for casting on. Pull the new loop through as before but keeping it on the right hand needle and slipping the end stitch off the left hand needle.

Place the right hand needle into the next stitch and work as before. Continue in this way to the end of the row.

When all the stitches are on the right hand needle, turn it round and hold it in the left hand.

When every row is worked in knit stitches it is called garter stitch. The finish is identical on both sides (Fig. 7).

The purl stitch

Hold the needles as before but with the yarn at the front. Insert the right hand needle from right to left into the front of the stitch. Wind the wool over and under the right hand needle (Fig. 8) and pull the new loop through the old one which is then slipped off the left hand needle (Fig. 9).

Working in all purl will also produce garter stitch but the tension will not be so even.

Stocking stitch

The right side of stocking stitch is smooth (Fig. 10) and the wrong, or purl, side more textured (Fig. 11). It is produced by alternating one row of plain knitting with one row of purl knitting throughout.

Sometimes the purl side is used as the right side and this is then called reversed stocking stitch.

Patterned stitches

All knitted stitches, however fancy, are basically made up of knitted or

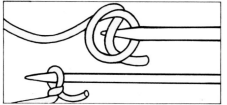
Fig. 1 Making a slip loop.

Fig. 2 Winding wool round fingers of right hand.

Fig. 3 Winding wool under and over right hand needle.

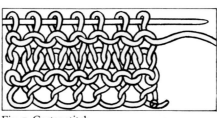
Fig. 4 Pulling new loop through 1st loop.

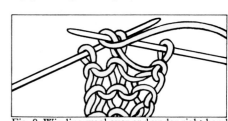
Fig. 5 Placing new loop over left hand needle.

Fig. 6 Inserting needle between 1st 2 stitches.

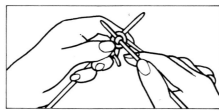
Fig. 7 Garter stitch.

Fig. 8 Winding wool over and under right hand needle for purl stitch.

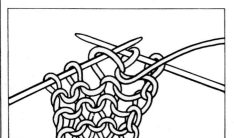
Fig. 9 Pulling a new loop through the old one.

Fig. 10 Right side of stocking stitch.

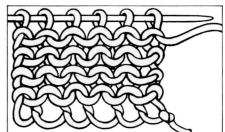
Fig. 11 Wrong or purl side of stocking stitch.

purled stitches. They are either knitted into the front of the stitch or they are knitted into the back of the stitch to twist it. Similarly, they can be purled into the front of the stitch or purled into the back of the stitch to twist it.

Moss stitch (or seed stitch)
A two row pattern. 1st row: begin with one knit, then one purl and alternate to end of row. 2nd row: reverse sequence and purl one, knit one to end.

Daisy stitch
A four row pattern. 1st row: knit. 2nd row: knit one, * purl 3 together, pass yarn round needle, purl same 3 stitches together again, knit one and repeat from * to end. Knit the 3rd row. 4th row: knit one, purl one, knit one, * purl 3 together, pass yarn round needle, purl same 3 stitches together again, knit one, repeat from * ending purl one, knit one.

Decreasing
The simplest method of decreasing is to knit two stitches together and this can be done either into the front or back of the stitches. Similarly, two stitches can be purled together, either into the front or back as instructed.

Increasing
One method of increasing the number of stitches is to knit or purl into a stitch twice. On a knit stitch, knit as usual without slipping it off the needle then knit into the back of the same stitch, keeping the yarn at the back of the work. On a purl stitch, purl as usual without slipping it off the needle and purl into the back of the same stitch, keeping the yarn at the front of the work.

Another way of making a stitch is to lay the yarn over the needle between two stitches then on the next row this extra loop is worked normally, thus producing an extra stitch.

Slip stitch
Sometimes stitches are slipped from the left hand needle to the right hand one without knitting or purling them. Insert the right hand needle into the stitch in the usual way and then slip it off the left hand needle without winding the yarn round.

Cabling
When one or more stitches are twisted around another stitch or stitches, the effect is like a twisted rope or cable. Slip the stitches on to a cable needle, which is a short double-pointed needle, work the next stitch or stitches and then work the stitches from the cable needle. The direction of the twist depends on whether the cable needle is held at the front or the back of the work.

Casting off
Casting off secures all the stitches on the last row of the work.

Knit the first two stitches, insert the left hand needle into the first of these and lift it over the second and so off the right hand needle. Knit the third stitch as usual and pass the second over the third. Continue in this way until the last stitch is left on the right hand needle. Break off the yarn and pull it through the loop to secure.

Intarsia
This technique is very important in picture knitting. It means knitting with two or more colours in any one row without taking the yarns across the back of the work. If a colour appears more than once in the row, separate balls are used and the back will be almost identical to the front.

Intarsia is usually knitted from a graph. This is very easy as each small square represents one stitch. Read from the bottom row upwards from right to left when the right side of the work is facing, left to right for the wrong side. Change stitch, colour or yarn as indicated on the graph.

At the join between two colours or different yarns, twist the two around each other firmly at the back of the work to link the sections before finishing the rest of the row.

Tension
The number of stitches and rows which, when worked on a specified size of needle, add up to a given measurement in either centimetres or inches is called the tension. When knitting garments this information, given at the beginning of the instructions, is crucial. Unless the knitter achieves the same tension as the designer, the garment will not fit for just one stitch out per centimetre (inch) can add up to a whole different size over the entire garment. This is why working a tension square is so important and why substituting yarns is rarely satisfactory unless the tension can be matched.

However, on projects such as the ones in this section, measurements are not vital and for this reason, none have been given. Although a needle size is given, this can only be taken as a guide because the yarn is only described in general terms. Quantities, too, may differ. Check on the ball band where the recommended needle size and tension may be given.

Abbreviations
cn	cable needle
dec	decrease
g st	garter stitch
inc	increase
K	knit
P	purl
psso	pass slipped stitch over
rep	repeat
RS	right side
sl	slip
st(s)	stitch(es)
st st	stocking stitch
tbl	through back of loop(s)
tog	together
WS	wrong side
wyif	with yarn in front
yrn	yarn round needle

Liquorice all-sort soft sculpture

This beginner's project produces quick, cheerful results which will encourage a child or first-time knitter. The garter stitch fabric is worked in thick wool with large needles.

Liquorice all-sorts make soft and colourful toys.

These liquorice all-sorts would be ideal as soft toys when packed with Kapok or crumbled foam. However, the cubes are a better shape if filled with a cube of solid foam and the cylinders are better with cardboard ends inside or filled with a thin flat piece of foam rolled up tightly and sewn in position.

If multiplied by three, the instructions would produce larger cubes and cylinders which, again filled with solid foam cut to size, would be suitable for do-it-yourself seating. A cube with a cylinder at the back would make a single seat, whilst two or three would make a sofa. The pink liquorice all-sort stood on end would make a pouffe.

To change colour on garter stitch, decide which side of the reversible fabric is to be the right side and always work the first row of a new colour on the same side.

You will need
- One pair 7 mm needles (no. 2)
- large bag of crumbled foam for filling or solid foam cubes
thick knit yarn, approximately:
  Black and orange cube.
- 100 g (3½ oz) black
- 50 g (2 oz) orange
  Yellow and black cube.
- 200 g (7 oz) yellow
- 50 g (2 oz) black
  Black and white liquorice all-sort.
- 100 g (3½ oz) black
- 50 g (2 oz) white
  Round black and white liquorice all-sort.
- 100 g (3½ oz) black
- 50 g (2 oz) white
  Round pink and black liquorice all-sort.
- 200 g (7 oz) pink
- 50 g (2 oz) black
  To make all five pieces.
- 350 g (13 oz) black
- 50 g (2 oz) white
- 200 g (7 oz) pink
- 50 g (2 oz) orange
- 200 g (7 oz) yellow

Instructions
Black and orange cube
Side pieces (knit 4)
Using black, cast on 22 sts. Work in g st.
K 8 rows black, 8 rows orange, 8 rows black, 8 rows orange and 8 rows black.
Cast off.
End pieces (knit 2)
Using black, cast on 22 sts.
K 40 rows.
Cast off.
To complete
Do not press. Sew up the cube leaving one seam open, fill with crumbled foam or solid foam and sew up the remaining edge.

Yellow and black cube
Side pieces (knit 4)
Using yellow, cast on 22 sts.
K 16 rows yellow, 8 rows black and 16 rows yellow.
Cast off.
End pieces (knit 2)
Using yellow, cast on 22 sts.
K 40 rows.
Cast off.
To complete
As given for black and orange cube.

Black and white liquorice all-sort
Side pieces (knit 4)

Using black, cast on 22 sts.
K 8 rows black, 8 rows white and 8 rows black.
Cast off.
End pieces (knit 2)
Using black, cast on 22 sts.
K 40 rows.
Cast off.
To complete
As black and orange cube.

Round black and white liquorice all-sort
Side piece (knit 1)
Using black, cast on 22 sts.
K 80 rows.
Leave sts on a holder with a length of yarn sufficient for sewing up.
End pieces (knit 2)
These round end pieces have a white circle in the middle of the black. Its position is indicated on Fig. 12(a). Each small square represents one stitch. Use two separate small balls of black and one of white, twisting the ends of the two colours where they meet. The back will look like a series of white running stitches around the inner edge of the black circle.
To complete
Neaten the four ends of yarn on the back of the intarsia circles. Sew up the cylinder. Sew in one end and half of the second end. Fill with crumbled foam or rolled up sheet foam and sew up remaining opening.

Round pink and black liquorice all-sort
Side piece (knit 1)
Using pink, cast on 22 sts.
K 140 rows.
Leave sts on a holder with a length of yarn for sewing up.
End pieces (knit 2)
Follow Fig. 12(b), using the intarsia method.
To complete
As given for previous cylinder.

Pegbag

This project introduces picture knitting using simple appliquéd shapes to form an image. Several new stitches are introduced but they are all very simple.

You will need
- Two pieces of bamboo garden cane each about 30 cm (12 in) long, for handles
- one pair 4 mm (no. 8) needles
- one cable needle, preferably the same size

Fig. 12 (a) Graph for black and white end and (b) for pink and black end.

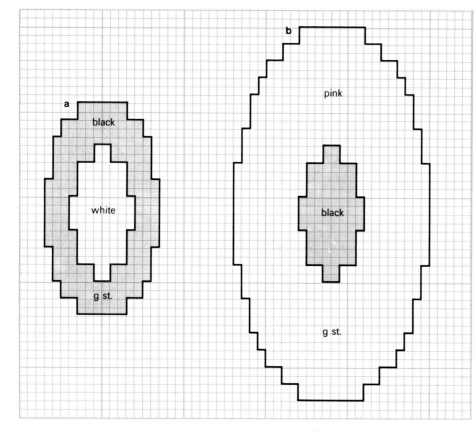

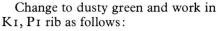

double knitting wool:
- 50 g (2 oz) pale blue for sky
- 100 g (3½ oz) dark brown for back, border, handles and tassels
- oddments of dusty green for hedge bottom, dark green for tree, mid-brown for tree trunk, beige, orange and dark blue for jumpers and mid-green for top of hedge and bits of tree

Instructions
Front
Using blue, cast on 52 sts.
Work in st st for 92 rows.

Change to dark brown and work in st st for 18 rows.
Cast off.

Back
Using dark brown, cast on 52 sts.
Work in st st for 92 rows.
Change to dark green and st st for 18 rows.
Cast off.

Hedge
Using mid-green, cast on 50 sts.
Work in moss stitch as follows:
1st row *K1, P1, rep from * to end.
2nd row *P1, K1, rep from * to end.
Rep 1st and 2nd rows five times more.

Change to dusty green and work in K1, P1 rib as follows:
*K1, P1, rep from * to end.
Rep this row three times more.
Cast off.

Tree trunk
Using mid-brown, cast on 7 sts.
Work 48 rows in mock rib as follows:
1st row (WS) K1, *P1, K1, rep from * to end.
2nd row P1, *sl 1 wyif (purlwise), P1, rep from *.
Cast off.

Tree top
Using dark green, cast on 13 sts and work in st st to the shape of Fig. 13. The surface texture in mid-green is achieved by wrapping the contrast colour around sets of 3 sts, marked on the graph, as follows:
1st row K.
2nd row P.
3rd row *K1, K next 3 sts then transfer them to cn, wind contrast yarn 6 times clockwise (looking down from the top) round these 3 sts under cn, return the sts to the right hand needle (called cluster 3) rep from * ending K1. Run the contrast colour yarn across the back of the knitting from one cluster to the next. Break it off at the end of each row.
Continue to work from the graph in this way.

Beige jumper (knit one)
Using beige, cast on 8 sts.
1st row *K1 tbl, P1 tbl, rep from * to end.
2nd row *K1, P1, rep from * to end.
K 6 rows in st st.
9th row Cast on an extra 4 sts and K across all 12 sts.
10th row Cast on an extra 4 sts, P across all 16 sts.
K 8 rows in st st.
19th row Cast off 4 sts, K to end.
20th row Cast off 4 sts, P to end.
K 6 rows in st st.
K 2 rows in K1, P1 rib.
Cast off.

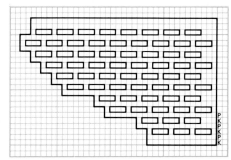

Fig. 13 Graph for tree top shape.

Left Soft sculpture knitted in garter stitch using bright colours and simple shapes.

Striped jumper (knit one)

Body. Using orange, cast on 16 sts and work in g st for *2 rows orange, 2 rows blue, 2 rows beige, rep from * then work 2 rows orange.

Cast off.

Sleeves (knit 2). Using orange, cast on 6 sts and work in g st for 2 rows orange, 2 rows blue, 2 rows beige, 2 rows orange, 2 rows blue.

Cast off.

Washing line

Using beige, make a thin twisted cord about 20 cm (8 in) long.

Front border

Using dark brown, cast on 192 sts loosely. Do this by knitting into each stitch, instead of between stitches.

K 8 rows g st.

Cast off.

Handles (knit 2)

Using dark brown, cast on 14 sts.

K 150 rows in st st to measure about 50 cm (20 in) long.

Cast off.

Facing (knit 2)

Using dark brown, cast on 40 sts.

K 8 rows in g st.

Cast off.

To complete

Pin out the back and front of the bag and turn over the contrast colour casing for the handles, using the reverse side of stocking stitch for the right side of the picture. Press under a damp cloth using a warm iron.

Press the beige jumper and the handles. Gently press the tree trunk and tree top but do not press any garter stitch.

Sew the handle casings in place. Sew the short sides of the border edge to edge and stretch it around the blue background.

Sew down the border with the tighter cast-off edge inside and the slacker cast-on edge on the outside.

Assemble the picture inside the border and sew down the tree trunk and the tree top. Place the hedge in position, easing up the rib base to fit and pulling up the top of the hedge into rounded shapes. When satisfied with the look of the hedge, carefully stretch and shrink it into place by pressing it under a damp cloth using a warm iron, then sew it in place.

Sew up the little jumpers and press the beige one flat. Press the striped one gently if it looks too 'fat'.

Lay the washing line across the picture. Catch it into place behind the border and on the tree trunk. Embroider the two jumpers on at the shoulders to represent pegs.

Sew back and front of bag together leaving about 8 cm (3 in) open each side below handles. Sew the facing inside to strengthen and neaten the appearance of the bag when open. Sew up the handles. Insert bamboo into the slots and sew the ends of the handles firmly around the ends of the bamboo.

Make two tassels in left-over colours and sew below the woollen handles, one on each side of the front of the bag.

Picture bedspread

This picture bedspread is simpler than it looks as it is made in several sections using thick Aran wool. The central picture is pure intarsia and a completely different image can be knitted by graphing the scene of your choice, real or imaginary, abstract or figurative. It does have to fit in with the border pieces though, so it must be in the same wool and have the same number of stitches and rows as the original.

Left The pegbag is knitted in simple stitches, with more advanced stitches in the appliquéd shapes. **Right** A bedspread gives plenty of scope for large picture knitting. The central section is pure intarsia and is knitted from a graph.

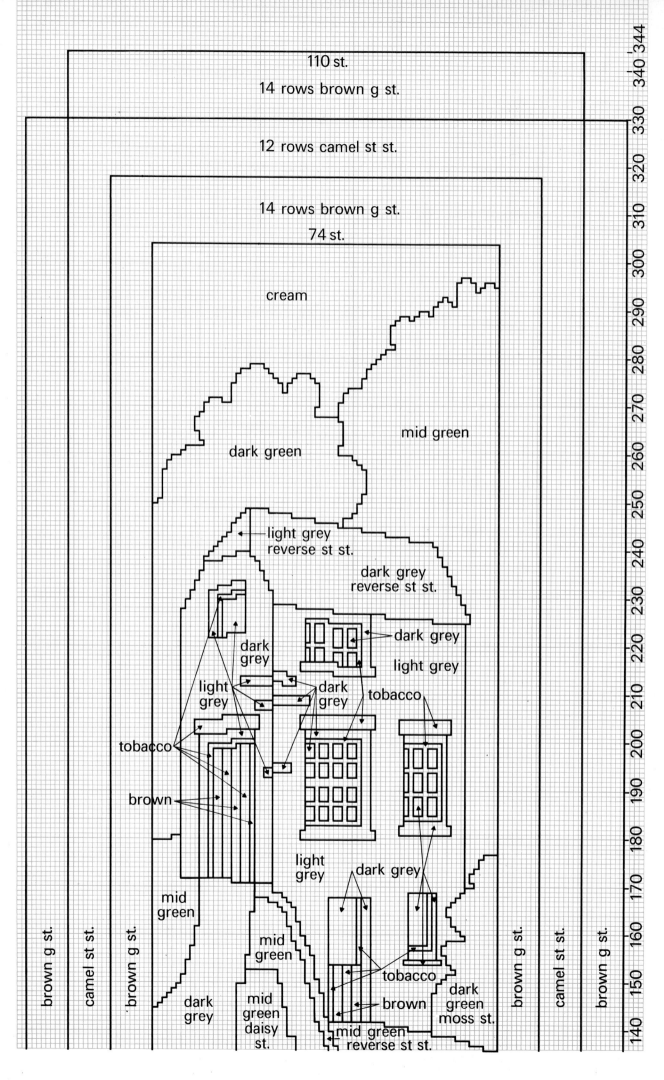

110 st.

14 rows brown g st.

12 rows camel st st.

14 rows brown g st.

74 st.

cream

mid green

dark green

light grey
reverse st st.

dark grey
reverse st st.

dark
grey

dark grey

light grey

light
grey

dark
grey

tobacco

tobacco

brown

light
grey

dark grey

mid
green

mid
green

tobacco

brown

mid green
reverse st st.

dark
grey

mid
green
daisy
st.

dark
green
moss st.

brown g st.

camel st st.

brown g st.

brown g st.

camel st st.

brown g st.

140
150
160
170
180
190
200
210
220
230
240
250
260
270
280
290
300
310
320
330
340 344

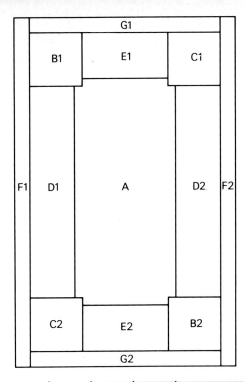

You will need
- Two pairs 6 mm (no. 4) needles

Aran wool:
- 1,350 g (48 oz) brown
- 1,000 g (35½ oz) cream
- 350 g (12½ oz) camel
- 200 g (7 oz) mid green
- 150 g (5½ oz) dark grey
- 50 g (2 oz) dark green
- 50 g (2 oz) light grey
- 50 g (2 oz) ginger

Fig. 14 **Above** Key to bedspread sections.
Fig. 15 **Opposite** and **below** Graph for section A of the bedspread in two sections.

Instructions
Fig. 14 shows the different sections in which the bedspread is worked.

Section A

Transfer Fig. 15 to graph paper joining the two sections for ease of working. Work from the graph taking care to cross the yarns firmly at the back of the work so that no loose stitches appear.

Sections B1 and B2

Work from Fig. 16 and starting at A, cast on 2 sts, using camel.

Working in st st, inc one st at each end of every row until there are 30 sts.

Dec one st at each end of every row until 2 sts remain.

Cross one st over the other and pull yarn through to form corner B.

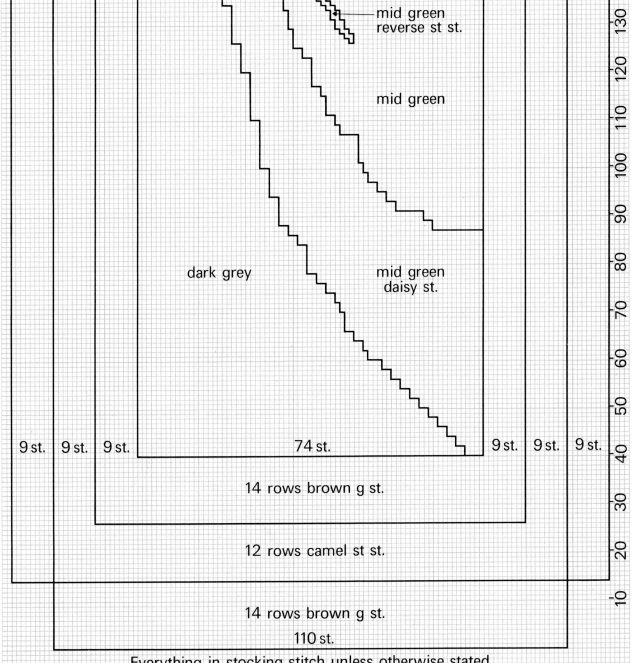

mid green
reverse st st.

mid green

dark grey

mid green
daisy st.

9 st.   9 st.   9 st.   74 st.   9 st.   9 st.   9 st.

14 rows brown g st.

12 rows camel st st.

14 rows brown g st.

110 st.

Everything in stocking stitch unless otherwise stated.
Fancy stitch instructions given previously.

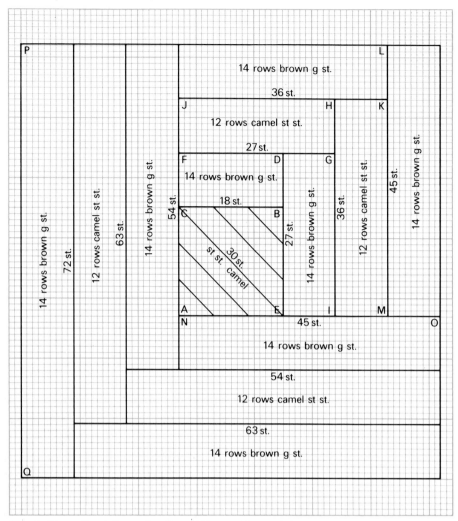

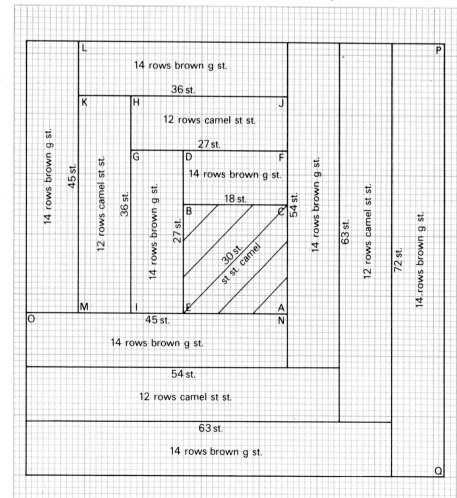

Fig. 16 **Above** Graph for sections B1 and B2.   Fig. 17 **Below** Graph for sections C1 and C2.

Using brown and with RS facing, pick up 18 sts along edge C to B.

K 13 rows in g st. Leave work on needle and break off yarn.

Using the second pair of needles and brown, pick up 27 sts along edge D to E.

K 13 more rows in g st, leave sts on needle and break off yarn.

Return to previous sts and, using camel, K 18 sts from F to D and pick up 9 more sts from D to G (27 sts).

Work 11 more rows in st st, leave sts on needle and break off yarn.

Using camel, pick up 9 sts from H to G and K across 27 sts from G to I (36 sts).

K 11 more rows in st st, leave sts on needle and break off yarn.

Using brown, K across 27 sts from J to K and pick up 9 sts from H to K (36 sts).

K 13 more rows in g st, leave sts on a holder and break off yarn.

Using brown, pick up 9 sts from L to K and knit across 36 sts from K to M (45 sts).

K 13 more rows in g st, leave sts on holder and break off yarn.

Continue the other half of this square as indicated on the graph, starting at N/O in brown and ending at P/Q in brown.

Sections C1 and C2
These pieces are a mirror image of corners B1 and B2, worked from Fig. 17.

Sections D1 and D2
Using cream, cast on 63 sts.

K 316 rows in st st and leave on a spare length of yarn.

Sections E1 and E2
Using cream, cast on 63 sts.

K 150 rows in st st and leave on a spare length of yarn.

Sections F1 and F2
Using brown, cast on 18 sts.

K in g st to fit top edge.

Cast off loosely.

Sections G1 and G2
Using brown, cast on 18 sts.

K in g st to fit side edges, including top edges.

Leave sts on spare length of wool.

To complete
Neaten off all the loose ends on the back of the work.

Press the picture carefully under a damp cloth, avoiding the g st areas. Press corner pieces, avoiding g st. Press the st st side pieces very firmly.

Sew up the pieces as carefully as possible, working from the central picture outwards. Do not spoil the final effect by rushing this very important finishing off process. Press.

Canvas work

Canvas work, as the name implies, is embroidery worked on canvas. It can include many different textured stitches but in this section we use only tent stitch – the simplest, most basic canvas work stitch of all.

Canvas work has been known in Europe since the early 16th century although from the middle of the 18th century until fairly recently, its popularity faded. It is also one of the most popular forms of embroidery in America today where it is known as Needlepoint if only tent stitch is used.

The simplicity of the stitch leaves wide scope for design and our four projects are intended to encourage the use of canvas work on a more adventurous scale than usual. They are mostly made up of small pieces of canvas, the advantage being that they can easily be carried around and worked on at odd moments. Larger pieces are more limited in this respect and have to be carefully handled and stored so that very often they become a half finished white elephant. The speed of results on something small is encouraging to a beginner and larger projects should be left until technical ability and confidence are established.

Materials and Equipment

The canvas used in all the projects is double thread canvas, either ten holes or five holes to 2.5 cm (1 in).

The thread used is 100 per cent tapestry wool, which is colour fast, moth resistant and available in a good range of colours.

Tapestry needles, both large and small, are used in canvas work: a darning needle may be substituted for a large tapestry needle. Always use a needle which can fall through the canvas holes without being pushed but which at the same time has an eye large enough to take the wool.

A canvas work frame is optional as the work can be done free hand but the larger the canvas is, the better it is to use a frame. However, even if the completed canvas has pulled out of alignment, it can be stretched back into shape.

White paper is used for designing.

Black felt tip pen is best to outline the designs on paper.

Laundry marker (ironed to fix the ink) and tailor's chalk are used to mark out the designs on the canvas.

Sewing needle and thread are used to help mark out the designs and also to lace the canvas over hardboard before framing.

A piece of wood or similar rigid material, slightly larger than the canvas, acts as a base for ironing the canvas. An ironing board could be used instead.

Two pieces of clean white cloth, which can take a hot iron, are required when ironing the canvas, one to cover the wood and one to cover the canvas.

Drawing pins or dressmakers' pins are used to secure the canvas and base cloth to the wood or ironing board.

Hardboard is used as a rigid backing for the canvas if it is to be framed.

Picture frames with their hard edges make a very good contrast to the soft surface of the canvas work. A well made wood or metal frame makes all the difference to the finished piece but it is best not to use glass in the frame as much of the quality of the embroidery would be lost. Avoid hanging the finished work where it would get dirty such as above an open fire or radiator.

Impact glue can be used for fixing the canvas to the hardboard at the back when framing.

General items can include small, sharp pointed scissors, tape measure and ruler.

Know how

Beginning a new thread
Do not knot the wool. If beginning a new canvas, leave a loose end at the back which can be threaded in later. If part of the canvas has already been worked, thread the needle through the previously worked stitches at the back before beginning work with the new thread. All rows are worked from right to left. Begin each area of colour in the upper right hand corner.

Tent stitch – gros point
Bring the needle up into a large hole at the upper right hand corner of the area to be worked. Pass the thread diagonally over the face of the canvas from that hole to another in the row below but one space to the left. Insert the needle in the hole and bring it out through the large hole immediately above and which is to the left of the first hole (Fig. 1). In the next row the tops of the stitches go into the same holes as the bottoms of the stitches in the previous row.

Tent stitch – petit point
This is a variation on gros point in which a stitch is made through every hole in the canvas, both big and small, thereby making four stitches where before there was only one. This makes a firmer surface which will wear better and creates a more detailed effect.

Bring the needle up in a large hole as before. Pass the thread diagonally over the face of the canvas and insert the needle in the small hole in the row below and immediately to the left of the first large hole so that it passes through where the vertical and horizontal double canvas threads cross. Bring the needle out immediately above through the small hole between the two vertical canvas threads in the same row as the first large hole (Fig. 2). Take the thread diagonally to the left as before, inserting the needle in the small hole between two horizontal canvas threads. Bring it out in the large hole immediately above.

On the next row the bottom of the stitches will be in the large holes.

Reinforced tent stitch
When making seat or cushion covers, it is advisable to use another stitch which strengthens the back of the canvas.

Bring the needle up in the second large hole of the second row in the upper right hand corner of the area being worked. Pass the needle and thread diagonally upwards and insert it in the large hole at the beginning of the row above, i.e. above and to the right of the first hole. At the back of the work take the needle diagonally downwards to re-emerge in the large hole immediately to the left of the first hole (Fig. 3).

Mixed stitches – gros and petit point
Some of the projects use a large stitch in a small area. Use a mixture of the gros and petit point to help work around tight curves and gentle slopes to give less of a stepped effect. To do this, stop the large stitch of gros point halfway across the stitch and use the small hole instead. Do the same thing when working towards the small stitch from the opposite direction in a different colour (Fig. 4).

Working the canvas
Work with the canvas stretched in the frame or freehand. If working in a frame, the canvas will not be so portable and the frames tend to be fairly large compared with the small sections of our projects. When worked freehand, finished canvas will probably have taken a diagonal 'set' but this is quite simple to straighten out when the work is finally pressed. Never pull stitches too tightly in the canvas as this

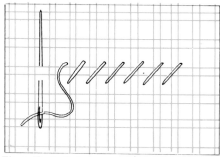
Fig. 1 Tent stitch – gros point.

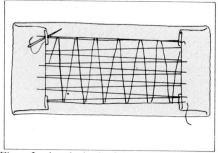
Fig. 5 Lacing the back of the canvas.

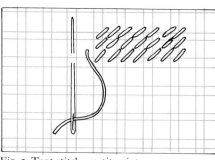
Fig. 2 Tent stitch – petit point.

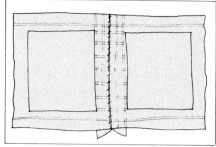
Fig. 6 Joining 2 pieces of double mesh canvas.

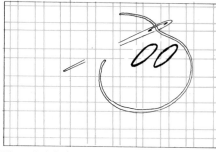
Fig. 3 Reinforced tent stitch.

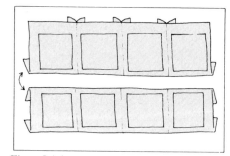
Fig. 7 Joining 2 rows.

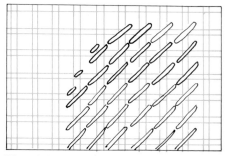
Fig. 4 Mixed stitches – gros and petit point.

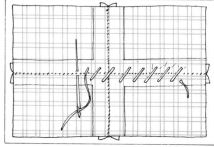
Fig. 8 Canvas work on top of oversewn joins.

increases the diagonal set and thins the surface of the work.

Designing

There is much more pleasure to be had out of canvas work if the design is one's own. The theme can be either abstract or figurative. If drawing is not a strong point, take a clear photograph or illustration and trace it.

The secret is to keep it very simple. First trace the design on to a piece of white paper with a black felt tip pen in clear, simple lines. Then lay the canvas over the paper. The lines of the design will show through the holes in the canvas. Trace these lines on to the surface of the canvas as smoothly as possible, preferably using a laundry marker as this will not rub off on to the wool after fixing by ironing.

If the canvas work is going to be in very pale colours, mark the canvas with a light coloured tailor's chalk instead of pen and then back stitch the lines into the canvas with a needle and pale coloured thread. This thread remains in the work as the stitches are worked over them. Once covered with stitches, there should be no canvas showing.

Pressing

When the work is finished, place the canvas upside down on an ironing board or piece of wood, which has been covered with a piece of clean white cloth. Use pins or drawing pins to pull the canvas back to its original shape and to attach it to the rigid ironing surface.

Cover the canvas with another clean white cloth and gently press with a steam iron or a damp cloth and an ordinary iron. Do not press too heavily or the canvas work will be flattened and dulled.

Leave the canvas as it is for 24 hours to dry completely and re-set the canvas. If still not right, repeat the process.

Framing

Stretch the canvas work over a piece of hardboard which fits the frame. Either glue the canvas edges to the back of the board or lace it with strong thread (Fig. 5).

Making up

When making up a piece of unmounted canvas work, sew just as for an ordinary fabric. However, it is important to catch some of the wool into the seam to make sure that bare canvas does not show through.

Joining

To join together a number of small canvases into one, place them in the correct sequence for the final project.

Decide how much border there will be between the squares and halve this measurement to find the point at which each of the canvases is folded for the seam line.

Start with the row of squares going down the left hand side and work only on their inner edges, not the edges which will form the outer border. Fold the surplus canvas backwards along the lower edge of the first section along a double thread line, also the top edge of the second section. Oversew these two folded edges tightly together with needle and sewing thread, lining up the threads of the canvases and the side edges of the canvas work (Fig. 6). The stitches will be covered with further canvas work later. Join the sections in pairs and then stitch the pairs together.

It is easier to handle the pieces if they are sewn two at a time.

When all the sections have been sewn together into vertical rows, press lightly along the joins.

Join the rows together, again folding the canvas backwards on a double thread line, the same distance from the edge as before and stitching tightly down the whole length, making sure that previous seams line up as shown in Fig. 7. Press lightly along the seams.

Once the pieces of canvas work are all sewn together, fill in the borders. Choose a contrasting colour or perhaps just black or grey and work in gros point (Fig. 8). Although the stitches will go through the double thickness at the seams do not work through all the width of the seam allowances as this would cause excess bulk. Trim the surplus canvas to within 3 or 4 squares of the seam.

Cleaning

If the canvas is only slightly soiled, use a domestic, aerosol dry-cleaning spray and follow the instructions on the container. If the canvas is very dirty, you can wash it, but this should not be done too often. You must check first for colour fastness and then put some soft warm water and soap flakes into a large shallow container and put the unmounted canvas work in it flat and face down. Sponge it very gently up and down. Rinse the same way until the water is clear.

Lay the canvas work face upwards on a flat surface. Sponge away all the excess moisture and pin the pieces into shape as for pressing.

Allow to dry completely.

Twelve small pictures

Each of these pictures is based on the same theme – land and sky. The design illustrates changes in the weather, giving an excuse for using many different colours within a fairly simple design. With only slight variations, the basic composition is the same.

You will need

● Double mesh canvas, ten holes to 2.5 cm (1 in), each piece 18 cm by 22 cm (7 in by 8½ in)
● metallized wooden frames 2 cm (¾ in) deep and hardboard
● canvas work equipment as given on page 179

Instructions

All the canvas work techniques required for this project are given on this and the facing page.

Enlarge the designs given in Fig. 9 on to white paper and transfer it to the canvas. The same basic outlines are used for each of the twelve pieces of canvas.

Fill in the details either freehand or by making twelve separate drawings on paper and transferring them in the usual way. Work the squares in gros point as shown in Fig. 1.

each square = 3 cm (1⅛")

Fig. 9 Designs for the pictures.

Press the canvases to the correct shape.

Cut the pieces of hardboard to measure 13 cm by 16.5 cm (5 in by 6½ in). Mount the canvases on the pieces of hardboard and place in the metal frames. They should push firmly into place.

Further suggestions

The idea of developing a basic theme could be used to create a series of pictures of particular personal relevance. For example, pictures for a child's bedroom could start with a drawing of his or her favourite toy, traced in clear outline on each canvas, then different details filled in. You might find a story book helpful for deciding what to do. For instance, a teddy could be shown bare, just a furry outline with eyes, ears and nose; going to school, copying the child's school uniform; at the seaside, with bathing trunks, hat, bucket and spade; in the rain, with mackintosh, wellingtons and rain; at a party, with party clothes and birthday cake; and in the winter, with snow, scarf, woolly hat and snowman.

For a more adult subject, make a study of the front of the house in all the different seasons.

Or simply take one window, changing the details – drawn curtains, open curtains, flowers, a cat, frosted panes.

Another possibility is to use an abstract theme, changing only the colours or the shapes slightly from one picture to another.

Presentation

There are many different ways of arranging such a collection of pictures, depending on how many there are and the wall space available.

Settee cushions

This set of cushions introduces a much larger scale of work with bigger canvas, larger needle and thicker wool so that the large areas can be worked in a comparatively short time.

When designing canvas work for cushion covers, it is important to consider the amount of wear they are going to get. Pale colours will show dirt fairly quickly, especially on a seat. Dark colours look dirty more slowly but will show every hair if you have a pale coloured pet. Reinforced tent stitch is used because the wear will be much greater than on pictures.

The designs are the same as those in the first project but have been enlarged to fit the cushions. They are best

used only on a plain background material as they are very colourful and will dominate the decor of a room. For a settee covered in a patterned fabric, consider reproducing that pattern in canvas work, on a larger or smaller scale, or in different colours.

Either make the canvas to fit existing cushions or make new ones.

You will need
- Double mesh canvas, five holes to 2.5 cm (1 in) to the required dimensions
- Sudan wool or 4 ply tapestry wool
- piping cord to fit around each cushion (optional)
- canvas work equipment as given on page 179
If making up new cushion:
- cushion filling e.g. feathers, sponge rubber, Kapok
- cotton or featherproof fabric lining to encase the filling
- furnishing fabric for base and gusset
- zip fastener (optional)

Instructions

All the canvas work techniques required for this project are given on pages 180 and 181.

If an existing cushion is to be recovered, remove the old cover and completely remove the piece of fabric that is going to be replaced by the canvas work by unpicking it along the seams. Press this flat and use it as a template for the canvas, remembering to add one extra row all round the edges to prevent any bare canvas showing after the work is sewn up.

To make a new cushion, cut a piece of canvas at least 5 cm (2 in) larger than the intended dimensions. Make an inner lining of cotton fabric for the filling so that the cover can be cleaned separately when necessary.

Enlarge the designs given in Fig. 9 and transfer them to the canvas.

Work in reinforced tent stitch.

When each piece is complete, press it lightly back to correct shape and leave to dry.

To complete

To renovate an existing cushion, turn what remains of the cushion cover inside out. Place the canvas in position, right sides together and pin all round. First tack the seams in place, rounding the corners of the canvas a little and sewing right through the last line of canvas work so that no bare canvas will show when the cushion is turned right side out. Turn the cushion right sides out to check that everything is

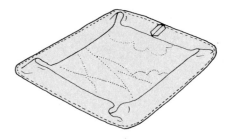

Fig. 10 Attaching gusset to canvas work top.

in the correct position. Sew either by hand or machine. Do not position the opening slit on one of the canvas work edges but instead unpick another seam at the back of the gusset.

If making a new cushion, stitch the gusset to all four sides of the canvas work top first, right sides together as before (Fig. 10). With right sides still together, attach the bottom piece, leaving one side open. Turn the cushion cover to the right side and insert the cushion pad. Finish the open side with a zip or slip stitching.

Friendship panel

This large piece of canvas work is actually made up of thirty-five separate squares and has been worked by twenty-one different people. It was stitched by a group of friends to commemorate a particular year, 1974, and passed from one to the other. This idea has quite often been used in the past, both in canvas work and patchwork and lends itself ideally to the production of a special gift to commemorate an important event.

Whoever organizes the project should provide each person with a choice of a large quantity of wool in lots of different colours so that they can choose their own combination. Provide each person, too, with their own needle and a marked piece of canvas.

You will need
- Double mesh canvas, ten holes to 2.5 cm (1 in) – as many pieces as required, allowing 2.5 cm (1 in) all round each piece for joining
- canvas work equipment as given on page 179

Top left The twelve small pictures are variations on a simple landscape scene.
Top right Details from the small pictures are enlarged for these settee cushions.
Bottom left Friendship panel worked as a joint venture to make an extra special gift.
Bottom right A box covered with canvas work makes an interesting three-dimensional project.

Measurements

Panel illustrated, approximately 90 cm by 60 cm (36 in by 24 in)

Instructions

All the canvas work techniques required for this project are given on pages 180 and 181.

To produce a friendship panel requires a lot of willing friends, a large frame and a great deal of time and patience to make up the small pieces into a single work. Each person should work in their own individual way, preferably without knowing what the other contributors are doing as this will produce a more varied and lively result. Some people will perhaps produce two or three squares, others will never finish theirs, so limit the number for each person but slightly overestimate the number of squares to be produced.

In the panel illustrated, nearly everyone used the simple tent stitch, both in petit point and gros point, and it is best to keep to a simple stitch, as the variety of colours and subject matter will be enough without having too many textural changes as well.

If an existing frame is to be used, work out the best size for the individual squares or rectangles remembering to leave at least $1\frac{1}{2}$ cm ($\frac{1}{2}$ in) between each piece and a border on the outside edge of not less than 2.5 cm (1 in). Alternatively, the size of the sections can be worked out first and a frame made specially. 10 cm (4 in) is a minimum for each section otherwise there would be little space for the subject matter of the design and. making up would involve a great deal more work.

Mark the outline of the section very clearly on each piece of canvas and make it clear to the contributors that their designs should go right up to the line but not beyond it.

When all the pieces have been completed, press each one to the correct shape. Arrange them into an attractive sequence, leaving space for the 'credits' and title. In the panel illustrated, the two centre squares hold the names of all the participants, in the order in which they finished the pieces and the date. However, information of this sort could be arranged in the border.

Lettering is obviously an important part of the project, so work it out carefully. Draw the letters on the canvas so that the spacing is even and the available area accurately filled. All letters and numbers can be fitted into

a depth of either five or seven squares.

Join all the pieces together and lightly press.

To work the areas between the individual sections, choose a contrasting colour or just black or grey, and use the simple tent stitch, gros point. Work any lettering in a colour that will show up against this background colour. Always fill in the lettering before the background, then stitch all the areas between the squares and the border round the entire panel.

Lightly press the whole piece for the last time, mount it and frame.

Covered box

The canvas work box is a special commemoration piece. It has solid silver panels set into the stitches, gold thread highlighting the lettering and silk and metallic cord running round the edges. The top of the lid is gently padded and it lifts off along the line of the battlements of the castle.

There are many uses for such a box – to hold sewing, cigars, jewellery, photographs or precious belongings and, handled carefully, it should last for a long time. It is best to start with a ready made box with a simple lift-off lid. Choose one that is well made and solid as the decoration itself will take a great deal of time and effort.

You will need
● Wooden box with a lift-off lid
● double thread canvas, ten holes to 2.5 cm (1 in) to fit all sides of the box
● Terylene wadding
● strong glue (a two-part glue with a twelve-hour setting time is ideal)
● leather to fit base of box
● hand drill
● 1.5 mm ($\frac{1}{16}$ in) drill bit
● piece of wood
● sheet metal, wood, leather or coloured card for insets
● metal snips
● clothes pegs
● canvas work equipment as given on page 179

Instructions

All the canvas work techniques required for this project are given on pages 180 and 181.

Measure the box to find the depth of the sides and the distance all round as shown in Fig. 11. Add 0.5 cm ($\frac{1}{4}$ in) to the length of the strip and draw the outline on a piece of canvas. (The extra measurement allows for the thickness

of the canvas work.) Cut the canvas at least 2.5 cm (1 in) all round from the outline (Fig. 11).

Measure the top of the lid and draw this on to another piece of canvas. Measure the depth of the lid and add this measurement to each side of the outline on the canvas (Fig. 12). Add an extra row to this to allow for the padding on the top which lifts the canvas work up. Cut with a margin of 2.5 cm (1 in) all round.

When designing a box, remember it is three dimensional and that only one or two sides and the lid will be seen at any one time. Think of the sides as linked together but each separate side being equally important. There could be a picture on each side as in the first project and the lid left plain or filled with clouds. There might be a pattern all over, but remember that it will have to join up perfectly on all the seam lines and is therefore slightly more difficult to work out.

Other materials than silver can, of course, be used as insets – wood veneer, leather or coloured card as long as they are thin and stiff enough to be drilled.

First decide where on the design the inset is to be incorporated. Trace the design on to the canvas, including the outline of the inset. Hold the canvas over the top of the inset material so that it is lined up with the appropriate area of the design. With a felt tip pen, mark through the large holes of the canvas on to the inset material along the outline of the traced inset shape (Fig. 13). Remove the canvas and, holding the inset material firmly over an old piece of flat wood, drill through the felt pen marks. These holes should line up exactly with the holes in the canvas and the marked line. Cut along the outside edge of the holes in the inset material, as closely as possible to the edges without going into the holes and no more than 1 mm ($\frac{1}{16}$ in) away (Fig. 14).

Place the drilled inset material on top of the canvas, lining it up with the lines on the canvas. Sew it in place, using a needle and thread, working through the canvas holes and then through the inset material holes in the same way as tent stitch (Fig. 15).

Work the side panels in tent stitch, using tapestry wool. At the edge of the inset material, treat the drilled holes just like holes in the canvas and stitch through them. You might need a slimmer needle for this.

To add gold or silver thread to the surface of the wool, start by pushing the end of the thread down through a hole to the wrong side of the canvas and sew it down. Lay the thread gently along the line it is to follow and sew it lightly in place with a complementary thread. At the end, cut the thread and again push it down through a hole and secure it to the back of the work.

When all the canvas work is completed on the side panel, wrap it tightly around the box and mark where the join will come, along a double thread line. Remove the canvas from the box, fold it and slip stitch the two edges tightly together, making sure to line up the upper and lower edge of the embroidery.

Try it for size – it must be tight – then remove it again. One or two rows of canvas will be unstitched, so complete the canvas work to cover the join in the canvas.

Fold over the top edge and bind it with an extra row of stitches (Fig. 16).

Make the canvas work for the lid in tent stitch.

When it is finished, cut diagonally into the corners being careful not to go too near the stitches (Fig. 17). Fold the side edges back along a double thread line and slip stitch as before. Check it for fit and oversew the joins with canvas work (Fig. 18). Cut away any surplus canvas on the inside, fold over the edge and bind as before.

To pad the top of the box, cut a piece of wadding the same size as the top. Cut further pieces, each 1 cm ($\frac{1}{2}$ in) smaller than the previous one, until the smallest possible size has been cut. Put these pieces of wadding on top of each other to form a pyramid and sew them lightly through all thicknesses to hold them in place (Fig. 19).

Use a good strong glue to attach the canvas work to the box, one that will give time to manoeuvre the canvas into place before it sets. Make sure that all

the sections fit well before applying the glue.

First stick the wadding to the top of the box and leave it to set.

Put a little glue all along the sides of the lid – too much will come through the canvas work. If in doubt, try a test piece on some scraps first.

Pull the canvas work down over the padding. Place a short strip of wood along each side and hold in place with a row of clothes pegs (Fig. 20). Check that all is in the correct position and leave to set.

Cut a piece of leather to fit the base of the box.

Glue the canvas work to the sides of the box as given for the lid.

When the glue has set, trim the bottom edge of the canvas and mitre the corners. Glue it down to the base of the box (Fig. 21). When dry, glue on the leather square.

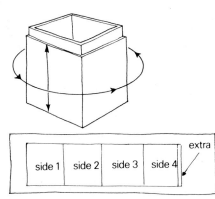
Fig. 11 Measuring canvas for sides.

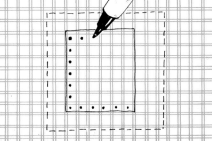
Fig. 12 Measuring canvas for lid.

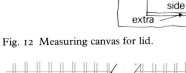
Fig. 13 Marking up inset material.

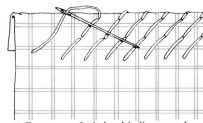
Fig. 14 Drilling and cutting inset material.

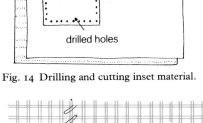
Fig. 15 Sewing down the inset material.

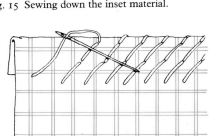
Fig. 16 Extra row of stitches binding top edge.

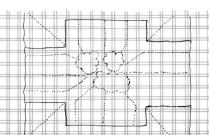
Fig. 17 Cutting into corners.

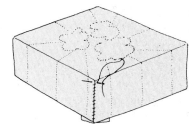
Fig. 18 Fitting and sewing the lid.

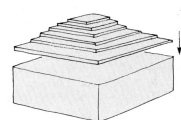
Fig. 19 Pyramid of wadding for lid.

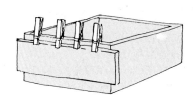
Fig. 20 Glueing canvas on lid.

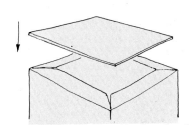
Fig. 21 Bottom of canvas and leather piece for base.

Index

Acknowledgements

Photographers

Simon Butcher: endpapers, 99; Melvin Grey: 9, 17, 23, 26, 29, 35, 43, 49, 63, 69, 77, 85, 91, 105, 113, 118–119, 119, 121, 127, 133, 139, 142 below left and right, 143, 147, 153, 161, 169, 179; Chris Harvey: 21, 45, 52 below, 65, 66 below left and above, 73 above right, 88–89, 115, 117, 123, 125 right, 130 left and right, 131 right, 137 below left, 151 above, 164; Spike Powell: 2–3, 13, 14, 15, 19, 20, 26–27, 27 above and below, 31 above and below, 33 left and right, 38, 39 above and below, 42, 47 left and right, 52 above, 53, 54 above and below, 55, 57, 59, 60, 61, 66 below right, 73 above left and below, 80, 83, 84, 90, 94–95, 101 left and right, 102–103, 103, 108–109, 125 left, 131 left, 135, 137 above and below right, 150, 151 below, 156–157, 157 above and below, 166–167, 170, 173, 174, 175, 183.

Illustrators

Mary Tomlin: 10–16, 24–28, 36–42, 44–48, 86–90, 92–98, 100–104, 114–120, 128–129, 140–144, 148–152, 162–168. Barbara Firth: 18–22, 30–34, 50–54, 56–60, 64–68, 79–84, 106–112, 134–138. Studio Briggs: 7–8, 70–76, 154–160, 180–185. Brian Mayor: 25, 172, 176–178. Janet Allen: 122–126.

Stockists

Many items can be obtained from general handicrafts shops or departments. Specialist items are available from the following by mail order.

Basket making
Cane and tools: Dryad, 178 Kensington High Street, London W8; Fred Aldous Ltd, 37 Lever Street, Manchester M60 1UX.

Leatherwork
Tools, hides and offcuts: S. Glassner, 480 Kingston Road, London SW20 8DX; J. T. Batchelor & Co, 39 Netherall Gardens, London NW3.
Hides: A. Paterson & Co Ltd, 12–15 St Andrews Square, Glasgow.

Pottery
Self-hardening clay and tools: (ColdClay) The Fulham Pottery Ltd, 210 New Kings Road, London SW6 4NY; (RealClay) Podmore & Sons Ltd, Shelton, Stoke-on-Trent, Staffordshire.

Marquetry
Knives, glues, veneers: Art Veneers Ltd, Industrial Estate, Mildenhall, Suffolk; Fred Aldous Ltd (see 'Basket making').
Information: Marquetry Society, 113 Kingsway, Petts Wood, Kent BR5 1PP.

Macramé
Boards, pins, threads: Fred Aldous Ltd (see 'Basket making').

Tatting
Shuttles, threads: Dryad (see 'Basket making').

Tie dyeing and tritik
Dyes: Dylon International Ltd, London SE26 5HD.

Appliqué
Machine embroidery and sewing threads: MacCulloch & Wallis Ltd, 25–26 Dering Street, London W1R 0BH.

Felt making
Carders, fleece: The Yarn Store, 89A Grosvenor Avenue, London N5; Frank Herring & Sons, 27 High West Street, Dorchester, Dorset.
Fleece: British Wool Marketing Board, PD Department, Oak Mills, Clayton, Bradford, West Yorkshire BD14 6JD.

Puppet making
Foam blocks and sheeting: Pentonville Rubber Co Ltd, 48–50 Pentonville Road, London N1.

Batik
Tjanting tools, wax and dyes: Candle Makers Supplies, 28 Blythe Road, London W14 0HA; Dryad (see 'Basket making').

Silk screen printing
Dyes: Selectasine, 22 Bulstrode Street, London W1.
Stencil paper, spray gun: Cowling & Wilcox Ltd, 26 Broadwick Street, London W1.
Squeegees, frames, mesh, Stenplex film, dyes: Sericol, 24 Parson's Green Lane, London SW6 4HS; Dryad (see 'Basket making').

Beadwork
Needles and beads: Ells and Farrier, The Bead House, 5 Princes Street, London W1.

Quilting
Frame: Fred Aldous Ltd (see 'Basket making').

Smocking
Embroidery threads, transfers: Dryad (see 'Basket making').

Metal thread embroidery
Metal threads: Mace and Nairn, 89 Crane Street, Salisbury, Wiltshire.

Needlepoint lace
Evenweave linen: Dryad (see 'Basket making'); Mace and Nairn (see 'Metal Thread Embroidery').
Linen lace thread, linen, paperweights: Mrs A. Sells, 49 Pedley Lane, Clifton, Shefford, Bedfordshire.
Information: The English Lace School, 42 St Peter's Street, Tiverton, Devon.

Canvas work
Canvas, tapestry wools: WHI Tapestry Shop, 85 Pimlico Road, London SW1

Weaving
Frames, yarns, thrums: The Yarn Store (see 'Felt making'); The Handweavers Studio & Gallery Ltd, 29 Haroldstone Road, London E17 7AN.

Crochet
Cotton yarns: Dryad (see 'Basket making'); Fred Aldous Ltd (see 'Basket making').

Knitting
Information: (Pingouin) French Wools Ltd, 7–11 Lexington Street, London W1R 4BU.

The publishers would also like to thank the following for kindly lending their products to be used in the photographs:
Title pages: Wooden Heart, 55 New Kings Road, London SW6 (pine furniture); Toby Mitchell, 17 Chalk Farm Road, London NW1 (lighting); Laura Ashley (wallpaper); Crossley York (carpet); page 17: S. Glassner (tools); page 105: Selectasine (dyes); Sericol (equipment); page 109: Neal Street Shop, 1 Neal Street, London WC1 (tray and crockery); Dennis Groves, Design Studio, 9 Sicilian Avenue, London WC1 (bed and screen).

Notes